Beyond the Veil of Knowledge

Is there a need to remodel constructivism to be more politically attuned? *Beyond the Veil of Knowledge* suggests that essentially contested concepts are a key medium that politicians use to try to minimize public resistance to their political goals. For constructivists, this means that the social construction of social knowledge and the social world ought better to be understood as the *sociopolitical* construction of *sociopolitical* knowledge and the *sociopolitical* world.

Intersubjective knowledge is very important, but so is background knowledge that is sociopolitically orchestrated in line with political agendas and by political and rhetorical means. The fixation of meanings closes off democratic contestation and, when it is successful, places democratic agency in limbo and degrades democratic deliberation and its beneficial qualities. Piki Ish-Shalom calls for an engaged academy: an academy that mobilizes its resources to engage society and the polity to prevent the watering down of democracy, while helping to create a space for criticism. In this book, he suggests several concrete measures for engagement, within the three spheres of individual theoretical work, the academic community, and society and polity.

Piki Ish-Shalom is Associate Professor of International Relations at the Hebrew University of Jerusalem.

Beyond the Veil of Knowledge
Triangulating Security, Democracy, and Academic Scholarship

PIKI ISH-SHALOM

University of Michigan Press ♦ *Ann Arbor*

Copyright © 2019 by Piki Ish-Shalom
All rights reserved

This book may not be reproduced, in whole or in part, including illustrations, in any form (beyond that copying permitted by Sections 107 and 108 of the U.S. Copyright Law and except by reviewers for the public press), without written permission from the publisher.

Published in the United States of America by
the University of Michigan Press
Manufactured in the United States of America
Printed on acid-free paper

First published January 2019

A CIP catalog record for this book is available from the British Library.

ISBN 978-0-472-13120-4 (hardcover : alk. paper)
ISBN 978-0-472-12466-4 (ebook)

*This book is dedicated to Emanuel Adler and Shlomo Avineri,
who took me soaring high above the clouds.*

Contents

Acknowledgments	ix
Introduction	1

Part I: Concepts and Politics

1	✦	Theoretical Framework	17
2	✦	Essentially Contested Concepts: Democracy and Security	43
3	✦	The Essential Contestedness of Concepts and Politics	69

Part II: Engaged Academia

4	✦	The Responsibility to Engage	97
5	✦	The Individual Level: Zooming In, Zooming Out	105
6	✦	The Second Level: The Community of Communities	117
7	✦	The Third Level: Structural Problems	133
8	✦	Traveling Forward in Time: Forecasting and Realizing the Spread of Democracy	151
9	✦	Moving Away from the Heart of Darkness: Advising the Security Sectors	175
		Conclusions: Having an Engaged Academia in a Conceptually Contested Environment	195

Appendix: "Megalim Olam"	205
Notes	211
References	219
Index	239

Digital materials related to this title can be found on the Fulcrum platform via the following citable URL: https://doi.org/10.3998/mpub.9852588

Acknowledgments

We live in (yet again) troubled times, in which democracy is on the defensive. When I started this project, sometime around 2010, my worries were mainly for the state of democracy in my own country, Israel. Since then more and more countries have entered the orbit of democracy in duress. This process lent urgency to my project, urgency that I could not face except in the tranquil and unhurried manner of academia. This is probably why it took me almost a decade to write and publish this book. I cannot but wonder how much longer it would have taken without the sense the urgency.

The years it took to write this book explain the long list of people I want to thank. I will start and end my acknowledgments with the same addressees of my first book, a good sign for some continuity in my way of thinking and living. I hope the book will prove that on top of the continuity there are also advantageous changes and development. Thus, my first thanks go to those known by the professional title of "anonymous reviewers." They are "us" in the broadest sense, in the amorphous way that academia is a community, an amorphous way I will try to concretize and morally argue for in the second part of this book. My gratitude, indeed, is to all of us who review and being reviewed, while keeping our sanity and sense of responsible scholarship. I am especially grateful to those many anonymous reviewers who met this project in its article and book forms, reviewed it, commented on it, and pushed me to improve my arguments and make the book what it is (though, as always, the mistakes still in it are my own personal intellectual property).

But there are also those I know by name who in various ways have helped me in writing this book. I offer my thanks to my two research assistants, Viki Auslender and Or Israeli, who might well have lost hope that anything would come out of this project but kept at it. And then there are colleagues, some of whom read parts of the manuscript, many of whom interacted with me in different ways to help me become the academic I am. I am indebted to Emanuel Adler, Jack Amoureux, Ofer Ashkenazi, Shlomo Avineri, Dan Avnon, Oren Barak, Ilan Baron, Corneliu Bjola, Felix Berenskoetter, Trine Villumsen Berling, Lothar Brock, Christian Büger, Emilee Chapman, Avner de-Shalit, Tali Dingott Alkopher, Annette Freyberg-Inan, Dalia Gavriely-Nuri, Anna Geis, Stefano Guzzini, Yoram Haftel, Ewan Harrison, Chris Hobson, Andy Hom, Patrick James, Patrick Jackson, Arie Kacowicz, Oliver Kessler, Roee Kibrik, Markus Kornprobst, Milja Kurki, Tony Lang, Anna Leander, Nava Löwenheim, Oded Löwenheim, Asa Maron, Alison McQueen, Dan Miodownik, Mor Mitrani, Harald Müller, Galia Press-BarNatan, Ariel Roth, Ken Schultz, Vered Karti Shemtov, Brent Steele, Giddon Tickotky, Vered Vinitzky-Seroussi, Jonas Wolff, and Steve Zipperstein.

As years go by in academia, one assumes managerial tasks that no one bothered telling us about when we started this career, such as serving on committees, directing institutes, and chairing departments. I do not have many kind words with which to discuss these roles, apart from the opportunity to better know the people who really manage us all, the administrative staff. Without their dedication and efficiency, there would be no university worthy of the name. Too often we take them and their work for granted, and not too rarely there is some animosity between them and the academic staff. A term or two in managerial positions teach us that this alienation is misplaced and that we belong to the same community. I am tempted to use Marx's battle cry: academic and administrative staff unite! But I will restrain myself and will only express my deep gratitude to all of them, first and foremost to Dorit Barak, Michal Barak, Rachela Caspy, Vered Eiss, Vicky Salant-Shlomi, and Chanoch Wolpe. They allowed me the peace of mind that enabled me to write this book while we all pretended together that *I* directed the academic unit.

Another set of thanks I owe to the two people with whom I initiated "Megalim Olam" (Hebrew: "Discovering the World") with www.ynet.co.il (see the appendix). Roi Simyoni, Ynet international desk's chief editor, warmly embraced my proposal to cooperate, and Mor Mitrani worked with me on the articles that were written for us in English, translating them and helping me in editing them. This project has lasted now for more than five years and is the closest I ever have gotten to discharge the responsibilities I burden others with. I thank them for making this project real.

Parts of the book have been published as articles in various journals and edited volumes: "Defining by Naming: Israeli Civic Warring over the Second Lebanon War," *European Journal of International Relations* 17 (3) (September 2011): 475–93; "Three Dialogic Imperatives in International Relations Scholarship: A Buberian Program," *Millennium: Journal of International Studies* 39 (3) (May 2011): 825–44; "Political Constructivism: The Political Construction of Social Knowledge," in *Arguing Global Governance: Agency, Lifeworld and Shared Reasoning*, ed. Corneliu Bjola and Markus Kornprobsts (New York: Routledge, 2010), 231–46; "Conceptualizing Democratization and Democratizing Conceptualization: A Virtuous Circle," in *The Conceptual Politics of Democracy Promotion*, ed. Christopher Hobson and Milja Kurki (New York: Routledge, 2011), 38–52; "Away from the Heart of Darkness: Transparency and Regulating the Relationships between Security Experts and Security Sectors," in *Capturing Security Expertise*, ed. Trine Villumsen Berling and Christian Bügers (New York: Routledge, 2015), 228–44; "Zooming In Zooming Out: Reflexive Engagements," in *Reflexivity and International Relations: Positionality, Critique, and Practice*, ed. Jack L. Amoureux and Brent J. Steele (New York: Routledge, 2015), 83–101; "Democracy," in *Concepts of World Politics*, ed. Felix Berenskoetter (London: Sage, 2016), 217–32; and "The Normative within the Explanatory: A Critical Take at the Democratic Peace Literature," in *Evaluating Progress in International Relations: How Do You Know?*, ed. Annette Freyberg-Inan, Patrick James, and Ewan Harrison (New York: Routledge, 2016), 139–55. Chapter 5 of the present book, "Zooming In, Zooming Out," started its life as the concluding chapter of my previous book, also with University of Michigan Press: *Democratic Peace: A Political Biography* (2013). I am indebted to all the publishing houses and journals for letting me use material originally published in their pages.

The research for this book was supported by grants from the Israel Science Foundation, Grant Number 1548/11 (2011–13), and the Israel Institute: Enhancing Knowledge and Study of Modern Israel (2015–16). Substantial parts of the book were written while on sabbatical at the Department of Political Science, Stanford University, where hospitality extended by Judy Goldstein and Ken Schultz helped me enormously.

I am also grateful to Ruth Freedman, who during the last decade or so has painstakingly, professionally, and caringly edited my texts, improving and refining each and every word in them, continuously rescuing English from me. I am thankful also to the editors at the University of Michigan Press. The book survived several of them, all of whom were professional and helpful, helping me to complete the torturous process of publishing a book: Melody Herr, Meredith Norwich, Danielle Coty, Elizabeth Demers, and Mary Francis.

And then there is my family. Whatever I will write here would not convey my true debt to them. So let me just express once again my gratitude to all of them, and specifically to Katty—my love for her is the most stable thing in my life—and to our three wonderfully and lovingly challenging kids: Noga, Shahaf, and Inbar, who is no longer little. It is on their behalf above all else that I am deeply troubled by current political processes and convinced that I have responsibilities outside the serenity of academia.

Finally, my gratefulness goes to the birdwatchers who kept me away from the computer and kept me company while looking for and looking at birds, especially to Professors Micha Mandel and Shlomi Segall, to Dudu Raved, who by now should have been granted an honorary doctorate from the Hebrew University of Jerusalem, to Eyal Shohat and Rony Livne, my desert and Pelagic Companions (respectively), and to Avner Rinot the walking field guide. And let us not forget the birds themselves, another source of global concerns and yet a personal and lasting spring of joy.

Introduction

After a decade of imprisonment in a fascist prison, Antonio Gramsci died in the Quisisana clinic in Rome on April 27, 1937, six days after being released due to further deterioration in his already frail health. In a sense, those few days in the clinic were a limbo of freedom: formally he was no longer a prisoner and therefore free. But in fact he could not enjoy liberty, and after a cerebral hemorrhage on April 25 he possessed no agential capacities in any meaningful sense. The Marxist in him would have said that freedom without resources is not freedom. But even non-Marxists would have difficulty convincing themselves that Gramsci's state in those six days was particularly free. Certain substantial constraints prevented him from fully enjoying his agency and freedom. In a similar way, our democratic lives also promise us liberty, but this promise is tainted by other aspects of our politics. Though those taints are far from those suffered by Gramsci in the Quisisana clinic, it may be that they are serious enough to be analyzed carefully and form the focus of emancipatory engagements. The "Gramsci in the Quisisana clinic" metaphor will help me establish the central objectives of this book, which are to examine some of the constraints on our freedom and propose engaged academia as an important measure for relieving the constraints that prevent full democratic agency.

The theoretical premise for this book is a constructivist framework nourished by an understanding that mainstream constructivism pays insufficient attention to everyday politics.[1] Thus, there is a need to remodel constructivism to make it more politically attuned. To this end, I will offer Gramsci's theory of hegemony, augmented by W. B. Gallie's (1956) framework of essentially contested concepts. In a nutshell, I would like to suggest that essentially contested concepts are a key medium that politicians use to try to minimize public resistance to their political goals. I argue that politicians try to fixate essentially contested concepts with one meaning or else empty concepts of all meaning, which frames the layperson's commonsensical understanding of the world in serving politicians' agenda. This means that what constructivism perceives as the *social* construction of *social* knowledge and the *social* world is better understood as the *sociopolitical* construction of *sociopolitical* knowledge and the *sociopolitical* world. Intersubjective knowledge is very important, but so is background knowledge that is sociopolitically orchestrated in line with political agendas and by political and rhetorical means. The fixation of meanings closes off democratic contestation and, when it is successful, makes the democratic citizen a "Gramsci in the Quisisana clinic": placing the person's democratic agency in limbo, degrading democratic deliberation, and causing the loss of its beneficial qualities. I argue that this agential limbo normatively calls for an engaged academia: an academia that mobilizes its resources to engage society and the polity to prevent democratic contestation and deliberation from being watered down, while helping create a space for criticism. I maintain that to do this, academics need to embrace a dual analytical gaze—one that is informed both by a keen Gramscian political perception of how politics impairs democratic agency and by a strong sense of Habermasian idealism regarding how we should regain this same agency. I will not remain in the abstract and will suggest several concrete measures that academia should commit to. We can divide these measures into three spheres: (1) the academic's individual theoretical work, (2) the academic community, and (3) the society and polity. In the first part of the book I will focus on the theoretical framework of politically attuned constructivism, and in the second part I will go normative to propose and analyze those measures.

Constructivism Goes Political

All too often, constructivism, which mainly deals with the social, does not take politics seriously enough. By politics I mean that mundane, human, social realm where lofty ideals are truthfully and honestly pursued and where considerations of power and earthly interests are practiced by (sometimes) dirty little means. This is politics as the social sphere, where agents and structures intermingle, producing consequences some of which are intended and some of which are not—politics, that is, as it really is (Ish-Shalom 2011a, 2011b).

Constructivism theorizes how our known social world came to be. The constructivist contention is that it came to be through social knowledge and social construction (Adler 1997; Guzzini 2000; Weldes 1996). Social knowledge refers to how people intersubjectively understand their physical and human environment. Those intersubjective understandings then form the building blocks of the construction of social reality because human beings act on the basis of how they understand their world and the expectations stemming from these understandings. Politically attuned constructivism agrees on those contentions but also stresses the political dimensions of social construction. This is not to say that politics is the only dimension at work in social construction but that politics does play an important role that is poorly appreciated (by constructivists). So, to rectify any theoretical insensitivity to power and politics, I plan to insert some Gramscian insights into the constructivist discussion, mostly by focusing on the medium of political concepts, which by and large are essentially contested.

Taking Antonio Gramsci's theory of hegemony, my argument's thrust is that one of the most effective political tools for political mobilization is the framing of the public common sense (Gramsci 1971, 1992, 1996, 2007) (for Gramsci's introduction to the study of international relations [IR], see Bieler and Morton 2001; Cox and Sinclair 1996; Davidson 2008; Gale 1998; Gill 1990, 1993, 2012; Hopf 2013; Ish-Shalom 2013; Joseph 2008; Puchala 2005). Framing the public common sense shapes how people intersubjectively understand their world, the expectations they develop about the world, and the processes they form a part of and take part in. This means that the public common sense is a key apparatus in the construction of social knowledge and social reality. And since the public common sense is sometimes framed politically, the construction of social knowledge is to some degree political, implying that we would be better off understanding social reality as a constructed *sociopolitical* reality.

Framing of the public common sense also shapes the public actions that people believe are possible, legitimate, and effective. Accordingly, rather than using brute force, a sophisticated and resourceful politician uses the third face of power and, if successful, sets the political agenda and thence public behavior (Lukes 2004). Gramsci, who was a Marxist, theorized hegemony as a totalistic condition where the common sense of (almost) the entire public has been framed, lulling the stupefied citizenry into conceding to capitalist interests. He means that the entire public, including the proletariat, unwittingly betrays its own true, objective interests in obedience to the interests of a small segment of society: the capitalists. My own understanding of hegemony is less ideological and hence less dogmatic and totalistic. I see hegemony as partial in terms of its grip on the public, and transient. Usually, its grip applies to certain groups rather than the whole public, and its content is limited, not totalistic. It is also transient and can change, for example, after exposure to successful political campaigning. This view is more germane to a pluralistic society segmented along different lines and interests. Because of this I prefer to use a term different from Gramsci's "hegemony," namely "public convention," to denote the public's partial and transitory framed common sense (Ish-Shalom 2011b, 2013). All the same, my own politically attuned constructivism does share with Gramsci's theory of hegemony an appreciation of the political effectiveness of framing the common sense, even when the framing is only partial and transitory.

Essentially Contested Concepts

William Connolly, following W. B. Gallie, has argued that language is a politically biased and biasing medium: "The language of politics is not a neutral medium that conveys ideas independently formed; it is an institutionalized structure of meanings that channels political thought and action in certain directions" (1974, 1). Concepts, being one of the most important components of the language of politics, are important in this channeling of political thought and action. A concept is "a mental representation of an element or phenomenon of the physical, social, or psychological world" (Davis 2005, 12). Concepts, as mental representations, are inherently vague, ambiguous, and fuzzy (Davis 2005, 5–6). Political concepts are not only inherently fuzzy, but also characteristically and essentially contested (Gallie 1956; in IR see Kurki 2010). Gallie argued that a concept must fulfill seven conditions to be considered essentially contested: (1) It must be appraisive or evaluative. (2) It must be internally complex, because it contains different principles and values. (3) Its internal complexity must allow differentiation of ranking; that is, its complexity creates a hierarchy of principles and values with greater or lesser importance for defining x as y. (4) It must be open; that is, it must allow the standard that is used to determine that x is y to be lowered or raised. (5) It can be used to defend one's own position. (6) It can be attributable to a host of historical exemplars. (7) Debate about its nature may not dispel its fuzziness but increase its vagueness, that is, its contestedness (Gallie 1956, 183–87). Highlighting the political nature and function of the essential contestedness of concepts, I will point out three additional conditions that must be met for a concept to be contested. First, the concept must have several reasonable and legitimate meanings. Second, there must be complex, irresolvable (actual or potential) disagreements over the appropriate meaning of the concept. Third, when becoming actual, those disagreements are important enough for certain interlocutors to be politicized (Ish-Shalom 2010, 2011b, 2015).

Political concepts are politically significant (see also Kibrik 2016). They are important for framing the public common sense politically. One way that people understand the world is by conceptualizing, using those mental representations of the world that we call concepts. By attaching meaning to concepts, we can conceptualize the world and decide what we should be achieving and how best to achieve it. Echoing Connolly, I maintain that conceptualizing concepts helps us to channel political thought and action, so that politics involves the constant effort to conceptualize political concepts and attach meaning to them. In order to mobilize public action unhindered by critical reflections, politicians frame the public common sense by fixating a contested political concept with meaning,[2] committing the public to a single, unreflected conceptualization, and making the public adhere to a particular set of public conventions, which act as road maps and guides.

Decontesting political concepts is therefore an exemplary political act. But since political concepts are by nature contested, it seems that politics entails an effort to decontest what cannot be decontested. And politicians, to fixate a political concept with meaning, try to present it as neutralized, beyond ideological debate, and with one natural meaning. Pierre Bourdieu grasps this attempt when he describes the performativity of concepts as acts of social magic understood as "the attempt to make things become reality by giving them a name ('nominating' them) and succeeding in the imposition of this new vision and division of social reality" (Guzzini 2013, 88). Calling those acts "social magic" points to an important feature of the classification and categorization through concepts, that the actions of the nominating agent, frequently the state, are seen not as political but as natural (Adler-Nissen 2013, 9). Similarly, Ian Lustick characterizes Gramsci's hegemony as "politics naturalized to be experienced as culture" (1999, 339). This is the Gramscian path to the creation of public conventions, and it is this process of constructing the sociopolitical world that politically attuned constructivism theorizes. Here the contestedness of political concepts plays a foundational political role by being both a political arena where winning is possible and a tool for achieving this outcome.

Take democracy, for example, one of the two concepts we will be returning to throughout this book (the other being security). Regardless of how complex and contested this political concept is, in the public arena it is quite an empty cliché, ossified, evaluated, and measured with a set of fixed criteria. These criteria are propagated, for example, by think tanks such as Freedom House and Transparency International, which use them as benchmarks against which the countries of the world can be compared and declared democratic or undemocratic (Löwenheim 2008; Steele 2010b, 63). Democracy as an empty or ossified concept has also been used politically as a yardstick for establishing those with "us" and those against "us" in the global war on terrorism that was declared by the Bush administration. This is an example of the political ramifications of concepts, of how a concept's meaning can be converted into political conviction, specific knowledge engendering a strongly opinionated view necessitating political action (Ish-Shalom 2013)—in this case the strategic necessity of promoting democracy, if necessary at gunpoint.

The adventurism of the Bush administration in Iraq and Afghanistan also exemplifies a more general conceptual phenomenon. Fixating the concept of democracy with meaning (or, for that matter, emptying it of meaning) spills over into the derivative concept of democratization: the conceptualization of democratization and policies of democracy promotion dovetail with fixating the meaning of democracy (see also Ish-Shalom 2012; Wolff 2012). If we understand democracy to be a structure, then promoting democracy may be understood as building the structural attributes of democracy, which is a relatively easy political act. Alternatively, if democracy is understood as a moral and cultural political phenomenon, then promoting democracy may be understood as disseminating democratic norms and values, which is an intricate, slow, daunting process. It was the fixated structural understandings of both democracy and democratization that blinded the Bush administration to the obstacles facing its attempt to democratize Iraq and Afghanistan and significantly contributed to its bogged-down adventurism. Other essentially contested concepts resemble democracy in that they are never islands unto themselves. Essentially contested concepts invariably get entangled with more derivative concepts. They form semantic fields that imply that concepts are actually a configured group of words and concepts linked by a common subject.

This Gramscian reading of politics and constructivism may convey a sense of pessimism about human and social fortune. It might seem to argue that humans are just captives of their irrationality, that Gramsci in the Quisisana clinic is not a metaphor but a true and accurate description of a deterministic reality where human society is forever locked in power struggles, and we are all just instruments in the service of manipulative politics and sectarian interests. I do not subscribe to this deterministic pessimism, and politically attuned constructivism should certainly not serve pessimism. I think that it might help if we supplemented a Gramscian reading with a Habermasian perspective. Politically attuned constructivists should be encouraged to adopt a dual analytical gaze (Ish-Shalom 2010), which, despite its difficulty, is actually crucial. It is important for the politically attuned constructivist to cultivate a Gramscian sensitivity to the way in which contemporary politics is practiced, alongside a Habermasian-inspired responsibility to change how it is practiced. It is, moreover, the social responsibility of every academic to be an active member of an engaged academia—the epistemological upshot that follows understanding the contestedness of political concepts, the contestedness of what was termed so aptly by Christopher Hobson and Milia Kurki "conceptual politics" (2011).

Jürgen Habermas's theory of communicative action can help us keep Gramscian pessimism in check and help us cultivate the dual gaze mentioned above (Habermas 1984, 1987, 1989) (for his introduction to the study of IR, see Anievas 2005; Checkel 2001; Diez and Steans 2005; Muller 2004; Mitzen 2005; Risse 2000; Weber 2005). Habermas's theory offers us a second strategy that can be used in decontesting political concepts, one that is committed to human reasonableness—or at least to the potential to achieve it. As we saw, meaningful political concepts are the building blocks for constructing social knowledge. The Habermasian ideal suggests that meaningful political concepts do not prevent rational argumentation, but actually help to produce it while elucidating for the public the aims and means, values and facts generated by such argumentation. The Habermasian vision maintains that attaching meaning to political concepts is both a reflective and a critical process and that the meaning of political concepts can withstand trial by reason and be elucidated in ideal speech situations through ideal speech acts. Accordingly, political concepts' meanings are not frozen into public conventions but rather subjected to ongoing critical public scrutiny and clarification. The communicative rationality, reason, criticism, and reflectivity enjoined by Habermas both enable the ideal speech situation and are enabled by it and consequently empower the participants in public deliberation to scrutinize and elucidate the meaning of political concepts, and not accept them at face value. The participants in public deliberation engage in a sincere and public dialogue that allows them to achieve a common understanding of each interlocutor's understanding of the meaning and conception of the political concepts under debate. Sectarian interests and power considerations are set aside, and, according to Habermasian argument, social knowledge becomes intersubjectively and truthfully constructed, paving the way to a reasonable public understanding of the public good and efficient and moral political action.

But how we can mitigate the gap between the Gramscian and Habermasian understandings of conceptual politics? How can we narrow this chasm between pessimism and optimism? Is there a strategy for saving human society and politics from fixating political concepts or emptying them of meaning, from using unreflected public conventions? Is there some group that can help human society move away from a Gramscian fixation on one meaning, toward a dynamic Habermasian elucidation of many meanings? I wish to argue that there is a group and a mechanism that can help achieve this, namely academia and academic discussion (or at least the ideal of academic discussion) regarding political concepts, the contestedness of political concepts, and the diverse meanings of these concepts. The meanings of the political concepts that we explore in this book, namely democracy and security, are especially important. Academia has the theoretical resources to understand the essential contestedness of political concepts, and may thus be equipped to mitigate the political manipulation of fixating meanings.

Note that this academic commitment to engage is morally grounded. In other words, I take morality seriously. I am not oblivious of the weaknesses of morality, to the theoretical lacunas in the various projects of justifying morality, to the contestations among philosophers regarding what morality actually dictates, permits, and prohibits, as well as to the exclusionary tendencies that have plagued moral thinking throughout its history. I understand morality to be human and social framework, and as such it suffers from the imperfection that typifies whatever is human and social. And yet I see no society worthy of its name without a moral framework, without ideas, deliberations, and standards for how we should behave toward each other. Poststructuralists often equate morality with the grand narratives that they deride, seeing it as yet another cynically devised instrument for power and domination. Morality, for poststructuralists, can be part of the problem. For me, imperfect as it is, morality is part of the solution. It is this understanding of morality that shapes my version of critical theory (some would describe it as a bit anachronistic); and it is this understanding that endows my perspective with some (very cautious) optimism that things and structures can be different and change for the better (or for the worse), that there is something to work for, and resources to work with. This moralism and cautious optimism may set me apart from many of the colleagues I otherwise share numerous critical sensitivities with.

Two caveats are in order. First, academia is not immune to the ramifications of decontesting what is essentially contested. As standpoint epistemologists have rightly noted, academics also have blind spots (see below). They sometimes are captives of a hegemonized common sense. Feminists have excelled in exposing the masculine blind spots operative in academia (Carroll and Zerilli 1993), and despite academia's universal potentiality (see below), it has regrettably never been immune to the maladies of nationalism and national chauvinism. The important point is not that academia does not suffer from these maladies but that it is equipped to engage with them and any blind spots. I also want to suggest that academics need to be *committed* to trying to engage with them. And like all sentient beings, academic scholars are morally committed and their moral commitments shape how they define essentially contested concepts. Consequently, and as we see below, notwithstanding the positivist search for objective definitions, definitions are the interpretative meeting point of empirical observation, experience, and moral commitment, and as such are essentially contested. They are heuristic devices that help us differentiate empirical phenomena and conceptual categories, and the delineation that we achieve is no less morally based than it is empirically based. Like other forms of labeling and categorization, academic definitions are morally founded to a degree and serve as acts of sociopolitical constructions of reality.

This understanding returns me to my normative call for engaged academia. Engagement is the normative stance dovetailing with a Habermasian-checked Gramscian sensitivity. If politics is the closure of discussion by fixating concepts with a single unreflected conceptualization or emptying them of meaning, then involved academia should be about opening discussion through conceptual engagement and reflecting on and disclosing the contested character of concepts, the contestation over them, and the ideological bases and normative significances of different conceptualizations.

Of no less importance, conceptual engagement should also be accompanied by an understanding that the definitions that theoreticians develop are also a certain kind of bounding practice involving the categorization of phenomena and conceptualization of essentially contested concepts. Thus, engagement calls for reflexivity in considering our own conceptualizations (Amoureux and Steele 2015; Hamati-Ataya 2011, 2013), namely that academic conceptualizations—let's call them definitions—are also normatively grounded and as such might be ideologically partisan. What this is saying is that if theoreticians are committed to participatory and deliberative democracy, then they need to engage as theoretician-citizens who don't just offer answers or try to impose their answers on the public but consider their main task to be asking questions and raising doubts. Theoreticians like this have the important social and political role of constantly opening up the intellectual space for criticism (see also Levine 2012).

The second important caveat is that accepting the contestedness of concepts does not imply moral or analytic relativism. By embracing an anything-goes attitude, relativism dodges all forms of engagement, either political or moral, with the essence of contestedness. This is because relativism results in sidestepping moral judgments, which are necessitated by the fact of contestedness. What I call for later is pluralism (see also Jackson 2011). Pluralism recognizes numerous legitimate meanings but limits them with the criterion of reasonableness. Pluralism is only maintained if we keep a commitment to our own moral groundwork. Therefore, pluralism does not ignore the ethical responsibility to morally evaluate different meanings. Unlike relativism, pluralism accepts and respects contestedness while valuing the reasonable meanings that people hold fairly. Relativism sidesteps meaningful dialogue; pluralism practices it.

Structure of the Book

The book is divided into two parts in the order of the argument presented above. The first part focuses on the theoretical arguments surrounding concepts, their essential contestedness, and political functions. Chapter 1, "Theoretical Framework," develops these themes and offers an analysis of concepts, their essential contestedness, and the two ways they can be de-contested: the Gramscian way and the Habermasian way. Both these routes involve distinct bounding practices, namely the acts and processes of delineating concepts (and their linguistic relatives) from each other and into distinct and identifiable categories. Common bounding practices include naming, labeling, and their academic equivalent, defining. This chapter will build further on these arguments and proposes a critical version of constructivism, one that, by focusing on essential contested concepts, is more politically attuned and well equipped to both theorize and engage conceptual politics.

Chapter 2, "Essentially Contested Concepts: Democracy and Security," focuses on the two concepts that form the backbone of the book: democracy and security. It analyzes them both as essentially contested concepts and as semantic fields and examines how the two concepts are conceptualized differently in different normative groundworks and how, notwithstanding bounding practices, both are interwoven with other concepts into different semantic fields. This analysis paves the way to the book's final movement (to be performed at the end of the second part), which weaves the two concepts into one semantic field—democratic security, in which an expanded and emancipatory security can uphold participatory and deliberative democracy and do this through legitimate, permissible tools.

The third and last chapter of the first part, "The Essential Contestedness of Concepts and Conceptual Politics," is empirical and takes us from the theoretical and abstract to the concreteness of the political realm. It analyzes several empirical examples to demonstrate three conceptual Gramscian tactics used by politicians to realize their agendas: (1) attaching a fixed meaning to essential contested concepts, which leads people to unreflexive action, (2) increasing conceptual fuzziness and ambiguity, which impedes effective opposition, and (3) combining the first two tactics into a third, which empties a concept of meaning and, having made it vacuous, uses it as a slogan and cliché to frame the common sense (this is especially attractive and politically effective for concepts that are commonly perceived as morally positive). In other words, this chapter demonstrates the relations of politics to construction and shows that construction is actually a sociopolitical process arising, so to speak, beyond the veil of knowledge. Highlighting the Gramscian tactics that prevail in the political realm also triggers the second and normative part of the book, in which I try to enlist academia in engaging society in a more Habermasian fashion.

The second, normative part of the book argues for an engaged academia, evoking the principles of self-reflexivity, communal setting and dialogue, pluralism, and commitment to transparency. These principles will assist academia to achieve a dual analytical gaze and discharge its substantive responsibility to society: its responsibility to engage. The rest of the book concretizes this normative proposal while suggesting several measures that engaged academia should undertake. Chapter 5, "The Individual Level: Zooming In, Zooming Out," concentrates on the individual scholar and how she should define the concepts she theorizes and theorizes with, and define them with moral sensitivity. Chapter 6, "The Second Level: The Community of Communities," turns to academia as an association of scholars. With the help of John Rawls's political liberalism, Will Kymlicka's multiculturalism, and Martin Buber's dialogical philosophy, it explains why and how dialogue and pluralism should be constitutive of academia, forming it as a community of communities. Chapter 7, "The Third Level: Structural Problems," analyzes certain structural problems that confront academia in facing the state, including basic versus applied research, transparency versus secrecy, and difference in time horizons. Understanding these structural problems paves the way to the next two chapters, which describe the concrete measures that engaged academia can use. Chapter 8, "Traveling Forward in Time: Forecasting and Realizing the Spread of Democracy," focuses on the academic practice of forecasting and the concept of democracy. I argue that forecasting creates three democratic dilemmas: (1) The legitimacy of injecting hidden moral commitments into policymaking—especially when the forecasters are outsiders. (2) The inequality of access to democratically grounded forecasters can potentially empower the powers that be and provide them with additional power resources. (3) Forecasts could be hijacked by skillful politicians and thus not only serve the powers that be but serve them by advancing agendas that clash with the agendas supported by the theoreticians-turned-forecasters. I recommend that theoreticians be conscious of these dilemmas, turn their attention from the state and engage with society, and produce their forecasts in the public sphere. By acting as theoretician-citizens, I propose, they can help empower a deliberative and participatory civil society.

Chapter 9, "Moving Away from the Heart of Darkness: Advising the Security Sectors," focuses on the academic practice of advising and the concept of security. I compare the contrasting ethics of academia and the security services, the former with its commitment to transparency, the latter with its commitment to secrecy, and argue that in order to escape cooption, academia must steer away from direct contact with the security services (state organs) and speak to civil society in the public sphere, as the proper arena for academic advice and engagement. I also recommend think tanks as the optimum intermediate institutions for transmitting academic ideas to help the state in a crisis.

In concluding the book, I weave together all the themes and advocate that an engaged academia commit itself to democratic security. By this I mean security that is emancipatory, democracy that is participatory and deliberative, and democratic security that seeks the removal of obstacles to citizens' democratic agency and opens up an intellectual space for criticism and true participation.

Part I ◆ Concepts and Politics

1 ✦ Theoretical Framework

Gramsci's main contribution to political theory was his development of the concept of hegemony (Gramsci 1971, 1992, 1996, 2007). Gramsci wrote his main body of work while incarcerated in a fascist Italian jail. Due to force of circumstance, his writing at the time was fragmentary and occasionally even clandestine and esoteric (Buttigieg 1992). Consequently, it tolerates a high degree of flexibility as well as application to different theoretical frameworks. Accordingly, the reading I propose of Gramsci's theory of hegemony highlights the crucial role of politics and concepts in constructing background knowledge. Later in the book, I juxtapose the Gramscian and the Habermasian readings of politics and suggest a concept-focused and politically attuned constructivist theory that is critical in orientation and well suited for an engaged academia (I elaborate this in the second part of the book).

Hegemony according to Gramsci

Gramsci's concept of hegemony arose from his attempts to explain the relative political stability of the capitalist order and the fact that the proletariat had not revolted against it, as long predicted by Marxists. His theory was an alternative to the orthodox Marxist claim that the capitalist order maintains its authority through forceful state organs. According to Gramsci, hegemony, as a noncoercive device of subtle domination through society, has hardly any need for the bayonet (Bates 1975). Gramscian domination occurs through civil society and is not necessarily imposed by political society. This is a major point where Gramsci differs from current liberal theory. Whereas liberal theory sees civil society as relatively autonomous from the state and its coercive organs, Gramsci sees civil society differently, as an integral state organ. The state perceived by Gramsci is a combination of coercive political society and civil society through which manipulative concession is accomplished. When considered thus, civil society is not the realm of individual freedom and voluntary social association, but another state device, in fact, the most efficient state device, as it works manipulatively and without necessitating force and coercion. Civil society is where hegemony is produced and reproduced by the media, academia, and cultural and religious institutions (Heywood 1994, 100–101).

The organic intellectuals of the capitalist order are those who disseminate capitalist values and norms through civil institutions and social artifacts like schools, churches, cultural establishments, and popular culture. Every person's common sense is thus framed through dissemination and socialization that influence his understanding of the world and perceptions of his interests in it. The proletariat can thus be manipulated to accept the capitalist order as the natural order of the world and the order that can secure its interests. This process of the naturalization of politics was captured aptly by Ian Lustick: "Hegemonic beliefs, as Gramsci put it, appear not as claims about the world but as 'common sense.' Hegemony is politics naturalized to be experienced as culture" (1999). And with these Gramscian insights in mind, Steven Lukes coined the phrase the "third face of power" (2004) to describe that aspect of power which manipulates public perceptions of objective interests in order to eliminate conflict from the political arena (see also Barnett and Duvall 2005, 53) and to dominate efficiently, without the need for force.

All this is well known. But, if we formulate it slightly differently, we can also understand Gramsci's theory of hegemony as a sociopolitical theory of background knowledge. Understood this way, the Gramscian theoretical framework could help to correct the inherent constructivist tendency to reduce the role of politics in constructing social reality (see also Adler 2005, 4; Ish-Shalom 2013; Weldes 1996). The Gramscian theory of background knowledge can complement mainstream constructivism with two crucial considerations. First, it penetrates the veil of knowledge to offer a political understanding of how background knowledge is formed and framed; often, background knowledge is not a result of spontaneous social processes but an outcome of deliberate, politically motivated effort. Second, Gramscian theory identifies different segments of society and theorizes their distinct behaviors and attitudes regarding background knowledge. Indeed, some people do not reflect on background knowledge but rather are passive recipients of its dictates. Others are far more active in engaging background knowledge. Some are theoreticians who reflect on background knowledge and construct theories about it. But, more important for our purposes, some participate actively in its creation. We can term these active segments of the public *organic intellectuals*, *political agents*, *political entrepreneurs*, or more old-fashionedly, *political elites*. But whatever name we give them (which is an important task, as we see below), background knowledge ceases to be understood as a naive social construct, becoming instead a highly political artifact reflecting the sectarian interests and power maneuvering that produced it. That is, it becomes a political entity and site of struggle and contestation.

Of course politics and the political have been discussed and defined countless times. Most discussions tend to identify politics with struggle or power distribution. Carl Schmitt (2007 [1927]) took this tendency to its extreme and identified the political with the distinction between friend and enemy. In his famous "Politics as a Vocation" Max Weber (1958 [1919], 78) defined politics with the struggle for power: "Politics for us means striving to share power or striving to influence the distribution of power, either among states or among groups within the state." And Harold Lasswell classically defined politics as involving the questions of who gets what, when, and how, questions usually determined by an official governmental decision-making process (1958). A similar definition was suggested by David Easton, who unsurprisingly added the component of the system to the definition of politics, but much to the same effect (1965). Nicholas Onuf has purposefully provided a fuzzier definition of politics: "Activities are political when members of a social unit construe those activities to be the most important ones engaging their attention" (1989, 2), and later connected "the most important ones" with rules that have the effect of distributing advantages unequally (22). The survey can go on and on, but the identification of politics with struggle and power is quite accepted, and thus I define politics as the public effort toward the allocation of material, ideal, and symbolic resources. Quite often this effort is conflictual and involves a public or sectarian struggle over said resources.

If we seek an exception to the almost consensual understanding of politics, Hannah Arendt linked politics morally to freedom, action, and coexistence: "For freedom, which is only seldom—in times of crisis or revolution—the direct aim of political action, is actually the reason why men live together in political organization at all; without it, political life as such would be meaningless. The raison d'être of politics is freedom and its field of experience is action" (1960, 28). However, this stress on the action involved in political organization may be seen as closely related, at least in certain periods, to the struggle to gain freedom. And moreover, my normative proposition for an engaged academia is not that different from the Arendtian normative program of struggling for freedom. Politics as conflict and politics as morally struggling against and within the constraints of the conflictual structure to gain freedom (and other values) are the obverse sides of the same coin. They provide, moreover, a justification for my call to a dual analytical gaze. But to be more attuned to the Arendtian notion of politics, we should also note that the resources being allocated include access to the process of allocation, namely access to the political process of contestation.

The public or sectarian struggle takes several forms, and, as Gramsci stressed, some of those forms are veiled. No less important, and as Gramsci theorized and demonstrated in his own life, at least some of the struggles seek social betterment and a more just society. Namely, they have a moral character. If the political tends to be adversarial, partisan, and sectarian and if it is where interests are shaped and sectarian conflicts arise over such interests, then the moral relates to the realm of the universal and as such determines values, principles, and norms. However, because of different conceptions of the just, namely, different value-sets, the moral aim of some struggles does not always resolve the conflictual disposition of politics (Rawls 1999a, 5). Likewise, the conflictual and political form of struggles for bettering society does not negate their moral content and intent. It is this understanding of politics and morality as being the obverse sides of the same social coin that informs the call for the dual analytical gaze that I develop further in the second part of the book.

Politics is frequently guided by conscious efforts to control the commonsense understanding of social reality. According to the Gramscian theoretical framework advanced here, common sense is the reservoir of background knowledge. It frames people's understanding of their environment and so is vital to the social construction of social reality. More precisely, it is the sociopolitical construction of sociopolitical reality.

Because common sense plays this vital role, political entrepreneurs wish to control it. They try to hegemonize it because they realize the usefulness of a hegemonized common sense as a powerful political tool. However, and here I part with Gramsci, though their aim is to achieve hegemony, the most political entrepreneurs usually achieve is a public convention, defined elsewhere as the "general background knowledge about the world that is taken for granted and shapes the commonsensical codes of thinking and behavior" (Ish-Shalom 2013, 5). Hegemony implies an all-embracing, fully framed common sense. Public convention, on the other hand, implies a more limited and partially framed common sense: limited in scope to certain sectors of society and partial in its grip on the common sense. Expressed in Gramscian terms, this political struggle is between hegemony and counterhegemony (or in the language adopted here, between institutionalized public conventions and oppositional public conventions). It is primarily a war of positions rather than a war of movement. And thus it is an ongoing struggle that gradually advances without violence (or hardly any violence) and is very incremental. With these parameters in mind, patience becomes a political virtue. This is especially true in the case of proponents of oppositional public conventions, because what they are up against are well-established sets of beliefs, values, and practices that jointly ensure the resilience of institutionalized public conventions, often backed by considerable governmental resources.

The main arena in the war of positions is civil society, with its educational, cultural, and associational institutions, and the tactical aim is to hegemonize the common sense and control it. There are several media to secure hegemony, some religious, some educational, some cultural. These media were aptly captured by Gramsci in his capacity as the literature and theater critic for the journal *L'Ordine Nuovo*. However, I would like to focus on different media, which are more linguistic in nature. Concepts and their linguistic relatives, such as tags, names, and labels, are important media in the war of positions, in the struggle to hegemonize the common sense. With the help of Gallie (1956; for more, see below), I will incorporate the theoretical framework of essentially contested concepts in Gramsci's concept of hegemony in order to overhaul constructivism, making it more politically attuned. By focusing on concepts and bounding practices, we will see how the deliberate decontestation of contested political concepts uses knowledge to construct sociopolitical reality. Rather than use the customary tools of domination and the monopoly over the legitimate use of force, political entrepreneurs prefer to use persuasion, dissemination and the socialization of values, norms, and practices in subtle campaigns in which rhetoric can be effective. Using rhetoric as the art of persuasion allows meaning to be attached to contested political concepts and concepts to be bounded and decontested.

Political Concepts and Contestation

A concept is "a mental representation of an element or phenomenon of the physical, social, or psychological world" (2005, 12). As mental representations, concepts are inherently vague, ambiguous, and fuzzy (Davis 2005, 5–6). As Gallie pointed out in 1956, they are not only inherently fuzzy, but characteristically and essentially contested (Gallie 1956). According to Gallie, there are seven conditions for a concept to be essentially contested: (1) It must be appraisive or evaluative. (2) It must be internally complex, because it contains different principles and values. (3) Its internal complexity must enable differentiation of ranking; namely, its complexity creates a hierarchy of principles and values with greater or lesser importance for defining x as y. (4) It is also open, in that it enables the standard that is used to determine that x is y to be lowered or raised. (5) It can be used to defend one's own stand. (6) It can be attributed to a host of historical exemplars. (7) Debates about its nature may not disperse its fuzziness but increase its vagueness, that is, its contestedness (Gallie 1956, 183–87). I point out three additional conditions, which highlight the political nature and function of the essential contestedness of concepts: First, there must be several possible meanings, or in Rawlsian terminology, several possible conceptions, of the concept. Second, there are irresolvable (actual or impending) disagreements over the appropriate meaning of the concept. Third, when becoming actual, the disagreements are important enough for certain interlocutors to become politicized, or in other words, to become contested (Ish-Shalom 2010, 2011b, 2015).

Contestation is a core feature of politics, involving the public and quite often conflictual effort to allocate resources—material, ideal, and symbolic. The very fact that political concepts meet the three conditions of contestedness makes them a central element of the political act. William Connolly made this perfectly clear:

> The concepts of politics do not simply provide a lens through which to observe a process that is independent of them . . . they are themselves part of that political life—they help to constitute it, to make it what it is. It follows that changes in those concepts, once accepted by a significant number of participants, contribute to changes in political life itself. It follows further that *proposals* for revision in some dimensions of our concepts carry similar import for political practice. (1974, 180)

The meanings attributed to concepts—or the different conception of concepts—as mental representations of the world are the media by which people understand the world. That is, to conceptualize concepts means to conceptualize the world around us: to fashion an understanding of the world *and* the ways we can act in the world in order to achieve our goals. Therefore, politics involves a continuous effort to conceptualize political concepts and attach meaning to them; this effort is the *political* action par excellence. Attaching meaning to concepts means making them useful vehicles of persuasion, making them a political road map able to direct people politically.

There are two ways to attach meaning. First, people may be aware of the contestedness of political concepts and critically reflect on the possible meanings, or conceptions, of those concepts that allow them to understand their world. As rational beings, people may participate actively in the cognitive process of conceptualizing concepts and form reasonable opinions and judgments as to possible meanings only following critical reflection. Conversely, it is possible that concepts' contestedness in the political sphere is rarely addressed and rarely evident at the level of the individual. Rarely, so the argument goes, do laypersons reflect upon the meanings of the concepts served up to them by interested political contenders, meanings they daily use. Moreover, they rarely comprehend that the meanings of the concepts they use are contested. In other words, individual adherence to meanings might be an unreflecting belief or—in Greek terms—doxa. Political concepts like state, nation, welfare, democracy, war, equality, liberty, and security are intensely debated theoretically and philosophically in academia and fiercely debated ideologically and along party lines in politics. Yet fiercely debated as they are, they can end up as mere clichés at the public level or—in Platonic terms—as shadows on the cave walls. Somehow the richness of political contestation fades away in the cognitive caves of citizens or in the "Quisisana clinic." This potential discrepancy is troubling both theoretically and democratically. Theoretically, we need to find a plausible account for the discrepancy and its consequences. Democratically, the process is troubling as it weakens the democratic mechanisms of popular participation and public reason.

The possibility of discrepancy lies at the crux of a dispute between two distinct traditions in IR. On the one hand, we have constructivism constituted on the philosophical conjecture that human activity is meaningful (Onuf 1989) and ruled governed (Kratochwil 1989, 11), that intersubjectively constructed meanings constitute humans' understanding of their surroundings and, consequently (at least to a large extent) their expectations and behavior. On the other hand, we have neo-Gramscianism, which is based on the political conjecture that human conduct takes place within the perimeters of hegemony and in orientation to it, that the everyperson is captivated by a structure of political beliefs created by intellectuals who are the agents of interested elites (Ish-Shalom 2013; Joseph 2008).[1] Constructivism is about the actuality and power of meaningfulness. Neo-Gramscianism is about the meekness and charade of meaningfulness. Constructivism is about long-term social processes. Neo-Gramscianism is about short and midterm mechanisms of political apparatuses of control and domination. With regard to attaching meanings to political concepts, constructivism posits the actions of argumentation and elucidation aimed at dynamically *reasoning* reflected meanings. Neo-Gramscianism posits claim-making and intentional and well-designed confounding that aims at *fixating* unreflected meanings (or alternatively, as I will later offer, emptying concepts of any meaning, making them vacuous). Constructivism is criticized for excessive idealism. Neo-Gramscianism is criticized for excessive materialism. I propose integrating the two in a manner that benefits from the merits of both traditions and offers us a sociopolitical theory of human behavior.

Constructivism

Constructivism is a social theory. It theorizes the way that our known social world came to be as it is. The constructivist contention is that it became this way through social knowledge (Adler 1997; Guzzini 2000; Weldes 1996). Social knowledge is defined as people's intersubjective understandings of their physical and human environment. Hence, the focus of constructivist research is the intersubjective intermediate, the sphere that links three aspects of human subjectivity and existence: (1) the relation of subject to subject, (2) the relation of subject to social system, and (3) subjective and objective states and conditions.

First, this sphere links the members of a society, in other words, the subjects. Accordingly, it is inherently related to social identity. Social identity, or the communal feeling of "we-ness" (Bar-Tal 1998, 94), is the social space where intersubjectivity rests and functions as the nexus in which social knowledge is produced and conveyed among the members of a society. At the same time, though, and in a reciprocated process, social knowledge produces a social space of "we-ness," or social identity, which it conveys in and across social identities. It is not surprising, then, that one of the main focuses of constructivist research is social identity, how it is produced, how it functions, and how it facilitates the production of social knowledge (Hansen and Wæver 2002; Katzenstein 1996; Risse 2010; Weldes 1996; Wendt 1992).

Social—or collective—identities lead to the second aspect of human existence that is mediated intersubjectively, namely the mutual constitutive relations between different subjects and their society (or social structure). As the well-known agent-structure problem states, there is no society without subjects, and there are no subjects (as opposed to individuals) without society. Subjects (as agents) and society (as social structure) constitute each other in a continuous, reciprocated process. And it is the intersubjective intermediate—in the form of social and collective identities—that links subjects and their society.

Third, intersubjectivity links the realm of the objective material environment and subjective ideal existence. In other words, whereas it is always necessary to study the subjective belief systems of a society's members and the objective backdrop against which social interactions take place in order to understand human experience, doing so is never sufficient. Rigorous social research should aspire to penetrate the intersubjective intermediate where social knowledge is produced and reproduced and produces. It is produced and reproduced through ongoing social practices and rituals and constantly produces social practices and rituals. And all this occurs in constant conjuncture with the objective world in which the social practices and rituals take place.[2]

Underlying all this is the fundamental apparatus of meaningful concepts. Concepts are the building blocks of intersubjective social knowledge; as mental representations of our world, they provide the interfaces for cognition, language, environment, and action. Concepts gain substance from the meanings attached to them, meanings that are the conceptions of concepts. Hence the constructivist interest in concepts and meanings (Davis 2005). Meaningful concepts are where abstract constructivist philosophy (in terms of both epistemology and ontology) and terminology can take root on relatively stable ground. Meaningful concepts lie at the heart of intersubjectivity and provide the key to viable social research that reaches beyond the necessary but insufficient focus on ideal and subjective intentions, on the one hand, and material and objective capabilities, on the other. And it is rigorous social research that will address the subjective and the objective (Pouliot 2007), the ideal and the material, and do this by studying the intersubjective sphere and investigating the meaningful concepts that link these three aspects of social and human existence.

Yet the question still remains of how these meanings are attached to concepts or, alternatively, how the contested concepts are reasoned. Two alternative models can be adduced from existing theories. The first model, which deals with reasoning, comes from Habermas's communicative action theory (Habermas 1987, 1984); the second model, dealing with fixating, can be adduced from Gramsci's political theory. Mainstream constructivism operates within the Habermasian understanding of the nexus of argumentation, social knowledge, and social reality. My aim is to explore the limitations of this understanding as social theory and offer a more Gramscian understanding—which brings politics into constructivism.

The Habermasian Route

As both Habermas and Gramsci have been extensively reviewed, interpreted, and applied to the study of IR, I shall refrain from addressing the full scope of their theories and selectively address elements that are relevant to my proposed theoretical framework.

Habermas defines an ideal speech situation as a social and political context in which individuals can optimally use the public sphere and apply their rationality in order to intersubjectively construct reasonable social knowledge. While Habermas does claim to pursue truth, his notion of it—according to Richard Bernstein (1983)—is beyond objectivism and relativism. His is a socially constructed truth, well situated in the social world and able to account for the material world. An ideal speech situation is a public forum in which politics and hidden interests are purified in order to prepare the ground for purity of argumentation. According to Habermas, argument "contains reasons or grounds that are connected in a systematic way with the *validity claim* of a problematic expression" (1984, 18). Arguments are the means by which "opinion . . . [is] transformed into knowledge" (1984, 25). Arguments are assessed on the basis of their merit and reasonableness, not for the force or power that may back them politically. It is not the speaker's reputation or legions of supporters that persuade the audience, but the merits of the argument. Habermas's theory is a discursive theory of democracy, wherein dialogue is the medium of mutual appropriation, deliberation is the core of ethical politics (or to use Habermas's terminology, "ethical-political discourse" [1993, 23]), and well-crafted argument is an illocutionary act.

Noticeable in Habermas is that both social structure and individual capabilities are important in creating the ideality of the speech situation. Within the social structure, the rules that govern deliberation and ensure the cleansing of nonrational factors from public deliberation, especially power considerations, are important. Yet it is individual capabilities that enable the favorable social structure to be used in constructing reasonable social knowledge. Individual capabilities are abilities that enable individuals to follow rules, act ethically, be willing and able to engage in dialogue, and possess the communicative competence needed to formulate ideal speech acts. Together, these capabilities engender public sincerity, which advances true and transparent arguments and a willingness to squarely assess opposing arguments and evaluate them solely on their merits. However, there is another capability, without which a favorable social structure could not contribute to achieving the ideal speech situation. Individuals must retain and entertain reflectivity: both self-regarding and other-regarding types of reflectivity. It is this reflectivity undertaken as a critical social activity that facilitates and encourages normative interest in questioning social knowledge and progressing toward a refined and improved intersubjective social knowledge that furthers the transcendence of existing social, economic, and political conditions.

As we discussed above, meaningful political concepts are the building blocks of social knowledge. In Habermasian terms, meaningful political concepts are the building blocks of ideal speech acts and rational argumentations that elucidate aims and means, values and facts. However, since the Habermasian process is both reflective and critical, the political concepts themselves withstand the trial of reason and are elucidated in the ideal speech situation. Because they undergo continuous scrutiny and clarification, the meanings of political concepts do not become political clichés. The rationality, reason, criticism, and reflectivity that facilitate and are facilitated by ideal speech situations oblige participants not to accept political concepts at face value but to scrutinize and elucidate them. The participants for their part engage in a dialogue that helps them reach a mutual understanding of what each one sees as the substance—meaning and conception—of the various political concepts under debate. Hence, political concepts are both elucidating and elucidated, and en route, social knowledge itself becomes intersubjectively constructed, paving the way to a reasonable public understanding of the public good and to efficient *and* normative political action. Returning now to the question posed above, whether meanings are fixated to concepts or whether concepts are reasoned, we can now see that concepts are supposedly reasoned and that they are reasoned by means of intersubjective, rational, reasonable, critical, and reflective social construction processes. Since this is a dynamic process, political concepts are not fixated with meaning but rather characterized by dynamism fueled by human reason.

Constructivists eagerly engage the Habermasian project because it is closely related to the constructivist theoretical agenda of studying the construction of social knowledge. Yet, generally speaking, they miss three important features in Habermas's theory of communicative action. First, although Habermas derives his ideal from seventeenth- and eighteenth-century European coffeehouses, salons, and literary societies (Habermas 1989, 31–43), the concept of the ideal speech situation is rather future-oriented in being a theoretical and philosophical normative schemata critically pointing the way to improving public deliberation. Second, Habermas contrasts communicative action with strategic action (Habermas 1984, 285–95). Strategic action is where power and interests are in action in the pursuit of instrumental rationality. And it is when exploring this dimension of modernity that Habermas reveals his social criticism and admits the resilience of politics in the social realm. Politics is linked to instrumental rationality and strategic action, which are among the targets of change for Habermas as a critical theoretician. Third, notwithstanding instrumental rationality and communicative action, Habermas completes his theoretical and philosophical schemata with a sociological account of the lifeworld. The lifeworld is the social and cultural background against which rationality operates and communicative action takes place (Bjola and Kornprobst 2011), where taken-for-granted social convictions, conventions, and beliefs are held. And it is this lifeworld that is a precondition for communicative action to construct social knowledge. As Habermas wrote, "The lifeworld appears as a reservoir of taken-for-granteds, of unshaken convictions that participants in communication draw upon in cooperative processes of interpretation" (1987, 124). Furthermore, the lifeworld engenders a "stock of knowledge [that] supplies members with unproblematic, common, background convictions that are assumed to be guaranteed; it is from these that contexts for processes of reaching understanding get shaped, processes in which those involved use tried and true situation definitions or negotiate new ones" (1987, 125). Habermas's analysis of the lifeworld also leads him, at times, to the Gramsci-like (or more fittingly, Bourdieu-like) observation that "on the basis of an already habitual communicative practice of everyday life, one subject inconspicuously harnesses another for his own purposes, that is, induces him to behave in a desired way by manipulatively employing linguistic means and thereby instrumentalizes him for his own success" (Habermas 1984, 288). This more "realistic" approach to unchecked political manipulation is even more evident in his later writing (1989, 175, 88).

It is this last theoretical assertion that makes Habermas more interesting and multifaceted as a theoretician than his superficial public representation. Habermas, after all, came to be identified with an omnipotent public reason that has the ability to purify rationality of dogmas, unfounded beliefs, and power considerations. Engaging with his account of strategic action and lifeworld problematizes this public representation of Habermas. Admittedly, though, Habermas's engagement with politics and power is lukewarm (Flyvbjerg 1998, 3; Fraser 1990). By stressing the distinctions between strategic and communicative action, he gives the impression that somehow politics and power are bonded solely to strategic action (Müller 2004, 414–15). Additionally, power and politics play too minor a role in his schemata of the construction of the lifeworld. And furthermore, his theory has been criticized for being too demanding even as an ideal (Baber and Bartlett 2005, 106–7). For these reasons, his theory, although indeed multifaceted, is too idealistic.

Yet, overall, constructivists fail to attain even those insights that Habermas reaches regarding power, strategic action, and the lifeworld. They seem mostly to have mistaken the ideality of Habermas schemata for a real-life social science theory, a ready-made tool for explanatory research (or for that matter, understanding-oriented research).[3] They also find it difficult to absorb the full importance of the lifeworld that Habermas depicts and his recognition of the resilience of power and instrumental rationality (see, for example, Checkel 2001; Diez and Steans 2005; Finnemore and Sikkink 2001).[4] These failures may be one reason why constructivism is criticized for excessive idealism. Confounding ideal-type theory with non-ideal-type theory is hardly likely to produce a realistic research agenda, and constructivism runs the risk of being unequipped to analyze the political manipulations and rhetorical tongue-twisting that is the bread and butter of political action. The fallibility of criticism and reflectivity opens the political space and political incentive to manipulative and abusive rhetoric. By relying too heavily on the faculties of criticism and reflectivity, constructivists can only fail to understand the nature and mechanisms of politics. What remains almost exclusively is inquiry into the long-term social processes of intersubjectively constructing social knowledge and social reality alone.

We find an exception to this rule in the thinking of first-generation constructivists, scholars such as Nicholas Onuf and Friedrich Kratochwil, who, in the late 1980s, initiated IR constructivism. Onuf (1989) and Kratochwil (1989) centered their social theory on rules, meanings, and language and were keenly interested in how politics and power make rules through which they construct social reality. Onuf (1989, 22), for example, links rules and politics, the social and the political:

> Whenever rules have the effect of distributing advantages unequally, the result is rule, which is the second general property of political society. . . . The paradigm of political society is aptly named because it links irrevocably the sine qua non of society—the availability, no, the unavoidability of rules—and of politics—the persistence of asymmetric social relations, known otherwise as the condition of rule.

This interest in and sensitivity to the role of politics led Onuf to embrace Gramsci (1989, 210) and Kratochwil to elaborate on speech act theory (1989, 33). But, in general, the first-generation constructivists focused on introducing constructivist conjectures and remained at the abstract level of metatheory. Their sensitivities were almost entirely abandoned by the second-generation constructivists, who focused their scholarly attention on norms and identities. Although at times they realized the role that power plays in the social construction of reality, they were more interested in the long-term processes and prospects of norm construction than in theorizing exactly how power plays a short-term, yet fundamental, role in those processes. Writing with Steven Bernstein, Emanuel Adler exemplifies this tendency by asserting that authority is involved in the constitution of the epistemes, though in the same breath he absolves himself of inquiring into this process (2005, 297–98).

Antje Wiener is yet another constructivist who takes contestation, and thus politics, seriously and develops a theory of contestation (2014). I share some of her assumptions and arguments, and our shared paths bring us to similar conclusions about contestation being constitutive for social change, the power of contestation in agreeing on meaning, and the theoretical necessity for weaving together fact and value, the normative and the analytical. But perhaps the importance of our concurrence lies in the normative: understanding the democratic importance of securing access to contestation (54). However, Wiener's theory lacks Gramsci's sensitivity to the conduct of politics and hence is mostly about bottom-up processes (81) where contestation almost seems to be the default mechanism of social activity, which, even if not equally accessed by all, has an unquestioned, almost guaranteed, existence. By adding the Gramscian layer, I render contestation a normative problematique. As I explained, politics, among other things, is the incessant effort to decontest the essentially contested; it is, quite often, the silencing of contestation. Thus, even with Wiener's important contribution to the constructivist literature, what I term below "the Gramscian route" has been seldom taken by mainstream constructivists. In a way, the endeavor I propose here tries to revive and concretize Onuf's and Kratochwil's. It is also, mostly in the second part of the book, a normative proposition for academia on how to discharge its responsibility to engage the wider public and ensure what Wiener seeks, namely to secure access to contestation because this is "crucial for just and legitimate political order" (2014, 10).

Gramscian sensitivity is indeed necessary to achieve this, by helping us understand that politics is not just about conscious and reflective reasoning over political concepts, but regretfully also about fixating meanings in every person's common sense. Fixating is a common phenomenon of the political world and a common political practice. To some extent, we are all captives of statically fixated meanings, of political concepts that frame our common sense because we fail to reflect on their meanings, and whose parameters influence our daily and political actions. Take, for instance, one of the most heated moral and ideological public controversies in the United States, abortion. Side by side with the philosophical discussion in academia, the public has split into two camps that seem to be stuck with the slogans "pro-life" and "pro-choice." Each camp values concepts that apparently prevent it from critically reflecting on its position and the concept that motivates the rival camp. Clinging to the two sloganized "pro-life" and "pro-choice" clichés renders a complex, multifaceted issue a two-dimensional conflict: you are either for life (i.e., against murder) or for choice (i.e., against enslavement).

Thus, the political and theoretical question is not just about elucidation and reasoning as the constituents of the conscious construction of social knowledge; it also involves confounding and fixating those meanings—in other words, the framing of our common sense that takes place beyond the veil of knowledge. Enter here Gramsci's theory of hegemony.

The Gramscian Route

Thomas Bates (1975, 352) defined Gramsci's conception of hegemony as "political leadership based on the consent of the led, a consent which is secured by the diffusion and popularization of the world view of the ruling class." This conceives hegemony as a political web of meanings that prevents the everyperson from reflecting critically on the social, economic, and political structure into which he is locked. The everyperson then is stupefied by intellectuals into consenting to the structure as given, as the product of natural laws, and to accepting his position there (even if lowly) as almost divinely ordained (Buttigieg 1992, 21; Gramsci 1992, 236). Thus, the everyperson is tamed into obedience that secures the existing structure.

In this Gramscian account, no room is left for rational argumentation or for reflection and criticism. At least not by the wider public. Much political reasoning is needed by political entrepreneurs, who design their campaign skillfully to produce the hegemony and counterhegemony they desire. But, within the wider public, rational argumentation, reasoning, reflection, and criticism are ignored and cloaked by a common sense framed by meanings diffused and fixated from above by private social institutions, namely civil society organs like schools and churches (Gramsci 1996, 200). The everyperson is therefore socialized into accepting a set of meanings, values, and ideals of someone else's making and choosing, and accepting them as undisputed truth. Political concepts are not critically reasoned over. They are politically fixated or rhetorically emptied and are in fact no more than political clichés. Whereas Habermas conceives of an ideal speech situation that allows ideal speech acts, Gramsci conceives what can be called veiled speech situations, which involve veiling speech acts. According to the Gramscian framework, politics is a harsh reality of silencing free thought, meaningful talk, and meaningful listening. This silencing can lead to what

Zali Gurevitch terms *repressive silence* (2001, 92–94). Whereas Habermas envisions power-free (but powerful) communicative action, Steven Lukes, using the Gramscian theoretical framework, asserts the third face of power: hidden power that confounds people's understanding of their real and objective interests and prevents conflicts (Lukes 2004).

Although we are bombarded by talk, it is not the speech of enlightened deliberation, but the cheap chatter of noise. This noise disrupts free thought and yokes the everyperson to the existing social structure. The argumentation and phronesis expected by Habermasian philosophy and every tenet of rational philosophy have no place in the Gramscian political world. The Gramscian world is controlled by organic intellectuals acting as sophists in the service of elites (Gramsci 1996, 199–210). They market their fuzzy claims and shrewdly succeed because phronesis is just a myth that cannot exist within the political web of fixated meanings known as hegemony. The pure argument's merit is not what carries the day, but rather the politically empowered claim. The public sphere is not and cannot be free from sectarian interests, since the public sphere's essence is the battle ground for sectarian and conflicting interests.

Thus, according to neo-Gramscian IR perspectives, political concepts are not consciously and critically reasoned (Ish-Shalom 2013; Joseph 2008) but fixated (or emptied) by interested agents to frame the common sense of the everyperson. If so, then social reality is the product neither of authentic social knowledge nor of long-term processes of reflective social construction. Social reality is the product of infusing the public common sense with distorted and unreflecting beliefs, or "doxa," as they are termed in Greek. And if that is what social reality is, constructivism should shed its naive approach of studying social knowledge separately from the politics that shape the processes of producing social knowledge. Constructivism should address the political dynamics and political mechanisms of producing social knowledge. Chiefly, it should study hegemony and counterhegemony, or institutionalized and oppositional public conventions,[5] how they are constructed and how they frame the parameters in which social knowledge is constructed by and constructs our social reality.

So far, we have stressed the Gramscian tactic of fixating meanings. But there are two more Gramscian tactics that have only been dealt with in brief. Concepts can be fixated and ossified into a single powerful meaning, translated into creed, political conviction, and thence action. But there is another possible route: to keep the concept fuzzy and almost meaningless, thus of no use in challenging institutionalized public convention. There is also a third tactic that involves emptying concepts of meaning and making them clichéd, vacuous, and ideal as political slogans whose rhetoric elicits uncritical, unreflexive support. These tactics are similar to the tactic of ossifying concepts with meanings in that they undermine the agential faculties of the democratic citizen and degrade public deliberation and democracy.

Naming and Labeling

The struggle over the common sense, or public conventions, involves media beside political concepts. These include tags, labels, and names. The struggle includes also bounding practices, namely the acts and processes of delineating concepts (and their linguistic relatives) from each other and placing them in distinct and identifiable categories. Bounding practices include conceptualizing, defining, tagging, labeling, and naming. Elsewhere, I have analyzed the notion of rhetorical capital (2013), which I define as the aggregate persuasive resources inherent in entities, and analyzed its applicability to theories. I examined why politicians are attracted to the mobilization of theories through rhetoric and how this mobilization is achieved. Metaphors are also entities that are rich in rhetorical capital and can potentially be employed by rhetorically minded politicians (for insights into the subject of metaphors in the study of IR, see, for example, Drulák 2006; Kornprobst et al. 2008; Carta 2014).

The symbolic substance of metaphor and how it links different ideas and objects makes it a robust resource for persuasion and a useful tool in the struggle for the common sense. As mentioned, concepts are also rich in rhetorical capital, and as social semiotics teaches us, symbols, signs, icons, and images can also be rhetorically useful in the struggle over common sense (see, for example, Brandist 1996; Dodds 2007; Peoples 2008; Vuori 2010; Hansen 2011; Schlag and Geis 2017). However, in this section I aim to focus on labeling and naming, and argue that (1) both are bounding practices equivalent to defining, and more common in the public and political arenas, (2) both are efficient political tools in the struggle over the common sense, (3) of the two, labeling is the more obvious arena and tool in the struggle over the common sense, as it is more publicly oriented, and (4) in unsettled, contested political events, parties can use naming as an indirect and subtle act of labeling.

In recent years, cultural geographers have shown increased interest in analyzing naming as a political process of domination or resistance (see, for example, Azaryahu 1986, 1996; Cohen and Kliot 1992; Herman 1999; Kearns and Berg 2002; Nash 1999). Naming is no longer considered a neutral, naive process, but a political act of appropriation, inclusion, and exclusion. A location's naming can be a significant aspect of power relation, and a means of resisting existing power relations. In the case of Mount McKinley, its renaming as Denali in 2015 by President Barack Obama was an attempt to rectify past exploitation, abuse, and cultural imperialism. In 1896, this mountain, which is the highest peak in the United States, was named after the presidential contender and later president, William McKinley, erasing its original Native American name, Denali. This was a powerful act of colonial appropriation and obliteration of local Native American heritage. Note that it took forty years to complete the act of renaming, which began in 1975 when the area surrounding the mountain was renamed Denali National Park and Preserve. At the time, however, the name of the mountain was kept as McKinley due to political resistance from Ohio, where McKinley was born. Political calculations and power considerations played a role in this drawn-out act of naming and renaming.

Thus, naming can involve a war of positions over the common sense between institutionalized and oppositional public conventions. I will also argue that the same insights can be applied to both social events and spatial objects. Naming events, or labeling them as belonging to one class of events or another, is a rhetorical and political act (see also Winkler 2008). Naming and labeling as acts of tagging and categorization are needed for human thinking and communication (see also Guzzini 2005, 499) and can often be rich in rhetorical capital. They are therefore suitable tools in the struggle for the common sense. For example, if labeling and classification link a given event to a positive class of events, then one side may gain the symbolic upper hand in the rhetorical struggle over the common sense. Some obvious examples from international politics are the classification and identification of a war as just or unjust; a violent political act as terrorism or guerilla warfare; a state as democratic or undemocratic; and elections as free and fair or manipulated. Claiming that one's war is just in fact justifies it while ipso facto painting the other side's war as unjust and unjustified. Likewise, we can identify a violent political act as legitimate guerilla warfare aimed at national liberation or as illegitimate terrorism and subversion.

Yet, as is common with rhetoric, the persuasive resources inherent to "naming" and "labeling" are neither universal nor comprehensive. Only specific names and labels in specific contexts with specific aims carry cultural resonance and may be rhetorically useful (Kubal 1998). The rhetorical usefulness of names and labels depends on the social and cultural structures external to those names, while the efficacy of their rhetorical capital depends on their linkage to these social and cultural structures. For example, names can link the public mind to a historical collective tradition. We find this in Israel quite often, for example, when a new settlement is given a biblical name (Cohen and Kliot 1992), which makes a statement of belonging and ostensibly establishes righteous appropriation. The same applies when labeling or classifying an event. Labeling is not in itself an attractive tool of persuasion. Only the specific content of the label, the linkage of one event to a certain class of events as opposed to another, can create cultural resonance and make labeling a tool of persuasion. Furthermore, "attractiveness" in the sense used here is highly contextual and depends on a political party's goal. For example, there is nothing positive in war, yet as I show below regarding the Second Lebanon War (2006), classifying a conflict as war can sometimes be useful rhetorically for internal political purposes. When politicians have rhetorical intentions, labeling and naming can be political maneuvers in the Gramscian struggle to hegemonize the common sense.

Philosophically, classification and naming can be treated either as two similar acts (in the tradition of Gottlob Frege and Bertrand Russell) or as two different acts (in the tradition of Saul Kripke and the latter Ludwig Wittgenstein) (see Clarkson 2003; Code 2006, 137). Russell (1956), in his theory of descriptions (descriptivism), equates naming with describing an entity. So naming performs a function similar to description in the sense that it comes close to an accurate reference to reality. In his thesis of rigid designation, Kripke (1980) suggests a contrasting account of the relationship between description and naming. As Carrol Clarkson pointed out (2003, 37),

> In Kripke's account, the descriptions we commonly associate with a name [of a person] cannot be taken as synonyms for that name. Instead, they serve as a handy way of picking that person out, even should those attributes later prove not to be true of the bearer. A rigid designator fixes the reference, even if it is on the basis of a contingent or mistaken attribute of the person in question.

Kripke's account is far more political than Russell's account and fits into the Gramscian framework of hegemonizing the common sense. According to Clarkson (2003, 37), "Once reference has been fixed (by way of ostension or an initial baptism) the name is passed on in the linguistic community, from link to link in a causal chain, each person using the name for the same bearer as that intended by the person from whom he heard it. And it is the mastery of this procedure, rather than the knowledge of a set of descriptions, that provides a more plausible account of how reference is determined." Two strands of Kripke's thesis fit in with Gramsci's theory of hegemony. First, according to Kripke, the reference (name) is fixed and not subjected to continuous reflection. One could therefore argue that the name takes over the common sense. Second, the point about mastering the procedure hints at the importance of the political factors associated with this process of hegemonizing the common sense. Some political entrepreneurs master the process and—with a Gramscian twist—manipulate it according to their political agenda.

In addition, the debate between Russell and Kripke not only concerns how closely naming and labeling are related. We can also reformulate the debate parameters and ask which comes first. According to Russell's theory, describing (and by allusion, classifying) precedes naming, and naming mainly constitutes a return to describing the entity. In Kripke's thesis, naming precedes and causally constitutes classifying, as it serves to fix a meaning that can be wrong or right but is always a fundamental step toward classifying an entity. This question of precedence can have political implications. In situations where a label is highly contested and no resolution of its meaning can be reached, a party might use naming to indirectly break a deadlocked question of classification. There are two possible ways to label by naming. The first is a stronger act. The party wishing to resolve the deadlocked issue of classification may turn to the act of naming the event, where the name is seen as a rigid designator that can fix the controversial definition. The party tries to name the event, hoping that it will be popularly accepted and thus rigidly designate the event. In such cases, labeling follows naming. A weaker act where naming is used to resolve a deadlock over classification happens in cases when a commonly accepted, popularly used name already exists. In such cases, the party can use a popular name as a power asset in political disputes over classification. Efficiently mobilizing a popular name is a way to prevail in the political struggle over classification and thus hegemonize the common sense. I will call these two political processes of labeling by naming (or naming as labeling) a Kripkean defining. The first mode is a strong Kripkean labeling, and the second is a weak Kripkean labeling.

Why does Kripkean labeling work? Why do parties rely on naming as an act of classification in a deadlocked political dispute? Classifying means relating one event or entity to a larger class of events or entities and is therefore an act of broadening and generalizing. Naming involves the opposite process, the delineation and marking out of a specific event or entity from a larger class of events or entities; it is thus an act of narrowing and specifying. Consequently, classification (and to a lesser extent, labeling) as generalization is more official and publicly oriented, whereas naming as specifying is more informal and privately oriented. On the whole, the state must engage in classification in order to link an event or entity officially to its rules and regulations. Law, for example, is the realm of general and public categories. State regulations and policies are expected to be generally applicable, and therefore relating one event or entity to a larger class of events or entities has important political implications and is thus a powerful political and public act. On the other hand, people need naming to establish social links and personal attachments.

I specifically use the terms *publicly oriented* and *privately oriented* and not *public* and *private*, as both labeling and naming can take place in public as well as in private, and can also be used publicly as well as privately. Their difference is their orientation. As explained above, labeling, and to a greater extent classifying, is more official and functions more on the organizational and institutional level: in an organization-to-organization, person-to-organization, or organization-to-person context. Thus, I claim that labeling is publicly oriented. Naming, on the other hand, is more informal and functions more on the person-to-person or persons-to-persons level. It involves intimacy, albeit mass intimacy at times. Thus, it is privately oriented. Names are essentially private and supposedly mark the personal space where negative liberty reigns and politics has no say. So, and as demonstrated below, classifying is potentially more contestable and political than naming and hence more likely to cause political deadlock. Consequently, sophisticated political entrepreneurs wishing to unravel political deadlocks can try to bypass an insoluble political contestation over classifying an event by resorting to the more informal act of naming. They can try to imprint a novel name on the common sense (strong Kripkean labeling) or harness an existing, informal, popular name to achieve the more official act of classifying (weak Kripkean labeling). This can be used to sidestep a deadlock. A successful outcome involves labeling by naming. A case in point was the naming of the summer 2006 events in Israel "the Second Lebanon War." What had been nameless and without classification following an unsettled political debate subsequently became named—using weak Kripkean labeling—and then classified (an event could hardly be named the Second Lebanon War unless it is a war).

But we should also note that neither naming nor labeling can be arbitrary since they are governed by epistemic criteria. As naming is more privately oriented and informal, it is less strict and its rules more fuzzy and flexible. But, to take root in the public common sense, a name cannot be arbitrary. It must fit the context its articulators seek to influence. A name can hegemonize the public common sense or convention when and only when its articulators seek its compatibility and resonance with existing conventions and the current context (context here refers to the amalgam of objective, material, and structural conditions [material factors] and the subjective or intersubjective processes of analyzing, understanding, and evaluating those conditions [ideal factors]). With all due respect to George Orwell and newspeak,[6] seldom do we find social and political contexts (and the conditions are extreme) in which "War is peace. Freedom is slavery. Ignorance is strength" (Orwell 1961, 17, 87). We see this below in the case of Israel's naming of the Second Lebanon War.

Definitions

The academic equivalent of labels and names is definition. The academic equivalent of labeling and naming is defining. The academic world delineates concepts and attaches meaning to them by defining them. Academia takes definitions seriously and sees defining as a necessary and fundamental research phase. For a definition to be academically accepted, it needs to be exhaustive and exclusive. Then the definition will be seen as accurate in the sense of covering all cases and phenomena relevant to the research and excluding all that are irrelevant. Concept definitions should also provide the foundation for research and hence be operationalizable, since operationalization is what enables us to collect, measure, and compare data and even repeat a study as required. Definitions enable us to work with colleagues and communicate our work to them. When the categories and concepts that we work with are defined accurately, our studies and theories are meaningful. That is, although definitions are more precise than labels and although they operate in different arenas, they have a similar function. Labels and definitions thus converge.[7]

The convergence of labels and definitions indicates that the same set of questions that were raised regarding the public and political attachment of meanings to concepts is also relevant to the attachment of meaning to academic definitions. Insofar as political concepts are contested, they will have several legitimate *academic* definitions inasmuch as they will have several legitimate *public* meanings. One of the reasons there are so many definitions for different concepts in academic literature is that they are contested. The next section explores the range of definitions of the concepts of democracy and security. But, first, a quick teaser of the discussion below to explain my argument in brief. It is legitimate and reasonable to define democracy structurally or normatively, as liberal or electoral, as elitist or participatory, and so on. And academia is no different than the public and political arenas. The same is true for the concept of democratization, with its many meanings and definitions. The definitions of democracy and democratization are linked: If democracy is defined in terms of election structure, division of power, and checks and balances, then democratization is conceptualized as building these structures, that is, as focusing on the formal, procedural, and structural. Policy scholars take this conceptualization as an invitation to study state apparatuses in "old" or institutional politics. If, on the other hand, democracy is conceptualized as a culture and morality of the type that creates a civic community, then democratization is conceptualized as constructing that community through the socialization and dissemination of democratic values in order to encourage the emergence of a democratic society and culture (mostly by empowering domestic agents of political and social transformation in the target country). In this case, policy scholars consider this conceptualization to be an invitation to focus on the social and individual levels and try to construct a civil society of informed, involved, and participating citizens. These two views are, of course, familiar and the basis of legitimate disagreements (Bridoux and Kurki 2014).

The interesting point is how these disagreements are approached in academia and less so the acknowledgment that there are definitional disagreements, since these are basically too obvious and too stark to be overlooked or ignored. Instead, two different and overlapping questions seem to be important and interesting. The first is where these definitional disagreements occur; the second is what their basis is. Regarding the first question, of where such disagreements are located in scholarly discussion, there are two possible answers: Definitional disagreements may be located at the methodological layer of the definition that the criterion of "operationalization" establishes. Alternatively, the definitional disagreements can occur in the more substantive layer that is concerned with the ontological nature of the defined phenomenon and is expressed and institutionalized in the criteria of exhaustiveness and exclusiveness. This is the layer that gives the concept its boundaries and makes the definition accurate. It allows us to determine which cases are classed under the heading of the concept studied and which fall outside of it.

As for the question of the source of the definitional disagreements, this question overlaps with the question of location but goes deeper than it and also has two possible answers. The first answer, which addresses the source of the disagreements, is that the disagreements, which are at the operationalization layer, are caused by inaccurate and flawed scientific procedures or technical and methodological errors. They can therefore easily be corrected. The second answer is that the definitions are different because they are based on different and unreconciled normative and ideological issues. In other words, the plethora of definitions used by the academic world is both legitimate and unavoidable due to the essentially contested nature of the concepts that academia studies and employs. Definitional disagreements are here to stay, then, and contestedness is as legitimate and necessary inside academia as it is outside.

The answers to the two overlapping questions point to two academic parties. The first consists of adherents of the positivist philosophy of social science. The second consists of adherents to postpositivism, especially the interpretivists and critical theoreticians. Interpretivists and critical theoreticians are interested in issues of morality and ideology and are conscious of their constitutive role in conducting research. Theory, after all, "is always *for* someone and *for* some purpose" (Cox 1981, 128). If that is the case, then the positivists have failed to grasp correctly the contestedness in which social reality and social research are embedded. They consequently confine themselves to strict and rigid bounding practices, which generate definitions that fixate concepts with particular meanings. They deny the essential contestedness of the concepts they study and use and thus accept their own definitions in a way very similar to how fixated public conventions are accepted. Positivists may fuss over the technical and methodological questions of definitions, but they fail to subject them to moral scrutiny (for a similar argument, see Hobson and Kurki 2011). They may ponder whether to use the Polity, Freedom House, or Transparency International index or to combine the three indexes in a better data set, but they ignore the possibility that these indexes may be based on fairly rigid understandings of democracy. Polity, for example, is mainly about democracy's structural features and therefore draws from structural understandings about it. Some positivist theoreticians may therefore find themselves unwittingly sacrificing their cultural understanding of democracy before the altar of structural measurement simply to meet the blind demand for definitional operationalization. Such dogmatic positivism may result in internal incoherency. This happened with William Dixon's version of democratic peace theory when he used structural indicators to test his normative theory (1994, 21; see also Ish-Shalom 2013, 58–59).

Interpretivists and critical theoreticians, on the other hand, do appreciate the contested nature of political concepts and the irreconcilable nature of definitional disagreements. They see that disagreement and contestation essentially stem from ideological and normative differences. Going back to one of the focuses of this book, democracy and democratization, critical theory understands what positivism can only fail to understand. The different academic definitions of democracy and democratization are firmly grounded in different normative and ideological groundwork. The minimalist structural definition of democracy is embedded in a conservative skepticism regarding human faculties, according to which it is not rationality that drives human action but a mix of perennial desires, instincts, and communal traditions; a mix that is extrarational and compels human beings to strive for power (more on that below). The normative and cultural definition of democracy is more comprehensive and based on a liberal optimism about human rationality. This liberal optimism conceives human beings as rationally driven creatures and the locus of indivisible civic rights. The normative and cultural definition of democracy therefore centers on the concepts of participation, deliberation, and rights and seeks to extend citizens' political participation (more on this below). Academic definitions are therefore intrinsically and unavoidably constituted on normative and ideological groundwork (as are their public conceptualizations).

The next chapter demonstrates these theoretical insights by offering a conceptual analysis of democracy and security and introducing the notion of semantic fields and its relevance to our discussion.

2 ✦ Essentially Contested Concepts

Democracy and Security

When we use concepts in academic work, we are expected to provide definitions. Definitions are what sets the boundaries of concepts, separating them from each other and making them identifiable and researchable. The boundaries of concepts are not set by academia alone. As Ian Hacking argued, the world does not come to us classified, it is we human agents who classify it (1999; see also Adler and Bernstein 2005, 295). Albeit less formally, every day everyone sets boundaries for concepts by tagging, labeling, categorizing, naming, and so on. These bounding practices all help people to differentiate concepts and make them appropriate tools for reaching out to and coping with phenomena, events, processes—in other words, the world. Without bounding practices, reality would seem even more chaotic and less manageable than it is. There is a catch, however. In the social world, definitions (and other bounding practices) involve rounding and bounding that which is unrounded and unbounded. In the social world, things do not fall neatly into human-made concepts. Boundaries are fuzzy at best. Social objects are connected by comparable features and differentiated by distinctive features. Therefore, defining involves the arbitrary delineation of social objects, including phenomena and processes. Definition also involves inflating the importance of some differences and distinguishing some phenomena and processes (rounding). Definition also undermines and even fails to consider the relevance of all existing differences, thus bringing together various other phenomena and processes (bounding). That is the only way for definitions (as well as categories, labels, tags, and names) and the concepts they bound and construct to be possible in the social world.

The questions now are, first, how does the definer, or any other concept bounder, manage to bound and round that which is unrounded and unbounded, and second, what are the implications of this act of rounding and bounding? The answer to these two questions concerns Gallie's framework of essentially contested concepts.[1] There is a gap between our need for bounding and the impossibility of actually doing so, at least regarding the social world. Nevertheless, there is an attempt to bridge this gap. In academia, we learn how to bound concepts by defining them and are taught how to define concepts rigorously and methodologically. But rigorous methodology can only take us so far, and bridging this gap calls for an extramethodological mechanism to help us sort and filter features of target phenomena, events, and processes. This process of sorting and filtering permits us to inflate the importance of certain differences while undermining and even ignoring other features in order to bound and round phenomena, events, and processes, and harness them in human-made concepts. This extramethodological mechanism consists of a priori normative, ontological, and epistemological assumptions. These assumptions are also the building blocks of ideological thought. In other words, there can be no bounding (using whatever bounding practice), and no concept, without ideological inclination and normative conviction. And it is the a priori assumptions that embed concepts within normative foundation, making them essentially contested. Thus although some of us may see them as razor sharp, objective and neutral, our definitions are actually the interpretative meeting point of empirical observation, experience, and moral commitment. And even though the more popular lay methods of bounding, including labeling, tagging, and naming, that one tends to find outside academia are less methodologically rigorous, they are also efforts to bridge the same gap while encountering these same fuzzy boundaries so prevalent in the social world.

And there is a related theoretical framework: the semantic field. The idea of a semantic field is that concepts are actually configured assemblages of words and concepts associated with a specific subject (Hobson 2015, 37). The idea of semantic field recalls Michael Freeden's observation that no single concept has a viable meaning in itself. Political concepts only acquire meaning, viability, and political significance in the context of a whole configuration of other political concepts (Freeden 1996, 75–91). Hence, we should not discuss a concept, be it democracy or security, in isolation, but as part of an assemblage of concepts. To optimize results, the correct level of analysis should address not just the concept alone, but the entire conceptual assemblage. In the case of democracy, this assemblage includes liberal democracy, social democracy, direct democracy, and so on, what

David Collier and Steven Levitsky call democracy with adjectives (1997). In the case of security, the assemblages will include international security, national security, human security, global security, social security, and so forth. This becomes clearer still when we move a step up the ladder from concepts to theories. Every theory of democracy or security is constituted by a different assemblage and has a different semantic field. Thus, no less than theoretical apparatuses, these theories are forms of political thought, which, as Freeden defined, are configurations of decontested political concepts arranged together, with each conferring meaning on the others and gaining meaning from them (Freeden 1996, 2).

The two theoretical frameworks of essentially contested concepts and concepts as a semantic field have the same starting point but make their way in different directions, only to finally meet and account for each other. Take, for example, democracy. Democracy as an essentially contested concept and democracy as a semantic field have similar starting points in that both argue that the concept of democracy is embedded in some sort of multiplicity. The two theoretical frameworks point in different directions in the sense that, as an essentially contested concept, democracy is a single concept and the multiplicity relates to its multiple definitions and conceptions. To discuss democracy as a semantic field involves taking apart the singularity of the concept and arguing that the concept is itself multiplicity, that is, actually an assemblage of several derivative concepts such as legitimacy, rule of law, representation, popular sovereignty, and so on. And these two theoretical frameworks meet and account for each in the sense that one source for the essential contestedness of democracy is the multiplicity of possible and legitimate configurations of the concepts that are related to democracy. This multiplicity is the outcome of (1) the different concepts that can be assembled and (2) the way that concepts associated with democracy bestow meaning on each other. And it is a two-way road, because the essential contestedness of democracy is also what makes possible the varied ways of assembling different concepts and conceptions (different semantic fields) into one configured concept—democracy. What this means is that the essential contestedness of democracy and democracy as a semantic field are constitutively interrelated and jointly constitute the concept and *phenomenon* of democracy. The same applies to security and other concepts.

This view of concepts as semantic fields has another implication. Let's take democracy again as an example. The concept of democracy not only comprises other derivative concepts, it itself is related to other concepts to form other semantic fields.² It is not only that concepts such as governance, pluralism, accountability, legitimacy, popular sovereignty, emancipation, representation, and political rights assemble to form this or that conception and theory of democracy or this or that semantic field of democracy. Democracy is related to other concepts such as peace (and/or) war, free trade, institutions both domestic and international, stability, alliances, and security, and thus forms part of different semantic fields at least some of which belong to international studies. Later, I argue that it is not so easy, and may even be impossible, to distinguish neatly between democracy as a semantic field that is configured by derivative concepts and democracy as a derivative concept that is derived from other distinct semantic fields. In a sense, the social world is one big semantic field, and our analytical task of cutting through it and rounding and bounding (defining) from it distinct and identifiable concepts may be both methodologically and heuristically crucial, yet a senseless Sisyphean ontological labor.

Democracy

Democracy is both an essentially contested concept and a semantic field. Etymologically, *democracy* is a relatively simple word. It comes from the Greek and means "rule by the people" (so its meaning is close to the word *republic*, which comes from the Latin and means "of the people"). But the definition of democracy as "rule by the people" does not go far enough. It leaves the concept shrouded in mystery and fuzziness: What does saying that "the people rule" mean? What domains do the people rule? What mechanisms can and should the people rule by? What is the normative foundation and justification for the people's rule? What are the conditions of rule by the people, and what are the limitations of that rule? Despite all the rhetorical potency of Abraham Lincoln's phrase "of the people, by the people, for the people," we are still left with definitional questions.

It should come as no surprise, then, that when Gallie penned his seminal article on essentially contested concepts, democracy was one of his paradigmatic examples. Gallie noted that democracy fulfills all the conditions of an essentially contested concept: (1) It is appraisive or evaluative. (2) It is internally complex because it contains different principles and values, such as majority rule, equality, and active participation. (3) Its internal complexity allows differentiation of ranking; that is, its complexity creates a hierarchy of principles and values with greater or lesser importance for defining an entity as a democracy. (4) The concept is open, in that it allows the standard used to decide whether a polity is a democracy to be changed. (5) The concept can be used to defend one's own state as democratic or attack other states as undemocratic. (6). It can be attributed to a host of historical exemplars, such as Athens and the First French Republic. (7) It is possible that debates about the nature of democracy do not help to disperse the fuzziness of the concept but rather increase its vagueness, its contestedness (Gallie 1956, 183–87; Kurki 2010). Simply put, defining democracy is not just a methodological act but an act grounded in normative commitments and political struggle. Or, with reference to the conditions specified here that stress the political essence of essential contestedness, defining democracy implies that there are multiple meanings—or conceptions—of a concept, at least some of which are reasonable and legitimate, and all of which are grounded in a distinct normative groundwork and are potential sources of political disagreement and contestation.

Democracy indeed has several reasonable and legitimate definitions and conceptions, and it is also a semantic field and an assemblage and configuration of several other concepts. Democracy can be conceptualized as participatory, deliberative, elitist, socialist, anarchical, cosmopolitan, and so forth (Collier and Levitsky 1997), and it can be the assemblage of such related concepts as governance, pluralism, accountability, legitimacy, popular sovereignty, emancipation, representation, and political rights. The next two sections will analyze the concept of democracy, first as an essentially contested concept and then as a semantic field.

There are several broad understandings of democracy, two of which dominate contemporary discourse. Each of these understandings stems from a different normative worldview, is based on a specific conception or definition of democracy, and is distinct from other bordering concepts, such as dictatorship, liberalism, or popular sovereignty. Each conception informs a different theory of democracy that explains, analyzes, or justifies the workings of democracy. I will start with the two dominant understandings and then analyze some of the other representative ones.

The first prevailing understanding combines several distinct conceptions and theories of democracy, including the normative and cultural conceptions and the deliberative and participatory theories of democracy. It is easy to overlook the commonalities between deliberation and participation.

When studying democracy simply as a political mechanism, one can argue that these theories are in conflict. Thus, Diana Mutz (2006) sees the demands for participation and deliberation as two opposing and conflicting demands. Widening participation may result in deteriorating conditions for deliberation and thus undermine its quality. Mutz argues that waiting for valuable, meaningful, and useful deliberations may require limiting participation and conducting discussions in limited circles of educated and politically motivated citizens, that is, elite deliberations. But once we examine the theories conceptually, delving into the conceptions and definitions that ground them, we find fundamental similarities. First, all of them emphasize individual citizens and their society—not the political system and the regime. Second, these theories do not settle for procedures and structures, and they all expect democratic norms and a democratic culture. Among other things, these expectations imply the consolidation of political rights, tolerance, openness, and participation, as well as the internalization of a sense of civic responsibility (see, for example, Pateman 1970; Mansbridge 1970; Barber 1984; de-Shalit 1997; Elster 1998; Habermas 1998; Dryzek 2002).

Thus, the normative and cultural definition of democracy is far-reaching and based on an optimistic and liberal view of human rationality. This definition sees human beings as rationally driven creatures. They don't lack emotions, desires, instincts, or communal bonds, but these are largely controlled by rationality and rational calculations, and this restraint includes controlled political behavior. Following the Enlightenment tradition, the rational individual is seen as the locus of indivisible civic rights and the best judge of her own interests and preferences. When understood normatively and culturally, democracy is based on participation and rights and seeks to widen the scope of political deliberations and thus extend the meaning of democracy.

The second leading understanding of democracy is narrower in its expectations of the citizenry and how it conceptualizes democracy. It combines the formal and procedural conception of democracy together with the elitist and structural theories of democracy. It tends to understand democracy in relatively minimalist terms (see, for example, Schumpeter 1962; Lippmann 1955; Przeworski 1999). A regime is democratic when it passes a certain structural threshold and has free, fair, open elections, autonomous branches of government, a division of power, and checks and balances. This precludes the tyrannical concentration of power in the hands of a small, unresponsive elite.

The minimalist structural definition of democracy stems from a conservative skepticism regarding human faculties. Joseph Schumpeter targeted what he called the classical theory of democracy, which he criticized for being based on an overly optimistic worldview and an unrealistic and utopist understanding of human nature (1962, 270). For Schumpeter and other elitist theoreticians of democracy, it is not rationality that drives human action, but a mixture of perennial desires, instincts, and communal traditions. This mixture is extrarational and compels humans to compete for power. Human beings are driven by what the great realist theoretician Hans Morgenthau called *animus dominandi* (1946, 191–96). And indeed, realism shares with conservatism and the elitist theory of democracy various fundamental and grounding ontological, anthropological, and normative assumptions (Ish-Shalom 2006b).

There are two major consequences of the conservative understanding that humans are arational (even irrational) power-seekers. The first is that because everyone seeks power, social and political organizations are in perpetual danger of destabilization. Among other things, this was the source of Aristotle's disdain for democracy, which he saw as a deviant version of the good polity (2009, 8). It was also why the great nineteenth-century British conservative Edmund Burke feared the French Revolution (1987). He predicted that the natural and only consequence of casting away the old regime by a horde of revolutionaries would be political chaos and a reign of terror. There is a second and obverse consequence of a conservative understanding of humans as lacking rationality. This is the constant danger of a dictatorial concentration of power in the hands of individuals who manage to seize it—an elite that serves its own sectarian interests in an unresponsive, unaccountable way. The outcome is a dictatorship and not necessarily a benign one. The conservative solution to these dangers is to have minimal and structural democracy. On the one hand, through regular elections, democracy guarantees that no power will last forever and prevents the concentration of power in a dictatorship. On the other hand, by confining political participation to elections only (along with a commitment to the rule of law), democracy precludes political and social destabilization.

As mentioned, the liberal and conservative understandings of democracy are the most widely accepted nowadays, at least in the West. They are also seen by contenders as the benchmarks against which to develop alternatives. This is why the alternatives to the liberal and conservative understandings are most often challengers that try to chip away at the more popular conceptions of democracy. Thus, while the liberal understanding of democracy focuses on individuals and human rights, and the conservative understanding focuses on elites and structures, the socialist understanding expands democracy to classes and the economic field (Luxemburg 1961). This move is dual. First, it argues that political equality is not enough. Political equality demands that all citizens have equal voting rights and (some) access to policymaking. Being economically minded, socialist theories of democracy argue that without true economic equality, the liberal insistence on political equality is just an illusion. Look at the American democracy, where massive funding is needed to run a successful political campaign. This benefits rich politicians and heavy donors, who may gain access to the ears of decision-makers. The same is true for mass-media corporations, which also have more resources and a greater capacity to promote their preferences and interests. Economic inequality also offers greater leeway to organized interest groups, which lobby to tilt policies to their side. Those lacking in material resources are naturally left by the democratic wayside without real political representation for their preferences or interests. Noam Chomsky voiced this critique from an anarchical perspective (see below), arguing that "democracy is largely a sham when the industrial system is controlled by any form of autocratic elite, whether of owners, managers, and technocrats, a 'vanguard' party, or a state bureaucracy" (1970).

More radical socialist thinking seeks to democratize socioeconomic domains other than the political ones. For example, revolutionary syndicalism wanted to democratize the workplace and give an equal say to workers, arguing that only economic equality and economic democratization (including in the workplace) can produce a real and effective democracy where the preferences and interests of all enjoy equal representation and political efficacy. This socialist worldview challenges the liberal separation of politics and economy, resulting in a welfare social democracy (Meyer with Hinchman 2007; Cohen and Rogers 1983) or more radical models of democracy.

But whatever democratic model socialism advocates, government and hierarchy will have vital roles in it, especially as devices and instruments for changing the current socioeconomic order. Social democracy is meant to herald real freedom, resolve social conflicts, and produce harmony, but as a hierarchical structure it may well be based on domination and sometimes force and violence. Hence, anarchism parts ways with socialism and

Marxism; anarchists insist that the aim and method must match and if the aim is equality and freedom, the road may not involve force and domination. Moreover, anarchists fear that even a benign elite will be corrupted by power and try to secure it. Anarchism argues that where there is rule there is self-interested abuse of power. In other words, wherever government exists, by definition so does dictatorship. This applies to socialist and Marxist democracy no less than capitalist representative democracy. The anarchist sees electoral and representative democracy as no more than a mechanism that gives popular legitimacy to a regime that serves the power and interests of property holders and power wielders (Chomsky 1970). Electoral and representative democracy also preserves adversarial society. Real democracy is anarchist democracy, which rejects notions of representation and advocates direct, participatory democracy in which sincere deliberation rules and consensual decisions are reached and inspired by communal voluntarism (Graeber 2002; on anarchism and world politics see Prichard 2010, 2012).

Other perspectives challenge other facets of the prevailing two understandings of democracy. For example, the individualistic drive of liberalism is challenged by the communitarian visions of democracy. Not surprisingly, some communitarian understandings of democracy come from non-Western traditions. Bhikhu Parekh, for example, who is an Indian-born British political theoretician and member of the House of Lords, criticizes the individualist assumption of liberalism as a culturally specific Western product, and as such not necessarily having universal moral appeal (1992; see also Bell's [2006] Confucian model of democracy). Parekh maintains that a culturally adjusted democracy should take multiculturalism more seriously and facilitate other, more culturally sensitive, models of democracy. He argues that democracy should not necessarily be based on representing individual interests and maintains that the antagonistic individual has become an idée fixe in this Western-based model. In non-Western polities, which are based on communitarian cultures, democracy can be less adversarial, more harmonious, and more representative of community preference and local cultural sensitivities. Such a democracy can follow the multicultural thrust, basing representation and popular sovereignty on collectives and communities.

The last understandings of democracy surveyed here fundamentally challenge the state and the state system as we know it. Cosmopolitan democracy challenges the assumption, which is almost taken for granted, that democracy should be confined to the modern state. The communitarian and structural (conservative) understandings of democracy normatively accept the state as the political embodiment of the national community. The liberal and many variants of the socialist understandings accept the state as a necessary political tool for realizing, maintaining, and distributing common goods.[3]

Cosmopolitan democracy looks beyond the confines of the state. The normative gist of democracy is that all individuals have the right (and responsibility) to be involved in shaping the decisions and policies that affect their lives. This norm is commonly translated into the "all affected" principle: the people who are affected by a decision have the right to be involved (directly or through representation) in making that decision. The common (almost natural) assumption is that our lives are most affected by the political unit of the state (along with some substate units, such as the city). Hence, it seems obvious that voting rights belong to citizens, not to foreigners, and that the state borders should also mark the borders of suffrage. What could be more obvious than that?

The cosmopolitan response to this is: could there be anything *less* problematic than this assumption? Consider environmental policies or law-enforcement policies, for a moment. In our increasingly globalizing world, the outcome of these policies is borderlessness. There are no boundaries to environmental hazards or unchecked crime organizations that prey mercilessly on citizens regardless of borders. The transnational impact of national policies is even more dramatic in the case of great powers, including economic powers. When the United States or European economies falter, the effect is not a ripple but an economic tsunami that hits other countries. When the United States announces its national security policy, the results are felt around the world. Therefore, how can the "all affected" principle justify state borders as the borders of suffrage? In our globalizing and dynamic world, it seems unrealistic to confine democracy to the state. This is the argument of cosmopolitans such as David Held (2010) and Daniele Archibugi (2008),[4] who argue that true and legitimate democracy can only exist on the global level.

Cosmopolitans believe that true democracy should be global, but that does not necessarily mean that the state should be rejected in favor of a cosmopolitan polity. Many cosmopolitans fear that a polity without states would be a cold, monstrous bureaucracy, so detached from its citizens that, without states to restrain it with checks and balances, it could develop into a frightful, global Leviathan. Held therefore argued (2010) that the global world should be organized as a multilevel framework where different polities crosscut each other's borders, and where cities, regions, states, and the whole world form a multilayered, decentralized democracy where everyone has what he calls "multilevel citizenship." This, he argues, would be the only democracy befitting the modern globalized world and modern (or postmodern) individuals with multiperspective identities.

To summarize the above: we have examined the normative groundworks that inform and constitute various understandings and conceptualizations of democracy. Each conceptualization has a specific normative groundwork, and hence the definitions of concepts are not objective, neutral derivatives of empirical and verified reality. Definitions are, rather, interpretative meeting points of empirical observations and moral commitments. As a consequence, they are essentially contested. Definitions are heuristic bounding devices that help delineate empirical phenomena and categories. They are thus crucial springboards for research. But, as we saw, these delineations are no less morally based than empirically founded. This is true for many of the concepts we define and use in the social sciences, and democracy is no different.

But democracy is not just an essentially contested concept. Every conception of democracy is interwoven with other derivative concepts, and each morally grounded (and essentially contested) conception of democracy configures and locates democracy within a distinct semantic field. Note too that semantic fields not only operate by relating democracy to other concepts, but also contrast it with other concepts or to their counterconcepts (Hobson 2015, 37). Semantic fields thus work on two prongs. On the one hand, they form a network of concepts that is based on similarities, sharedness, and family resemblance. On the other hand, they separate concepts by establishing delineations based on differences and contrasts. For example, the semantic fields of democracy indicate not only what democracy is, but also what it is not; and what democracy is not varies between the different semantic fields.

The normative and cultural understandings of democracy link democracy to normative concepts such as rights, tolerance, and openness. These norms (and others) then become part of the semantic field of democracy. So we cannot understand democracy without these norms, and we cannot understand democracy without conceptually relating it to these normative concepts. The same is true for deliberation, which becomes not only a necessary political activity, but a necessary derivative concept, like participation. Participation relates democracy to active citizenry, deliberation relates it to rationality and reasoning (and reasonableness), and both relate it to civic responsibility,[5] as both an expectation from citizens and an inevitably derivative concept. Rationality and reasonableness in turn can link democracy to enlightenment and optimism and surely to the concepts of progress and liberalism. Thus, democracy is enveloped by a rich semantic field of varied concepts, making it not only essentially contested but also conceptually networked and located. This also shows us which concepts do not belong in democracy's semantic field and, therefore, what democracy is not. Surely dictatorship and totalitarianism do not belong to the semantic field of democracy. In a sense, they are the conceptual "other" of democracy, and probably the same goes for conservatism and pessimism.

The structural understanding of democracy has lower expectations of the citizenry. As noted before, the underlying attitude is one of disbelief and skepticism, and it is indeed skepticism that is interwoven with democracy conceptually in its semantic field—skepticism and the concept of power. Democracy is the skeptic's mechanical antidote for the dictatorial aspirations that motivate individuals, Morgenthau's *animus dominandi*. It also counteracts dictatorial aspirations by offering a structure of checks and balances and elections. I have already analyzed this view and used it to show the normative groundwork underpinning democracy as an essentially contested concept. We saw how the normative groundwork creates a uniform and coherent conceptualization of democracy. I now want to highlight the multiplicity within the unitary form of democracy. These threads can now all be seen not only as political acts, practices, beliefs, and values, but also as concepts. As concepts, they are interwoven and configured as a semantic field. And the same is true for conservatism and elitism, which I analyzed as political ideologies, and with democracy form a conceptual triangle that distinguishes the structural understanding of democracy from the comparable triangle of democracy, progress, and liberalism.[6] This structural understanding contrasts the concept of democracy not only with dictatorship and totalitarianism, but also with many of the concepts, such as participation and deliberation, that form the backbone of the normative semantic field of democracy. According to the structural understanding, democracy is not participation and deliberation—it works purposefully and structurally against them.

The same is true for the other understandings of democracy analyzed above: The socialist understandings of democracy relate it to such concepts as equality, welfare, and syndicalism, and interest groups and capitalism can loom large as the conceptual "others," conceptually indicating what democracy is not and which social phenomena should be struggled against. Accordingly, socialists see capitalist democracy as a political malfunction and conceptual oxymoron. Democracy thus forms a triangle with socialism and equality (or egalitarianism). At the same time, this conceptual relating of democracy to equality can be used by ideological opponents (mainly libertarians) to criticize socialist understandings of democracy as forming a semantic field lacking any internal coherence. For these critics, the socialist semantic field of democracy includes such concepts as dictatorship and, even more problematically, totalitarianism. It is democracy emptied of all conceptual clarity and normative substance.

To some extent, this criticism, based on the conceptual analysis offered by the semantic field perspective, can also be shared by anarchists. Anarchists believe that democracy should be detached from the organizing principles and concepts of hierarchy and domination (which are related to the semantic field of dictatorship) and should be positively equated conceptually with harmony, directness, consensus, community, voluntarism, and mutualism (which libertarians see as clearly belonging to the semantic field of totalitarianism). In triangular terms, democracy is linked to anarchism and consensus. Community also plays a central role in the semantic field of the communitarian understanding of democracy, combined with the concepts of culture and multiculturalism. According to this understanding, democracy forms a conceptual triangle with communitarianism and multiculturalism. Consequently, it also becomes conceptually detached from individualism and contestation, expelling the two—which may be conceptual necessities in the liberal semantic field of democracy—from the semantic field of democracy. And according to the cosmopolitan understandings of democracy, the semantic field of democracy is necessarily linked to such concepts as cosmopolis, humanity, globalism, and multilevel citizenship. The cosmopolitan semantic field of democracy contrasts it with borders and national partisanship. Here democracy forms a conceptual triangle with cosmopolitanism and humanity.

Note, though, that these triangles lead us to yet another observation. The triangles are not semantic fields of democracy. The two accompanying concepts are not derivative concepts of democracy. In these triangles, democracy itself is the derivative of other concepts, a conceptual member of various other semantic fields. Democracy and elitism are concepts in the semantic field of conservatism, democracy and progress are derivatives of liberalism in its own semantic field, democracy and equality are essential conceptual members in the semantic field of socialism, and so on. Thus, democracy (and other concepts) can be a semantic field in its own right but also (simultaneously) an integral semantic organ in other conceptual fields. No concept is an island to itself, and no semantic field is fenced or bounded.

And if we consider the democratic peace theories, we are reminded that the (generic) concept of democracy is similarly related causally and conceptually to such paradigmatic IR concepts as war and peace. Namely, what we learn when we study essentially contested concepts alongside semantic fields is that, in a sense, the social world is a single, all-inclusive semantic field, and that our analytical task of cutting through it and carving (defining) distinct concepts from it is both methodologically and heuristically crucial and a senseless Sisyphean labor.

Security

The concept of security has been widened, deepened, broadened, extended, reconstructed, but it is still as elusive as ever. Though it is a fundamental concept for understanding social reality and constituting the discipline of IR, security has no consensual definition (Buzan and Hansen 2009, 8; Peoples and Vaughan-Williams 2010, 1). While this may be disappointing, it is not so surprising considering that security is an essentially contested concept. The lack of a consensual definition is a constitutive and definitional feature of being an essentially contested concept. To reiterate briefly, the three politically attuned criteria for a concept to be essentially contested are these: (1) The concept must have several reasonable legitimate meanings. (2) There must be irresolvable (actual or impending) disagreements over the appropriate meaning of the concept. (3). On the way to becoming actual, the disagreements are important enough for certain interlocutors to become politicized. As we see below, security indeed fulfills these conditions and therefore qualifies as an essentially contested concept.

Let me be clear on this. The dictionary definition of security is relatively straightforward. It means the absence of threats. However, that definition is good only as far as it goes, and like the etymological understanding of democracy as "rule by the people," it really does not go very far. As the wideners, deepeners, and extenders saw, defining security as an absence of threats leaves us with a mass of unresolved fundamental questions: Who is secured and by whom? How are they secured? And no less importantly, what are they secured against? When discussing security, it is these questions we must answer, making this a comprehensive phenomenon and concept that must be studied and understood in all its dimensions.[7] In other words, saying that security is the absence of threats tells us very little if we are seeking a complete grasp of the phenomenon and concept of security. A comprehensive understanding of security not only involves the facticity of the phenomenon, but also the a priori normative groundwork with which to study the facticity and give it meaning by defining it as a concept and a category for analytical study. Thus, a comprehensive understanding of the concept of security demands no less than understanding and analyzing its essential contestedness.

There is another crucial point for understanding the essential contestedness of the concept of security: just like democracy, security forms semantic fields and is part of other semantic fields. Therefore, security is an assemblage and configuration of several other concepts, and as argued already, it can also be understood, following Freeden, as configurations of decontested political concepts arranged together, with each conferring meaning on the others and gaining meaning from them (Freeden 1996, 2).

The following sections analyze security both as an essentially contested concept and as a semantic field, preparing the way for the end of the book, which analyzes how these two qualities should interrelate and form one semantic field.

As early as 1952, Arnold Wolfers described security as an ambiguous symbol and pointed the way to critical theoreticians who at a later stage identified security as an essentially contested concept (see, for example, Buzan 1983, 6; Smith 2005; Fierke 2007; Peoples and Vaughan-Williams 2010, 2). Wolfers should be recognized for his early observation of the difficulties of defining security. But declaring a concept essentially contested goes much deeper than just highlighting an ambiguity. It means delving into the heart of a concept, exploring the fundamental beliefs that constitute it, and understanding how inherently and necessarily constitutive those a priori, basic beliefs are. In fact, they are so inherently and necessarily constitutive that security is too elusive a concept to be conclusively and consensually definable, as it is shrouded in layers that are a priori and founded on moral commitments that can vary from one researcher to the next (Smith 2005, 28) and one theoretical camp to the next. Put differently, these a priori moral commitments constitute the researchers' understanding of security and are fundamental to the way theoreticians define security. It is the constitutive role of a priori moral commitments in defining security that underlies these three conditions, and each set of moral commitments informs and constitutes a different conceptualization of security such that each party attaches critical importance to its own conceptualization of security, insisting on its reliability and legitimacy.

One important caveat must be mentioned here. My purpose is not to offer a full survey of the security literature. This is beyond the scope of one chapter. My more modest goal is to demonstrate the essential contestedness of the concept of security by exploring the normative groundwork of each of the security schools. As discussed below, every categorization is an exercise in social construction, which is also true with regard to dividing theoreticians into schools and approaches. This should be borne in mind when delineating different security schools and approaches, even more so than with the approaches to democracy. However, the provisional analysis offered here contributes real insights into the essential contestedness of the concept of security and the normative groundwork that constitutes its conceptualizations and definitions. It thus establishes the basis for later arguments concerning the epistemological and methodological strategy of *zooming in, zooming out.*

I will begin the analysis with the most mainstream perspective of all: realism, a perspective that (especially in its neorealist variant) adamantly adheres to positivist objectivity. Next I move on to more novel and critical perspectives, which by virtue of their critical nature recognize and even enhance the role of morality in their understanding and conceptualization of security. These perspectives are critical security studies, human security studies, feminist security studies, and poststructuralist security studies. I aim to argue that one of the fundamental reasons for the differences between these security studies is their divergent normative groundwork.

Realist security studies have been the focus of criticism for the past two or three decades. Many critical theoreticians have targeted realism for being conservative and serving the status quo. Armed with Robert Cox's oft-quoted assertion that "theory is always *for* someone and *for* some purpose" (1981, 128), they link realist security studies with the powerful, arguing that the realist perspective serves the interests of the powerful and powerful states. Revising Cox, Ken Booth argues forcefully that "realism ('*for someone* and *for* some purpose') has been a theory *of* the powerful, *by* the powerful, *for* the powerful" (2007, 158). I have no qualms with this critique (see Ish-Shalom 2006b), but my intention here is to ground theory in a normative approach. And the realist security conceptualization is grounded in the ethics of consequentialism and its Weberian variant, the ethics of responsibility.[8] This is the ethics that judges morality by consequences, by how the consequences of acts affect the lives of the greatest possible number of people. It is not the lofty intentions or lives of individuals that count, but the actions whose results enhance the life prospects of the greatest numbers and diminish the sufferings of the multitudes. For realists, this is the only viable ethics in politics, especially international politics. The instrument for achieving this goal is international stability, which is attained by and between states through mechanisms such as alliances and the balance of power. Hence, security is statist and international, and realist security scholars cannot allow themselves to get involved in such issues as human security and economic development. Stephen Walt defined security and security studies as the "*study of the threat, use and control of military force*" (1991, 212). In Walt's definition, we can see the consequentialist's urge to focus narrowly on military force, since military force is what helps stabilize or destabilize great-power relations and world politics, and thus safeguard the lives of the greatest possible number of people. Walt cautions us that defining the field any other way "would destroy its intellectual coherence and make it more difficult to devise solutions to any of these important problems" (1991, 213). Note that while pollution, global warming, disease, child abuse, and economic recessions are important problems to ponder, the way forward is by concentrating our intellectual efforts on military force, the rest being simply derivatives of international stability.

The same consequentialist ethics drive Kenneth Waltz's interest in international stability and bipolarity, which are characterized not so much by peace as by the absence of war between the superpowers (Waltz 1979). Waltz also argues that well-intentioned statespersons will only harm international stability through chasing peace while applying categorical-imperative modes of administration (1959, 1, 190). It is on consequences, not intending and chasing, that Waltz, the arch-neorealist, judges the realities of world politics. Therefore, consequentialism and the Weberian ethics of responsibility are the normative groundwork of realist security studies and their definition of security.

Now this normative approach is not unreasonable. It has a long, prestigious heritage in moral philosophy, strong contemporary adherents, and a commonsensical appeal. However, it is far from the only normative approach, and it is morally unpersuasive to many security scholars. Foremost among is the group that established what became known as critical security studies (or the Aberystwyth school). Spearheaded by Booth and then Richard Wyn Jones, these scholars embraced another normative approach, namely Kantian-originated deontology. Deontology is best captured by the two famous formulations of the Kantian categorical imperative. The first formulation reads, "Act only according to that maxim by which you can at the same time will that it should become a universal law" (Kant 1969, 44). The second formulation reads, "Act so that you treat humanity, whether in your own person or in that of another, always as an end and never as a means only" (Kant 1969, 54). Both these maxims, and especially the second, counter the consequential logic that it is reasonable and permissible to sacrifice lives to save a greater number of lives. The willingness and permissibility of sacrificing the few for the many runs deep in conventional military reasoning and conventional security studies. However, this is impermissible according to deontologists and critical security scholars. Therefore, they reject the narrow, stability-prone realist security agenda. For Booth and his allies, the only way to secure the absence of threats—in other words security—is by advancing the Frankfurt school's agenda conceptualizing security as emancipation. According to Booth's definition,

> As a discourse of politics, emancipation seeks the securing of people from those oppressions that stop them carrying out what they would freely choose to do, compatible with the freedom of others. It provides a threefold framework for politics: a philosophical anchorage for knowledge, a theory of progress for society, and a practice of resistance against oppression. Emancipation is the philosophy, theory, and politics of inventing humanity. (2007, 112; italics removed)

Security involves not only the absence of military threats but a total transformation of life, political organization, and international order, so that people find themselves emancipated according to the general Kantian vision of autonomy and the Frankfurt school's mode of immanent critique (on immanent critique, see Levine 2012).

But this reasoning can be taken further. If the absence of military threat is an inadequate definition of security, and if security involves the total transformation of society and the emancipation of life, then a series of transformative measures is required. A group of scholars and practitioners have taken this insight seriously and conceptualized security as human security. This movement was begun by practitioners both inside and outside the United Nations' institutions (Buzan and Hansen 2009, 202–13). However, it quickly gained supporters in academia, such as Caroline Thomas and Peter Wilkin, who refined the conceptualization and grounded it in epistemic and normative commitments (Thomas and Wilkin 1999). If critical security scholars supplemented Kantian deontology with Frankfurt school criticism, human security scholars (aligned with development studies) complemented their Kantianism with the capability approach to ethics (see also Peoples and Vaughan-Williams 2010, 123). This approach, developed by Amartya Sen, who was joined by Martha Nussbaum and other philosophers, reoriented distributive justice toward the ethical imperative of ensuring people's (both individuals and communities) capabilities so they can function freely as agents.[9] As Thomas wrote, "Human security is about the achievement of human dignity which incorporates personal autonomy, control over one's life and unhindered participation in the life of the community" (2001, 162). The operative scheme of the capability approach is to provide and ensure those human and social capabilities that enable people to convert primary goods into an ability to achieve their chosen ends (Sen 2000, 74). In other words, human security scholars advocate the support of human and social capabilities that allow people to gain freedom and achieve agency. It is this ethical approach that serves as the groundwork for human security in its plea to eradicate global poverty. And, unsurprisingly, human security scholars find little in common with realist scholars of security (see Wilkin 2002).

It is in this approach to security that Freeden's observation that concepts gain meaning and viability as part of a whole conceptual configuration is most helpful. Security gains its meaning from the human with which it is assembled; likewise the human gains its meaning from the security to which it is attached in the conceptualization of human security. In a way, this is security with a human face, involving humans who can be purposeful agents because they are positively secured. It is almost senseless to talk about humanity without talking about security apprehended as human security (see especially Etzioni 2007); and it is meaningless to talk about security if it is not tied to humans as referent objects (both on the individual and the community levels). There is a stark difference between this assemblage and the international security of realist security studies, which define states as referent objects and conceptualize security in military terms and content. Barry Buzan and Lene Hansen aptly capture this conceptual phenomenon with their contention that security is a hyphenated concept (2009, 10)—for security to be meaningful, it must be hyphenated and assembled with a joining concept such as the human, the international, the global,[10] and so on.

The deontology of human security and critical security studies and the consequentialism of realism share a universalist drive. The two other approaches I will discuss run counter to the universalist drive in which deontology and consequentialism are rooted. The two approaches are feminist and poststructuralist security studies. Feminist security studies are grounded in the ethics of care developed by philosophers such as Carol Gilligan (1982), Susan Okin (1989), and Iris Marion Young (1981, 1986). The ethics of care rejects central suppositions and principles of modern political theory, as well as the ethics of rights. It challenges their emphasis on the principles of universality, autonomous rationality, and impartiality. In particular, ethics-of-care advocates reject the distinction deontologists make between rationality and emotionality, and the resultant attempt in modern moral philosophy to expel emotions, care, desires, sympathy, and empathy from the realm of moral reasoning. For ethics-of-care advocates, emotions, sympathy, and empathy are an inherent dimension of moral reasoning, and care is a constitutive element of morality and justice. Furthermore, excessive autonomy and individualism, leading to atomism, ignore the real and concrete social nature of human life. Concrete normative theory, that is, the ethics of care, must take all these precepts and observations into account, along with the real experiences of concrete people (see, for example, Robinson 1999).

We can see how the ethics of care provides the normative groundwork for feminist security studies. An example is Annick Wibben's *Feminist Security Studies*, in which she argues, "Staying attuned to varied everyday experience, through the telling of women's stories in this case, is central to feminists' resistance to abstraction. It provides a corrective to the generalizing and universalizing tendencies in traditional science that work to institute bias and obscure responsibility" (2011, 2). No wonder, then, that Wibben went on to develop a narrative approach to security.[11] For her, "Narratives are essential because they are a primary way by which we make sense of the world around us, produce meanings, articulate intentions, and legitimize actions" (2011, 2). It is the particularity of narratives that brings her to center the study of security around them. Narratives are the best means for capturing the real experiences of real people, along with their real desires, wants, and social relations.[12] Feminist security studies also focus mainly on women's experiences because women are marginalized in world politics and by mainstream and malestream security studies (see also Tickner 1988, 430; Hutchings 2008, 99). Narratives can also elicit empathy, which increases the potential for change and security, especially for those who are currently marginalized.

Poststructuralism goes further than feminism in its attack on the universality, autonomous rationality, and impartiality of modern moral theory.[13] This it does to such an extent that its thinkers question the core modern themes of subjectivity and foundationalism. This radical questioning leads to relativism, since poststructuralists eschew universal ideational schemes (or metanarratives, to use poststructural language), including morality, which they tend to see as a power-serving apparatus masquerading as benevolent universalism. Their moral relativism is closely linked to their epistemological antifoundationalism. This antifoundationalism is evident, for example, in arguments propounded by Jef Huysmans, who, following James Der Derian, gives up on the practice of defining: "Its main function [that of definition] is to identify the subject of research, to clarify for the reader what one is going to talk about. This act locates the text within a particular research agenda and identifies it by separating it from other understandings of security. In that sense one could argue that definitions operate as a rite of passage, a ritual of purification through which one makes the research a legitimate part of a body of literature and a research community" (1998, 230). Poststructuralist relativism, therefore, causes its adherents to shy away from the academic practice of defining.

However, as various scholars have rightly argued, poststructuralists do feel some degree of unease at their own moral relativism (for example, Steele 2013; Amoureux 2015; Lowenheim 2014). Consequently, in its search for a way out of its moral relativism, poststructuralism has taken an ethical turn (Smith 2005, 51; Wyn Jones 2005, 219). Some poststructuralists, such as David Campbell, have found Emanuel Levinas's thinking and his view of ethics as responsibility to the Other a suitable, nonfoundational, and ethical course of action. Campbell explains that Levinas shows him an ethics that does not dictate rules or maxims and is not founded on any reified notions of subjectivity. For Campbell, the helpful lesson offered by Levinas is "the recognition that *'we' are always already ethically situated; making judgments about conduct, therefore, depends less on what sort of rules are invoked as regulations, and more on how the interdependence of our relations with others are appreciated*" (1993, 93). This nonfoundationalist poststructural ethics spares Campbell and his fellow travelers from being charged with moral nihilism without their having to commit themselves to a structured system of moral rules and maxims. They can continue to celebrate resistance to power, violence, and oppression and conduct their deconstruction of security, war, hegemonic power, and other related concepts. And, as in the case of Huysmans, they can continue to do this without suggesting any foundational definitions of these concepts to their readers.

To summarize, this section has presented the various normative groundworks that constitute the different security schools. Each security conceptualization is grounded in a normative groundwork. The a prioricity of the normative assumptions morally commits theoreticians to their own conceptualization of security. As Steve Smith so aptly wrote, "The concept of security is therefore a battleground in and of itself" (2005, 57). And, as Michael Sheehan forecast, it is "likely to continue to be an intellectual and political battleground" (2005, 179). Security, then, fulfills the three conditions for being an essential contested concept.

We now turn to the analysis of security as a semantic field that reveals the multiplicity of concepts that are interlinked with the concept of security. Part of this multiplicity concerns the observation of Buzan and Hansen, quoted above, that security is a hyphenated concept (2009, 10) and that in order to be meaningful, security must be assembled with associated concepts such as the human, the international, and the global. But this observation does not cover the entire question of semantic fields. As we will see in the next section, concepts form part of the semantic fields of security not only when they are explicitly hyphenated to it.

Let us begin with the realist semantic field of security. The realist view links security to concepts such as the state, the states system, balance, stability, military, secrecy, threat, deterrence, power, force, and resources. It also links security to normative concepts such as the ethics of responsibility and consequentialism. In terms of emotional concepts, it is connected mostly with fear, and politicians know how to misuse this conceptual association to great effect in mobilizing support for security policies and, Copenhagen school scholars will add, for their general agenda. When an issue is conceptualized as security related, fear helps to remove it from the domain of normal politics, out of democracy's reach and into the domain of extreme instrumentality. Critical perspectives also add judgmental concepts like chauvinism, militarism, and masculinity to the realist semantic field of security. Security is thus left solely in the hands of the political and security elites. Any consultation with the concerns of the wider public will be considered inappropriate, destabilizing, and harmful to national security. This view appears to imply that democracy should be conceptualized narrowly to accommodate security. Moreover, explicating the realist semantic field of security helps to identify what security is not, and it is not what the other schools of security argue it must be: health, development, and environment. On the other hand, security is also not emancipation and hope, and it should definitely not be confused with participation and transparent deliberation.

Critical security studies tie security conceptually to a whole different semantic field. It is not stability or states that form security's semantic field, but concepts like the individual, emancipation, progress, and transformation. Hope is the primary emotional concept here, not fear, and normative concepts such as deontology and imperatives are more relevant to security's semantic field. Critical security scholars also argue that the effort to achieve security binds us to immanent criticism and the whole conceptual apparatus of the Frankfurt school, such as dialectics, emancipation, reason, reification, and culture. Security is not about the search for stability or the fortification of public and political lives, because fortifying the state and stressing secrecy can only lead to oppression and domination or the authoritarianization of the political. Security thus cannot be separated from democracy in its broadest conceptualization of participation and deliberation, that is, consulting the public reason and the concerns of individuals.

Human security shares some concepts with critical security studies, in particular the concept of emancipation conceptualized as freedom and autonomy. Yet by emphasizing the conditions for freedom and autonomy, human security introduces other concepts to the semantic field, especially distributive justice, primary goods, capabilities, agency, autonomy, and ends. It also links security with humanity, community, and participation and, by linking it with the capability approach, clarifies what security is definitely not: it is not poverty, whether domestic or global, relative or absolute, because poverty stifles the necessary conditions for freedom and autonomy and destroys the capabilities and agency of individuals. Poverty is thus insecurity par excellence. In democratic terms, human security is better suited to participatory conceptualizations of democracy because it is related to participation and the achievement of agency.

But the semantic fields of critical security and human security can also be criticized from more radical perspectives, for being excessively attached to rationality, imperatives, and universality. According to the feminist school, the semantic field of security should include emotional entities and concepts such as care, sympathy, and empathy. As we saw in Wibben's thinking, security is also related to narratives, experience, concreteness, desires, wants, and empowerment. Insecurity points to the conceptual Other of security, which is marginality, minority, and abstractness. Abstractness and its conceptual relation with universality and rationality leave power and decision-making capabilities in the hands of the traditional closed elite, which is, of course, masculine. Mainstream and malestream security conceptualizations are a handy instrument (not unlike securitization) for leaving women and other minorities outside the power circles of democracy. Masculine democracy that promotes national security is a democracy that ignores the concrete concerns and thus real security of women and other minorities. The result is indeed a masculine democracy, which equals nondemocracy and insecurity.

With poststructuralism, the semantic field of security grows even more removed from the concepts of universalism and rationality, to become a conceptual field that tries to evade concepts and their definitions altogether. It is actually a conceptual field that ignores its own existence. However, it remains an identifiable semantic field populated by concepts like relativism and antifoundationalism and probably also discourse, subjectivity, Other, and performativity. Security, like democracy, becomes a forceful tool of productive power (Barnett and Duvall 2005) that, with the aid of rituals, discursive practices, and performances (as practices and concepts), produces subjects who fail to recognize that they lack subjectivity and agency. And what in realism was the core emotional concept, namely fear, in poststructuralism becomes an instrumental concept that helps the state mobilize society against itself in a move that is ultimately dictatorial and even totalitarian. Once more security is an empty concept that fills political life with totalitarian content, and democracy is a mask hiding the most powerful form of agentless dictatorship.

We now have the resources to analyze security as a concept derivative from other concepts and position it in conceptual triangular structures within relevant semantic fields. Thus, in realist terms, security is bound together with elitism as part of the semantic field of conservatism; in critical security studies, it is bound with emancipation to form the semantic field of immanent criticism; in human security, it is attached to human autonomy as part of the ethics of capabilities; in the feminist conceptualization, security forms with care the conceptual triangular structure of feminism; and in poststructuralist conceptualization, security joins relativism; forming the conceptual triangular structure of postmodernism. These triangles reinforce the argument that semantic fields are intertwined and not fenced, and that they shape each other conceptually into wide, fuzzy, and undistinguished semantic fields. But here I want to introduce another twist in this argument, which highlights the immanent and unavoidable conceptual relationship between democracy and security and suggests that they have a different conceptual relationship in each conceptualization of security and democracy and each of their semantic fields. Realist conceptualizations of security are rooted in elitist and structural understandings of democracy, while in critical security studies and human security studies democracy can only be understood in its wider sense of participation and deliberation. And, of course, that is a two-way conceptual route in which the conceptualization of security stems from a certain understanding of democracy, and a given understanding democracy produces a concomitant conceptualization of security. The conceptualization of participatory and deliberative democracy cannot accept a national security dominated by elites and secrecy. The notion of elitist democracy is intertwined with national security in being attuned to the military and security apparatus.

Conclusions

Semantic field analysis and the theoretical framework of essentially contested concepts are not mutually exclusive. They in fact complement each other and provide a rich conceptual analysis of the social world. What is more, the two analytical perspectives account for each other constitutively. One source of a concept's essential contestedness is the multiplicity of the possible and legitimate configurations of its related concepts, namely the concept's plausible semantic fields. Similarly, it is the essential contestedness of a concept that allows it to be assembled into different semantic fields all referring to the same subject, and at least some of which relate to it reasonably and legitimately. And this is so, of course, for democracy and security, which are essentially contested and have many different semantic fields.

Together, these two analytical perspectives allow us to understand the all-inclusiveness of the social world—how social phenomena relate to the concepts that represent them mentally and how different essentially contested concepts are related through semantic fields, none of which is fenced. Different semantic fields are intertwined to mutually and conceptually form a single intertwined semantic field. In this sense, at least, the concepts representing social phenomena are inseparable from each other, and, arguably, so are the social phenomena themselves. Consequently, it indeed transpires that the act of defining, that is, academically bounding concepts and distinguishing them from each other, is both a heuristically and methodologically crucial task and a senseless Sisyphean ontological labor.

Bounding practices are essential not just in and for academia. They are also heuristically important for managing life in the social and political realms. Yet bounding practices are not necessarily the same as academic defining in all spheres. Especially in politics, bounding practices are different. I turn now to this aspect of conceptual politics. The next chapter empirically examines some of the discursive methods that politicians use to mobilize the essential contestedness of concepts and harness the conceptual features of essential contestedness and semantic fields, their purpose being that of carrying out an effective conceptual politics that involves politically constructing social reality.

3 ✦ The Essential Contestedness of Concepts and Politics

Concepts, those essential building blocks of our sociopolitical existence, are essentially contested, and academia has its own bounding practices—some reflexive, some less so—for managing that contestedness. Academic bounding practices, or definitions, strive to clarify the content of concepts by bounding them from one another while seeking to establish order within the conceptual realm. The success of these practices may be limited, but that is their aim. In the continuum between Gramsci and Habermas, academia tends toward Habermas. This is especially true for the more reflexive approaches. These approaches are supposedly open to the plurality of conceptions and the ideal of communicating across understandings. True to themselves, reflexive theoreticians aim to create an institutional and cultural environment as close as possible to the Habermasian ideal situation. They aim to use this environment not so much to establish a definitional consensus as to foster understanding over the sources of the difference in understandings and the limits of what is and is not legitimate. This is surely an ideal, and I will have more to say on this later. But the ideality of the academic world exists in stark contrast to the political world, which is driven by different motives and a different set of objectives, not least being to gain the upper hand in public struggles. Concepts are one of the tools for gaining the upper hand, and to follow Gramsci, they are an extremely efficient tool. To make concepts a tool, not to mention a weapon, politicians steer clear from definitions to embrace labeling, categorizing, naming, and the like. These are bounding practices that build on the essential contestedness of concepts and facilitate various politically advantageous tactics: (1) attaching fixated meaning to concepts to induce unreflexive action in the public, (2) increasing fuzziness and ambiguity of concepts to impede effective opposition, and (3) frequently combining (1) and (2) in order to empty the concept of meaning and, once it is vacuous, use it as a slogan or cliché to frame the common sense. As explained below, this tactic is especially attractive and politically effective in relation to concepts that are commonly seen as morally positive. Hence, democracy is often used this way in the political arena. These tactics transform concepts and their bounding into a tool for framing the common sense. Concepts thus also become the arena in which politicians vie with each other for success. This kind of politics is captured nicely by the notion of conceptual politics, defined by Christopher Hobson and Milja Kurki as "the ways in which contested concepts—like democracy—are interpreted, used, and fought over by actors, and how certain meanings and definitions come to influence real world phenomena" (2012, 3; italics removed). Accordingly, instead of the Habermasian ideal situation, what we often get is the Gramscian veiling situation. This chapter first delves into these Gramscian bounding practices and veiling situations and then analyzes their effects.

The Fighting of Summer 2006

In the summer of 2006, there was or was not a war in Lebanon. This is not an outrageous Baudrillardian statement. There was of course a fierce armed conflict, which claimed the lives of hundreds of people, both combatants and noncombatants, on both sides. But, in Israel, a fascinating public debate arose over the question of naming and labeling this event, a debate centering on the question, Was the fighting a war, or was it merely an extended military operation? The public debate that emerged was a civic struggle over the war, a political campaign that tried to make sense of the summer's events. The government labeled the fighting not a war and despite fierce opposition tried to leave the event in a fuzzy conceptual state.

What is so interesting about this public debate is that the stakes were not self-evident; or stated differently, what comprised the instrumental rationalities driving the debate were not obvious. The warfare had ended, so no one could claim there were security interests involved in defining it one way or the other. Economically speaking, the Israeli government had decided as soon as July 30, 2006, to pay compensation to Israelis harmed during the event, as would have been expected following a war (see also Israel Government 2006b). This decision did not resolve all legal consequences of declaring war, but it did go a long way in that direction, at least materially speaking. The government simply insisted on not labeling this warfare as war. Opposing the government stance was an array of parties, prominent among these being the bereaved families, who led a fierce struggle to label the warfare as war. This civic conflict, I claim, was a struggle over symbols important to the issues of status, political capital, and social prestige. On the one hand, the government attempted to limit its political loses. The outcome of the conflict was judged in Israel to be somewhere between a failure to secure an unequivocal victory and all-out defeat. It is one thing to fail in a limited conflict but quite another to lose a war. The government therefore had a political interest in labeling the violence as something other than war, since this affected the political price it would pay. Ipso facto, the political opposition had every political incentive to attach the label "war" and thus reap the political benefits of the government's failure in conducting the military campaign. The bereaved families had a different stake in the civic battle over labeling. In a nation where death in battle commands the highest respect, the families of the fallen, to secure for their loved ones the highest status in collective remembrance, needed to label the circumstances of death as a war rather than as a limited clash. Two camps thus faced each other in a political struggle over symbols and symbolic rewards.

But before analyzing in depth the civic struggle and political maneuverings, let us return to the warfare itself. On the morning of July 12, 2006, under cover of a diversionary rocket attack on two Israeli villages, Hezbollah conducted a surprise assault on an Israeli border patrol, killing three soldiers, wounding three more, and capturing two (who died soon after from wounds suffered in the attack). An Israeli tank that entered Lebanon in hot pursuit drove over a powerful bomb, killing all four crew members. Another Israeli soldier was killed trying to rescue the tank. The same day, the Israeli cabinet authorized "severe and harsh" retaliation against Lebanon (Israel Government 2006a). This decision was understandable given the gross violation of Israeli sovereignty. According to just war doctrine, Israel had just cause to go to war. However, the choice of the target for retaliation—the state and citizens of Lebanon—was strategically awkward and morally flawed. The perpetrator was not the state of Lebanon, but a substate actor with its own quarrels with the Lebanese government.[1] Israel's strategic reasoning was that devastating blows would force the Lebanese people to recognize Hezbollah's adventurism as a threat and that the Lebanese would pressure their government to assert sovereignty over southern Lebanon, end Hezbollah's rule, and maybe even smash Hezbollah. Yet none of the parties to which Israel assigned roles in its strategy—that is, the Lebanese people, their government, or Hezbollah—was willing (or able) to cooperate in this grand design. Soon, all-out warfare had erupted. The Israeli Air Force devastated southern Lebanon and parts of Beirut. Hezbollah pounded northern Israel with thousands of surface-to-surface rockets and missiles. Israel launched an extensive (yet hesitant) ground incursion seeking to squash Hezbollah but failed to achieve decisive outcomes.

By mid-August, after thirty-four days of escalation and intense fighting, little was gained, though impermissible violence had been inflicted on both sides. The distinction principle, that is, the distinction between combatants and noncombatants, was ignored by the Israel Defense Forces (IDF) and by Hezbollah, which bombarded cities and villages. Dozens of Israeli noncombatants and hundreds of Lebanese noncombatants were killed and many more injured. Vital Lebanese infrastructure was intentionally destroyed and Israeli hospitals intentionally targeted. Hundreds of thousands of Israeli and Lebanese civilians fled their homes, becoming internal refugees. Serious environmental damage also occurred on both sides of the border.[2] In the wake of the morally impermissible violence, the international community launched a concerted effort to stop the fighting. On August 11, 2006, UN Security Council Resolution 1701, which was approved by both the Lebanese and the Israeli governments, introduced a ceasefire and ended the warfare.

During the fighting, politics was operative as the struggle over the common sense. Realizing the impossibility of crushing its rival, each side tried to create an impression of victory or, more precisely, the impression of defeating its enemy. In other words, the warfare involved a struggle over hegemonizing the public common sense, of framing a consciousness of triumph and defeat. This kind of politics had both internal and external/bilateral features. I will deal with the internal first. As Dalia Gavriely-Nuri (2008) shows, the Israeli government attempted to exclude the conflict, portraying it as a short, limited military operation, practically a normal occurrence. In its efforts to do so, the government used metaphorical annihilation, namely, a discursive strategy that systematically uses a fixed series of metaphors to exclude a subject, event, or situation by blurring its basic characteristics while stressing, if not creating, others (Gavriely-Nuri 2008, 8). In the first two weeks of the fighting, the media went along with the government, continually referring to "the fighting in the north." Then the (as yet unofficial) name "Second Lebanon War" began to surface in the media, gradually (and one might add counterhegemonically) supplanting the popular discourse and hegemonizing the common sense (Gavriely-Nuri 2008, 7–8). The public conventions were framed by naming the popular understanding of the events as war, thus frustrating the government's efforts.

Another feature of politics as the struggle over the common sense involved both sides' efforts to dominate the external/bilateral conflict. In their attempts to defeat their opponent (or at least create that impression), each side attacked the other's symbols. Hezbollah successfully targeted what it considered a symbol of unrivaled Israeli power, an Israeli missile boat, the *Chanit* and, above all, did it live during a broadcast by Hassan Nasrallah, Hezbollah's charismatic secretary-general. The effect of the strike was to unsettle the Israeli public. The IDF, too, decided to attack the enemy on the symbolic and metaphoric front. The most obvious case was the battle to capture and destroy Bint Jbail, the southern Lebanese Shiite town considered Hezbollah's regional capital. It was from this town that Nasrallah delivered his famous speech of May 2000, calling Israel as weak and fragile as a spiderweb. The IDF took special pains to conquer Bint Jbail, even naming this operation Steel Webs (Kober 2008), an allusion to Nasrallah's metaphor. The fierce battles over Bint Jbail left many dead and large-scale devastation. These examples illustrate the Gramscian logic of politics and the importance and efficacy of using symbols, metaphors, names, and labels in warfare.

Let us now examine the postwarfare events of August 2006. The antiwar protests in Israel had several facets. The first demonstration, which took place four days into the fighting, was organized by small groups on the left and attracted only a few hundred demonstrators. These people were easily marginalized by labeling them "radicals." Basically, a goodly majority of Israelis supported the warfare and its aims. But, as the fighting escalated with no results, unease began creeping in as to its contours, especially the handling of the conflict by the government and the IDF. Bungled IDF operations, IDF failures to secure the goals of the fighting (including the rescue of the two kidnapped soldiers and preventing the rocket bombardment against Israel), mounting numbers of internal refugees, and an inept government response to them, intensified by comprehensive live coverage of the problems, combined to fuel public apprehension, transforming it into all-out opposition. When the warfare ended, criticism of the government performance was channeled into civic protest led by four groups. The first group consisted of reservists who, although demobilized, refused to simply go home and put everything behind them. The second group consisted of bereaved families, who called for the resignation of those responsible for the failures. The third group was the Movement for Quality Government in Israel, an active social movement, seasoned in heading civic protest. The fourth group consisted of public figures and intellectuals concerned about the immoral conduct of the conflict and the ineptitude of the civic and military leadership that the war highlighted. Key among these was renowned Israeli writer David Grossman, whose son Uri was killed in the final, most disputed stage of the warfare. Together, these four groups (backed by the political opposition) demanded the resignation of those responsible and the appointment of a state commission to investigate the war. Some of the leadership did resign, including Minister of Defense Amir Peretz and several senior army officers. These were joined later by Chief of Staff Dan Halutz.

Although these resignations eased some of the pressures on Prime Minister Ehud Olmert, mounting protest left him no choice but to agree to an official investigation. However, through skillful political maneuvering, Olmert managed to diffuse some of its explosiveness. Rather than establish a state commission, the government appointed a governmental inspection probe, also referred to as a governmental commission, which lacked the legal authority of a state commission and could only produce nonenforceable recommendations. Since its members were government selected, the committee also carried less weight in the public eye, where it was perceived as less autonomous than a state commission appointed by the Supreme Court, which in Israel is usually headed by a Supreme Court judge. The civil protest movement opposed the government commission and was wary of its inferior status and lack of legal punch, but to no avail. After several minor obstacles and changes in composition, the commission, chaired by retired judge Eliyhau Winograd, began its work on September 18, 2006. On April 30, 2007, it delivered a scathing preliminary report, and nine months later, on January 30, 2008, its final report was published. The final report was far more moderate than hoped for by the protestors and lacked recommendations regarding the leadership (for both reports see Winograd 2008). From Olmert's standpoint, the commission was a success. The passage of time since the war, the commission's lack of bite, and its decision to make no recommendations about individuals in the leadership left Olmert almost intact politically.

The maneuvering and countermaneuvering seen in Israel after the summer of 2006 illustrates the world of politics in all its might and pettiness. Yet politics runs deeper than that. It goes to where a struggle is fought for the hearts and minds of the public, a struggle over hegemonizing the common sense through the media of symbols, metaphors, political concepts, names, and labels. And it was on this last front, names and labels, that Olmert and his government proved less successful in their tactic of sustaining fuzziness.

The bereaved families had two aims. The first was to ensure an inquiry to determine responsibilities and ensure that those responsible for failures were held accountable. Second, on a more emotional, symbolic level, they demanded that the country officially and legally classify the violence as war. Under Israel's Basic Laws, the government of Israel does not have to declare war to go to war. Therefore there was no formal declaration when the hostilities began in July 2006. The warfare was not declared a war and was not referred to as a war by the government or the IDF, and at least not in the first two weeks, nor by the media (Gavriely-Nuri 2008, 8). And even though the state compensated those who suffered damages as though it was a war, it refused to classify it as such officially. As argued above, the stakes involved in classifying the fighting as a war or otherwise were not financial or related to security; they were mostly symbolic and political. Faced with demands to assign responsibilities for the war and with civic campaigning for a state commission, the government tried to minimize the gravity of its failures to the maximum degree. It established a governmental commission, not a state commission, and referred to the warfare as fighting or a military campaign, but not as war. For the bereaved families this was not enough. They wanted their loved ones accorded the highest honors bestowed on Israel's fallen; they wanted them recognized as having been killed in war, not in some kind of unclassified fighting.

So for the families of the fallen soldiers this was the symbolic meaning of the civic struggle over the classifying and labeling of the fighting—they wanted to see it carved onto the tombstones of their loved ones, the soldiers, that they had been "killed in war," not just "killed in a battle in Lebanon"—because this carried meaning. As the mother of one fallen soldier explained in a newspaper interview, "It was a matter of principle for the bereaved parents to define the northern campaign as a war. Our sons fought in a war and the fact that it was not being called a war was really inappropriate. Our sons believed they were going to war to defend their homes. I now hope that when our sons listen in heaven they will rest easier" (quoted in Rada 2007).

On the one hand, then, the government tried to shore up its poor public standing by not labeling the warfare as war, but it was challenged in this by the bereaved families, which fought to secure the highest possible social status, respect, and honor for their loved ones by classifying as a war the event where they gave their lives. Moreover, the bereaved families were backed by the political opposition, which hoped to underscore the government's failures by having the failed campaign classed as a war. The government had two assets in this struggle: it had the legal authority to declare the event a war or not a war, and it could point to the conservative understanding of traditional war as extended warfare between *sovereign polities*. Since the battle in Lebanon was fought mainly against Hezbollah, which was not a sovereign polity, the government could deny that this confrontation was a war (see, for example, Givati 2007). But, the bereaved families had other assets that proved more powerful. First, they had the social standing and political capital that comes in Israel with having made the greatest sacrifice of all for Israel's security. As Udi Lebel (2007, 71) writes, "Representatives of many bereaved families have become opinion leaders and movers and shakers in Israeli society." In other words, they are very powerful actors in the Israeli public arena and strong enough to secure their goals vis-à-vis other political actors. Second, they were backed by the popular discourse that had already a name, the "Second Lebanon War." That is, the public discourse had unofficially yet unmistakably imprinted the name "Second Lebanon War" on the public consciousness. The common sense was therefore en route to being framed by the oppositional public conventions and to perceiving the warfare as war. It consequently became an uphill struggle for the government to sustain the conceptual fuzziness it desired and to overturn the commonsense perception of the warfare as a war. In fact, the government's handicap was so great that when it finally agreed to the legal classification of a war, the popular news website Ynet wrote sarcastically, "In case you had not realized, the Ministerial Committee for Symbols and Ceremonies has news for you—last summer we had a war" (Sofer 2007).

Moreover, the bereaved families had another asset in their civic war of positions: the by-now well-developed understanding of new war. By this time it had become accepted that war has many faces, including asymmetric clashes between organized armies and substate guerilla groups (for seminal works on this see Kaldor 1999, 2006). Hence, the warfare in Lebanon fitted in with the understanding of new wars and was therefore grounded in reality that made the demand to classify the fighting a war no arbitrary matter. Nor was the alternative classification arbitrary, since its advocates had the conservative understanding of traditional war to back them. In other words, neither of the labels was Orwellian newspeak. Both labels were politically legitimate and viable, as they were grounded in reality and the current understanding of reality. The civic struggle over labeling the fighting was actually an example of paradigmatic maneuvering to win the public common sense. But it was maneuvering with a twist: One party, the government, tactically cherished conceptual fuzziness. It wanted to sustain the fuzziness by denying the alternative label. The goal of the opposing parties was to clear the conceptual clouds and wage an effective attack by conceptually labeling the event a war.

Under pressure from public conventions, the government struggled to sustain its refusal to call the fighting a war, until finally on March 19, 2007, seven months after it ended, the Ministerial Committee for Symbols and Ceremonies decided to classify the events as war. The government having yielded over the labeling, the second act now began in this theater of the political. Having accepted that they had bowed to the common understanding of the violence, politicians now clashed over who would take the credit for naming it. Here too, the stakes were entirely political. Once the fate of the debate was sealed, the politicians started to vie for the kudos of being the name-giver: for naming the war in line with the public will. The Ministerial Committee for Symbols and Ceremonies under Minister Yaakov Edry of the Kadima Party, and a committee nominated by the Defense Minister Peretz from the Labor Party, both claimed the authority to name the war. The compromise reached was that Edry's committee would chose the name in consultation with the Defense Ministry committee. The obvious name chosen from a list that was drawn up was the "Second Lebanon War." A week later, on March 25, the government approved both the declaration and the name. The civic conflict was resolved in a weak, Kripkean labeling by naming. The popular name worked against the official position of the government, helping the opposition to prevail in the civic battle over labeling. The events of the summer of 2006 were retrospectively designated the Second Lebanon War.

Beyond the Second Lebanon War

In the case just cited, there seems to be a troubling discrepancy between the theoretical framework and the empirical analysis. Following Gramsci, the theoretical framework involves some grand theorizing about the sociopolitical world. However, the empirical analysis simply presents a microcase and conducts a microanalysis of seven months of domestic politics. We could therefore ask ourselves, Is that all there is to it? Is the effort to develop and embrace this theoretical framework worth all the work? To which I would unequivocally answer yes! The theoretical framework, this politically attuned constructivism, lends itself to this kind of microanalysis, or in other words, to the analysis of microcases (see also Goldfarb 2006). That is not simply a methodological assertion, but an ontological one. As soon as we understand the constructed foundation of the sociopolitical reality, we will also realize that it stems from numerous interrelated microprocesses and struggles, such as the ones we saw above. Ontologically speaking, the most theoretically rewarding analysis is the kind of microanalysis offered here.

To validate this bold assertion, let us consider some cases in which this type of microanalysis would be appropriate. To this end we will examine several microcases taken from the Israeli context, a recent paradigmatic global microcase, and finally a brief examination of a regional case from the Balkans. Given that Israel's official national ideology, Zionism, is intimately linked to the revival of Hebrew as a spoken language, it comes as no surprise that language, words, labeling, and names play a key role in constructing Israel's sociopolitical reality. The Israeli sociopolitical arena abounds with examples of conflict over labeling and naming. One example was the 1948 war, which in Hebrew is *Milchemet Haatzmaut* (the "War of Independence") and in Arabic the *Nakba* ("Catastrophe"). While the first name indicates the celebratory nature of the event and is preferred by Jewish Zionists, the latter name, which is embraced by many Israeli Palestinians, memorializes their national tragedy. There are other examples. Jewish settlers in the occupied territories are called *mityashvim* by the political Right, linking them semantically to the description of the founding fathers of the Zionist movement who settled the land of Israel. The political Left, on the other hand, calls them *mitnachalim*, indicating the semiclandestine nature of this act of settlement, its break with Zionist history, and its inconsistency with Israeli law and sovereignty. A similar struggle is waged over the geographical territory itself. Should the area be called the "West Bank," an older name linking the region to the former Jordanian rule; the "Occupied Territories," denoting unlawfully held territory forcefully seized from others; or Judea and Samaria, the biblical name for the region that captures the national, religious, and historical attachment of the Jewish people to the land, and supposedly legitimizes Jewish-Israeli sovereignty? In order to regularize naming and labeling, the Israeli Broadcasting Authority has issued ethical guidelines, known as the Nakdi Briefing, to deal with these controversial names and labels. Siding with the Right, the Briefing orders that broadcasts should refer to these areas as Judea and Samaria (Israeli Broadcasting Authority 1998, 27). It also instructs that the settlers should be referred to as they refer to themselves (Israeli Broadcasting Authority 1998, 37). Needless to say, this decision gives the settlers political leverage in hegemonizing public conventions.

And then there is the interesting case of one tiny and beautiful bird that fell victim to the political importance of names: *Cinnyris osea*, or *tzufit boheket* in Hebrew. The *tzufit* is a passerine bird, about 10 cm long, and not unlike the hummingbirds of the New World in appearance and feeding behavior (though the latter belong to a different order, the Apodiformes, in which they constitute a family of their own, the Trochilidae). The male is metallic blue, the female a drab gray. Originally an African bird, it spread throughout Israel in the first half of the twentieth century and symbolizing the transformative power of the Zionist project, the triumph over the wasteland and the harnessing and cultivation of the land of Israel, making it blossom with introduced flowers and European-style gardens (ecologically speaking, this was, of course, a disaster). As gardening and nectar-producing flowers spread throughout the Jewish settlements, so did the *tzufit*. Originally secluded in the oases along the Dead Sea, it is now found nationwide as one of the most common and beloved birds in Israel. Its popularity elevated it to the short list of candidates in a 2007 campaign to elect an Israeli national bird for Israel's sixtieth Independence Day. While the *tzufit* was indeed among the more popular candidates, it had one thing against it—its common or English name: Palestinian sunbird. How could the Israeli national bird be called "Palestinian"? Would there be implications for the authenticity of the Zionist project and its embeddedness in the land of Israel? What ramifications would this bird have over the struggle for legitimacy over the land, and was the country "Israel" or "Palestine"? Finally, this delightful bird lost in battle to the hoopoe (*Upupa epops*), which has a neutral-enough name (albeit the name of an IDF unit,[3] whose veterans supposedly voted for it en bloc). There are even some nonverified and probably unfounded rumors that there was an Israeli campaign to rename the Palestinian sunbird, to make it sound sufficiently Zionist or at least not explicitly anti-Zionist, a rumor that aroused a Palestinian uproar and a countercampaign spearheaded by the Palestine Wildlife Society.

Another example of the political struggle regarding naming and labeling that is more directly linked to discussions about war and security is the First Lebanon War, fought between 1982 and 1985. Since both the First and Second Lebanon Wars were fought on the same territory and had multiple similarities, we can use the first war to take our analysis back in time for a deeper understanding of the history of the political struggles over naming and labeling and their long-term implications. The First Lebanon War is an example of a failed act of naming. Officially, the warfare was named *Mivtza Shlom Hagalil* (Operation Peace for Galilee) and was never officially declared a war. Its popular name, nonetheless, was the Lebanon War, and, popularly, Israelis perceive it as a war. Nothing shows the perception of this operation as a war more clearly than the naming of the Second Lebanon War. Obviously a "second" war implies a first, which was Operation Peace for Galilee, or the First Lebanon War. Ironically, naming the 2006 warfare the Second Lebanon War, retrospectively classified the 1982 warfare (albeit unofficially) as a war.

But why did the popular naming of Operation Peace for Galilee fail to secure its official classification as a war? Why it is still officially classed as an operation even though it is popularly considered a war? Why did a Kripkean labeling by naming fail to materialize? The answer concerns the relative weakness of Israeli civil society during the 1980s. At that time, the Israeli government had far more leverage and power over Israeli civil society than it does today. And when civil society is relatively weak, the Gramscian framework is less relevant or, more accurately, provides other terms of analysis. Hegemony could contain some aspects of what Gramsci called Caesarism or Bonapartism. Gramsci applied these terms to political strategies in situations where opposing political forces "balance each other in a catastrophic manner; that is to say, they balance each other in such a way that a continuation of the conflict can only terminate in their reciprocal destruction" (Gramsci 1971, 219). Gramsci, who was more attuned to autocratic regimes, believed that Caesarism or Bonapartism allows a society to avoid a violent war of movement and mutual destruction by accepting the arbitration of a great leader. However, as Ian Lustick argues (1993), there is another political alternative that can prevent a catastrophic balance—a national unity coalition. Israel had a unity government in 1984 after the First Lebanon War (Alimi 2007, 96; Korn 1994; Shenhav

2004, 100), and it allowed Israel's political system to shield itself from civic pressures. To paraphrase this in the Gramscian terms we explored in the introduction: Israeli civil society has failed to meet liberal expectations of assuming an associative autonomous position vis-à-vis the state and has remained, if not an integral state organ, at least an ineffective and feeble sphere dominated by the political system and state. Gramsci's triangle of state, political society, and civil society appears a more efficient theoretical framework for understanding 1980s Israel than the liberal associative understanding of an autonomous civil society. And the triangular relationship of the sociopolitical scenario at the time the coalition of the main political parties allowed the government to resist the popular naming of the Lebanon warfare as "war." Thus, civic opposition to the war and the oppositional public conventions could not materialize into institutionalized public conventions. With the First Lebanon War, then, labeling by naming did not occur. Probably, however, the failure of civic opposition in the 1980s and the awareness of the failed policies that mired the IDF in the Lebanese mud for eighteen years provided the momentum to strengthen Israeli civil society and transform the government-civil society equilibrium. This led to a more pluralistic Israel and a powerful and relatively associative autonomous civil society that could pressure its government in 2006 and achieve obedience to its will through a weak Kripkean labeling by naming.

Campaigning for the Climate

The year 2007 was Al Gore's year. Stepping on and off podiums around the world, he both raised global public awareness of the issue of global warming and gained prestigious awards. Al Gore was not alone in this campaign. He was preceded by countless scientists generating vast quantities of alarming data for decades. From the mid-1980s, many were part of the Intergovernmental Panel on Climate Change (IPCC), an IGO that was Gore's Peace Nobel co-laureate. Both parties had important—and differentiated—roles to play in the global campaign against global warming. Studying these differentiated roles shows how Gore mobilized the second tactic that is available to politicians using concepts as political tools. In contrast to the previous section, which considered how the Olmert government tried to sustain conceptual fuzziness to its advantage, I now show how Gore tried to attach meanings to concepts in a way that served his agenda.

Watching *An Inconvenient Truth* is a moving experience. Gore has a gospel to deliver and is a talented presenter who uses every available rhetorical device to get his point across: he is humorous, witty, sentimental, emotional, and fierce. He regards the issue as a story—or a narrative—that he must convey to the audience (on the importance of narratives in political communication and discourse, see Shenhav 2005a, 2005b, 2006, 2015). Gore talks about his personal history, alongside contemporary events and summaries of scientific data, kaleidoscoping personal and national tragedies into a single heartrending narrative. He describes the car accident that nearly killed his six-year-old son Albert, and Hurricane Katrina's deadly impact on New Orleans. The mobilization of anxieties in Gore's rhetoric is clearly a resource in his global warming campaign. Furthermore, to marshal public anxiety, Gore adheres to what may be termed the logic of securitization à la the Copenhagen school of IR (Graeger 1996). This involves linking environmental issues to security hazards. To cap it all, Gore has an enemy, a "They" to struggle with—namely the oil lobby and its White House allies who together distort evidence, harass scientists, and desire to veil the inconvenient truth regarding global warming. Their success is our doom. Yet Gore proves to be no saint in his campaign. For Gore, scientific data (which have been gathered by IPCC members and others) are but a means to be mobilized, bent, even misrepresented as required. Gore's inaccuracies led to controversies that were aired and litigated in the British High Court after a Kent school governor, Stewart Dimmock, tried to ban the film from secondary schools. On October 10, 2007, High Court judge Michael Burton declined to ban the film from schools but, noting its inaccuracies, ruled it could only be shown with guidance notes to prevent political indoctrination (Burton 2007). Especially relevant to our interest is Justice Burton's judgment that the film "is substantially founded upon scientific research and fact, albeit that the science is used, in the hands of a talented politician and communicator, to make a political statement and to support a political programme." Gore doesn't distort the data, necessarily, he just represents and misrepresents information to suit his ends.

However, the point of this section is not to expose Gore's rhetoric or criticize him personally. The point is to highlight the political preeminence of fixating as opposed to reasoning over meanings. When we are in the throes of a public debate over something with a potentially tragic impact on humanity's fate, we are actually locked into a political struggle over labeling; a war where one of the key battles is whether an environmental phenomenon should be conceptualized as "global warming" or "climate change" (the former being Gore's alarm call; the latter being the reassuring message of the other side—Gore's "they").

In this war of labels, the aim is to gain control over public conventions by using Gramscian tactics and vernacular. Elsewhere, I define the term "commonsensical descriptory vernacular" as the loose expression of unreflective accounts that unfold the narratives in which the world is captured and figured out by the public common sense (Ish-Shalom 2013). This vernacular is imbued with Gramscian tactics. Common sense, as its name indicates, is a public medium. It is a synonymous term for unreflecting intersubjective social knowledge, and as such it is the site of political contestation, a struggle between institutionalized and oppositional public conventions. Successfully using the commonsensical descriptory vernacular means succeeding in framing the common sense, that is, winning politically by institutionalizing public conventions.

Indeed, the instrument used by the two sides in the global warming / climate change debate does not seek to elucidate the public good by addressing public reason. If it did, the IPCC would be the best agent, armed as it is with data and theories (graphically charted and at times executively summarized (Intergovernmental Panel on Climate Change 2007). Since its establishment, the IPCC has employed the theoretical explanatory vernacular, an academic subset of the Habermas-like vernacular. This vernacular presents a strong argument that addresses public reason, and by reasoning through relevant political concepts, attempts to elucidate public good. The IPCC's use of the theoretical explanatory vernacular is evident not only in the dry, rational tones of the reports and the richness of the data and models, but also in the language of probability employed. Although probability is a salient scientific feature, it has little rhetorical standing in public discourse and no place in the Gramsci-like vernacular. And indeed, the IPCC's three first reports, along with its gathered data, projections, and recommendations, have failed to raise global awareness. It took the combined efforts of the IPCC (with its fourth report) and Gore to achieve a significant impact. The IPCC could no longer rely solely on producing reports conforming to the strict rules of the theoretical explanatory vernacular in order to succeed in utilizing the commonsensical descriptory vernacular. It had to engage itself with a more public-efficient vernacular, allying itself with a talented rhetor and a more Gramsci-like vernacular. And that rhetor was Gore.

The relative success of the fourth IPCC report in raising global awareness can be attributed to this coalition (see also Callaghan 2008, 7; Newman 2007) and, in terms of the conceptualization of this book, to Gore's use of Gramsci-like tactics and vernacular. It was not insignificant that the Nobel Peace Prize Committee declared, "He is probably the single individual who has done most to create greater worldwide understanding of the measures that need to be adopted" (Norwegian Nobel Committee 2007). It is not that the IPCC abandoned its use of cautious, meticulous argumentation. Rather, it willingly cooperated with Gore's rhetoric (or even aligned itself with Gore's campaign). Thus, what we are now witnessing is a concerted attempt to construct oppositional public conventions by mobilizing Gramsci-like tactics and a commonsensical descriptory vernacular. This side's victory, so to speak, involves labeling the environmental phenomenon as "global warming." Thus, global warming has become a (securitized) political concept conceptualized as a human-made phenomenon that can only be reined in by a sufficiently strong (democratic) political will. Its meaning was fixated in an attempt to crush an opposition that was richer in material resources. There are those today who similarly attempt to dub it "global heating," further stressing the active role of humanity in causing this trend (see, for example, Angliss 2007; Henderson 2006). As noted earlier, the alternative political concept of "climate change" involves the fixation of the same climate phenomenon's meaning as a circular natural phenomenon, which is unaffected by either human action or political (democratic) will.

Gore's pursuits have helped to make this issue politically salient. The political salience of climate change did not change its global nature or the transnational advocacy and campaigning for it. However, it did make the domestic and national struggles over climate change particularly intense. Moreover, although the most visible milestones in the struggle were global, in the form of international summits and agreements, the real, substantial war of positions was within national political systems. As we discussed, the struggle involved efforts by all sides to conceptualize the issue. Nowadays, no serious party or aspiring politician can afford to ignore or be apathetic toward climate change. The winds of change have even blown through the American Republican Party, which played a central role in challenging concerns about climate change, and Republican leaders like John McCain, Rudolph Giuliani, and Mitt Romney also tried to address it (Santora 2007).

Even President George W. Bush and politicians who held fast to the notion of climate change needed to show concern. They had several techniques for this: the first was to field their own scientists, those climate skeptics whose data and theories could generate skepticism regarding human responsibility for climate change and the disastrousness of its consequences (the most outspoken of them being Bjørn Lomborg).[4] Another technique was to add the issue to their own agenda and political platform and simply pay lip service to it. A third technique, which Bush used, was for America to pretend sincere American participation in world summits on the subject while organizing alternative international meetings to legitimize less than full adherence to the Kyoto Protocol or pressuring for compromise on the Bali Road Map. Thus, Bush organized a meeting of this nature in Washington, DC, following the preparatory UN world summit in September 2007, and a second meeting in Hawaii following the Bali Summit in December 2007. The struggle over the meaning of the climate phenomenon and the resultant social knowledge has become political through and through and is conducted through political vehicles, including the attempt to fixate concepts with meanings and frame the common sense.

Gore's successes paved the way for incremental domestic gains in the United States and elsewhere, later capitalized by President Obama's endorsement of the 2015 Paris Agreement. But in politics the seal is hardly ever permanent and the moving finger keeps on writing the pages of history. Succeeding Obama, President Donald Trump has assumed a reactionary and dismissive attitude toward global warming, trying to undo Obama's environmental legacy. Concerning his accomplishments and conceptual tactics, the juries are still out.

The Balkans

The Balkans are an example of the third tactic by which concepts that are commonly seen as morally positive, such as just cause, are emptied of real meaning and transformed into vacuous concepts to be used as forceful political slogans. In the 1990s the Balkans were a hotbed of historical narratives, secessions, and wars, where parties exploited just cause as a conceptual vehicle to enlist just war theory in their struggle for international and, to a greater extent, domestic legitimacy. Radovan Karadžić, who was president of the Republika Srpska during the bloody events of the 1990s and was convicted of crimes against humanity and genocide by the UN War Crimes Court in The Hague, declared during the trial: "I will defend that nation of ours and their cause that is just and holy, I stand here before you not to defend the mere mortal that I am, but to defend the greatness of a small nation in Bosnia-Herzegovina, which for 500 years has had to suffer. We have a good case. We have good evidence and proof" (BBC News 2010). In this example, Karadžić used just war and the concept of just cause (or in his terms just "case") to justify the crimes against humanity perpetrated under his leadership. However, his is a vacuous version of just cause, a concept bereft of any meaningful meaning, and so dysfunctional. Note that the purpose and function of just cause and the entire just war framework is to check violence and war. The principles of just cause and just war achieve this by establishing a series of very strict conditions that must be met for the resort to war to be permissible. The jus ad bellum facet of just war establishes six such principles: (1) just cause, (2) right intention, (3) legitimate authority, (4) last resort, (5) probable chances of success, (6) proportionality. Our interest here is with the first principle, just cause, which establishes two main grounds for permissibility: self-defense against military aggression and the protection of defenseless third parties against large-scale systematic victimization. It is understood that in order to guarantee that violence and war are kept in check, the condition for self-defense arise only under dire circumstances, namely clear and present danger. So Karadžić's argument that his country had just cause with roots stretching back five hundred years was completely nonlegitimate. His political demagoguery that emptied the moral concept and then abused its vacuous version. Karadžić attempted to transform the understanding of just cause through unacceptable arguments—citing longue durée historical processes (which as we will see in a moment can be shrouded in mystery) as just cause, which in fact eliminates the function of checking violence. He created a vacuous version of just cause and just war by turning them into apparatuses that sanction and justify the Bosnian Serbs' resort to war. Karadžić utilized this conceptual tactic to portray himself as the savior of the Bosnian Serbs, who were allegedly victims of an offense by the evil international community.

And this tactic, of transforming just cause into a vacuous concept and subsequently trying to justify unnecessary and thus impermissible acts of violence by using it, was even more striking with Slobodan Milošević. A good example of this was his address to the Serbian people on June 28, 1989, at an occasion marking the six hundredth anniversary of the Battle of Kosovo:

> Today, it is difficult to say what is the historical truth about the Battle of Kosovo and what is legend. Today this is no longer important. Oppressed by pain and filled with hope, the people used to remember and to forget, as, after all, all people in the world do, and it was ashamed of treachery and glorified heroism. Therefore it is difficult to say today whether the Battle of Kosovo was a defeat or a victory for the Serbian people, whether thanks to it we fell into slavery or we survived in this slavery . . .
>
> Six centuries later, now, we are being again engaged in battles and are facing battles. They are not armed battles, although such things cannot be excluded yet. However, regardless of what kind of battles they are, they cannot be won without resolve, bravery, and sacrifice, without the noble qualities that were present here in the field of Kosovo in the days past. (1989)

In his speech, Milošević sets the stage for the bloody events that followed the speech, orchestrating them and legitimizing the use of force as a defensive act against the harms inflicted on Serbians for more than six hundred years. The historical act of aggression that, according to Milošević, justified resort to war was a battle of whose historical facts Milošević himself confessed ignorance, while admitting its unimportance. For Milošević, just cause was a vacuous concept, devoid of meaning, that he could sloganize and abuse to justify war rather than try to avoid it and reduce violence. This Gramscian move, even if morally disastrous, was politically sound and domestically successful. By using this vacuous concept, the Serbs could look themselves in the mirror and see victims of ugly circumstances misunderstood by an uninformed and biased international community rather than perpetrators of crimes against humanity.

The third tactic, that of emptying concepts of real meaning and transforming them into vacuous concepts that are used as forceful political slogans, is especially attractive and politically effective for concepts commonly perceived as morally positive. As morally positive concepts, they are loaded with rhetorical capital and can be manipulated to justify what is often morally impermissible. This dual feature makes such concepts especially vulnerable to the tactic of emptying and transformation. This is often so with democracy, which, like just cause, is also used publicly and politically as a vacuous concept that has been emptied of meaning, sloganized, and abused. The complexities and essential contestedness of democracy as a concept, which have been discussed extensively in academia (the Habermasian way), are nowhere to be seen when democracy is discussed politically. In the political context, the meaning of democracy is taken for granted and hardly questioned or discussed. Israeli politicians often boast that Israel is the only democracy in the Middle East and the IDF is the world's most moral fighting force. These assertions are now self-evident truths in the Israeli common sense, facts that are never reflected upon, questioned, or challenged. But when you probe deeper into the conceptual map that allows the common sense to be framed in this way, you find a distinct lack of discussion combined with empty concepts that stifle public deliberation and leave little room for dissent and criticism. When the idea of democracy is emptied of its meaning, it undermines democracy, or at least some of the civic engagements that certain understandings of democracy consider to be democracy's real essence.

This was the fate of some educators in Israel who tried to start discussions about Israeli democracy. In the summer of 2015, civics studies coordinator Adar Cohen was fired following complaints from the political Right about his educational conduct and for authorizing of the use of a textbook that was not sufficiently patriotic. Two years later, Adam Verta was fired from his high school teaching position for holding a critical discussion in class that disputed the public common sense of the meaning of morality and the accepted public truth that the IDF is the world's most moral military. One of his students used Facebook to arouse a public furor over this discussion, and Verta was fired by a frightened school management. It seems that politicians and, following them, bureaucrats find it more convenient and politically effective to allow the vacuousness of a concept to persist than to permit lively civic discussion and criticism. Yet surely, both morality and democracy thrive on conceptual discussions, and to quash discussion by dismissing those who ask questions fails to recognize the contestedness of the concepts and, worse still, does no service to their richness either as concepts or social phenomena.

Conclusions

So far we have considered a duality that is both interesting and disturbing. Although concepts are essentially contested, which raises the question of the plurality of legitimate conceptualizations and definitions, their essential contestedness does not necessarily translate into ideal speech situations. The Habermasian road is scarcely taken in the public sphere. The public sphere is dominated by rhetors who manipulate the essential contestedness of political concepts. They do not discuss the plurality of legitimate meanings and conceptualizations. What they do is either (1) sustain and mobilize the ambiguity of concepts, (2) bound concepts and fixate them with an attached meaning, or (3) empty concepts, especially those that are seen as morally positive, of any meaning and use their vacuous version as political slogans. And they use these tactics to deliver forceful rhetorical claims. It is not necessarily the better argument that wins the public discussion, but the argument (or claim) that attracts the political forces and resonates with the public—and not necessarily by speaking to the reasonable side of the public but to its emotions. It is these bounding practices that undermine democratic agency and keep the citizens in the "Quisisana clinic" (which is not unlike the Platonic cave). This should not come as surprise to the constructivists who for years now have been studying identity, emotions, and other social features that have real and true ramifications in politics and international politics. But this unsurprising inference will not sit well with the uncritical Habermasian reading of international politics found quite commonly in constructivist circles. And this is one important implication of the book so far: constructivism should go political.

The IPCC and Gore's cooperation, the discursive warring over defining the Second Lebanon War, and Milošević's appropriation of the Battle of Kosovo all show that, rather than studying the force of the better argument alone, constructivists should focus too on the relations between power and social knowledge construction: in other words, it is important to embrace a more politically attuned constructivism and study the sociopolitical construction of knowledge behind the veil. This is because the Habermasian ideal speech act is not what dominates the public sphere but rather the Gramscian veiling speech act and the commonsensical descriptory vernacular. The Gramscian veiling speech act achieves its results by sustaining ambiguity, fixating meanings, or emptying concepts of substantial meaning. Therefore, social knowledge is not authentic from the point of view of being a public good that is freely elucidated by public reason and potentially results in the intersubjective equivalent to the authenticity of being "true to oneself." Rather, it is political in the sense of being a common sense framed by a power-dominated hegemony (or institutionalized public conventions): an unreflecting and uncritical common sense that is a poor arbitrator of public good. Politics is part of the social process of constructing social knowledge, and social knowledge is indeed implicated with power and interest. In other words, when social knowledge is constructed this way, it becomes the intersubjective equivalent to the Marxist notion of false consciousness. Social knowledge is a political site where institutionalized and opposing public conventions contest in a discursive struggle to frame the common sense. This means that social reality is largely an outcome of a political discursive contestation between institutionalized and oppositional public conventions and constructed politically no less than socially. Constructivism would fare well indeed if it were melded with Gramscian theoretical frameworks.

However, a different set of more normative issues still needs to be addressed and will form the basis for the second and normative part of the book. It is very doubtful whether the "worldwide understanding" of the sort created by Al Gore, the new institutionalized understanding of the summer of 2006 as war, and Radovan Karadžić's rhetorical use of just cause are something we ought to embrace or laud. For that matter, we can also ask whether Gore is really worthy of the Nobel Peace Prize, and we should surely embrace the fact that Karadžić was tried for his crimes. If Gore's efforts have produced a "worldwide understanding" that is simply an intersubjective false consciousness, then we are faced with the question of whether we actually wish to embrace intersubjective false consciousness as a state of mind. Put differently, not only is the manipulability of political argumentation at stake, so is the nature of its sociopolitical outcomes.

One way of reducing this concern would be an act-consequentialist response that argues that at least in Gore's case, his Gramsci-like vernacular is the most effective means of promoting a good cause (combating global warming). Yet this is a questionable stance. First, it lessens the potential for human rationality and reasonableness and instrumentalizes humanity in what Kantian deontologists would argue is an impermissible tactic even in the service of a good cause. Second, and according to rule-consequentialist logic, embracing Gore's tactic could help to reify this sort of politics and consolidate the resilience and dominance of the Gramsci-like vernacular still further. That, of course, raises the specter of rhetors successfully employing manipulative tactics, not to advance good causes, as Gore seemingly does, but bad causes. Milošević and Karadžić spring to mind here. But they are not alone. Consider, for example, how the Bush administration mobilized public fear to smooth the way for the Patriot Act and surveillance politics after September 11, 2001. This marked a paradigmatic case of Gramsci-like vernacular undermining the democratic nature of a polity. Third, and based on act-consequentialist reasoning, should Gore's movie and reputation ever become discredited (and it is not that difficult to point out various problems with the scientific soundness of the movie), the entire global warming agenda could crash in flames. But if the warnings of *An Inconvenient Truth* are true, then that defeat could prove tragic for planet Earth and humanity as a whole.

We need then to seek an alternative way to influence the world's understanding of the possible disastrous changes taking place in the earth's climate. And we should seek a different political framework for oppositional democratic campaigns such as the one surrounding the events of summer 2006 (aka the Second Lebanon War). And this democratic alternative might be a commitment to what Walter Baber and Robert Bartlett call deliberative environmental politics (2005). Baber and Bartlett (2005, 12) argue that deliberation, in the form of contemplative decision-making and collective inclusive discourse, is necessary for ecological rationality, substantive democratic governance, and policy reasonableness. Understood thus, deliberative environmental politics is the remedy for the normative problems analyzed above with regard to the Gramsci-like vernacular employed so successfully by Gore. This means that the alternative to Gore's illegitimate rhetorical tactic is not political inaction but deliberative environmental politics more in line with a Habermasian vernacular. But given the success and resilience of the Gramscian vernacular in politics, we must also ask whether a deliberative environmental politics is possible. In other words, are there any prospects for a Habermasian vernacular in our politics?

To answer this challenging question, I wish to claim that although Habermas and Gramsci have different theoretical frameworks, they share several important understandings to positive effect. As shown above,

Habermas demonstrates a keen awareness of the political manipulability of existing political processes for forming the lifeworld, and he is no stranger to the political processes described here. We also find some affinities between Gramsci and Habermas in their vision of the ideal future society. Both are critical theoreticians seeking a reasoned, consensual, and transparent society that is devoid of substantial schisms. In other words, Gramsci does believe in the unfulfilled potentiality for reason in the everyman. However, it is in their vision of the pathway for getting from the here and now to the there and (future) then that Gramsci and Habermas differ. Gramsci conceives that a counterhegemony will achieve change through the mobilization of the public's uncritical common sense. Habermas, on the other hand, maintains that the vision of an ideal society will materialize through public reason and rationality. Put differently, it is not in their views of the present or future that the two thinkers differ. Where they differ is in terms of the political dynamics and modes of argumentation that could link the present to the future. And although this difference is not minor, it does offer enough of a common language and basis for scholars who are committed to an engaged academia, such as advocated here, to adopt a kind of analytical dual gaze. It is a duality of gaze that is difficult yet crucial to attain. The constructivist who goes political should try to cultivate both a Gramscian sensitivity to how politics is conducted and a Habermasian responsibility toward changing how present-day politics is conducted. Constructivists, that is, should go political and critical. A critical vocation is not possible without being politically attuned.

Habermas's theory of argumentation is far from worthless for this purpose and vocation. It has a proper and important role in prescribing how the democratic public sphere *should* be organized to improve the prospects of a working ideal speech act, how an ideal speech situation might come about, and how the potentiality for reason and communicative competence in the everyman can be fulfilled. And it is in the interests of constructivists who are going political and critical, no less than of the political theoreticians, to work this out. The latter's interest springs from their engagement with the quality of the polity. The former should be interested because they fully understand the constitutive relationship between social knowledge and social reality. And for that reason they should also understand that the quality of the latter depends on the soundness of the former. Furthermore, as scholars who immerse themselves in the world of ideas and knowledge, democracy and security, constructivists are familiar with the way sociopolitical knowledge is constructed. This familiarity, I argue, is one of the things that burdens them with social responsibility to think about how to devise a construction of social knowledge that is as power-free as possible. After all, lifting the veil from social knowledge construction processes and cleansing power as much as possible from the constructing of social knowledge might bring about a less distorted social reality, whatever that may mean.

It is to this aim that the book now turns, of cultivating a dual analytical gaze that will benefit from both Gramsci's sensitivity to the political and Habermas's political responsibility.

Part II · Engaged Academia

4 ✦ The Responsibility to Engage

In Part I I showed that politically attuned constructivism is epistemologically better positioned and equipped for handling, studying, and addressing conceptual politics when theorizing the sociopolitical world. In Part II, I propose that conceptual politics also allows for a normative investigation of academia's social and political roles and responsibilities. This investigation concludes with a call for an engaged academia, the cultivation of a dual analytical gaze, and several measures and principles. The main principles to be embraced and implemented are self-reflexivity, communal setting and dialogue, pluralism, a commitment to transparency, responsibility, and civic (and conceptual) engagement. A social science committed to these principles can fully engage conceptual politics, improve academic research, and participate in the civic struggle to improve the world outside academia. I will explore these measures and principles, first generally and abstractly, and then more concretely and on three analytical levels: the level of the individual theoretician, the level of the community of theoreticians, and the level of society, where academia forms a part—an engaged part.

A caveat is in order. While I consider my arguments concerning the responsibilities of academia to be universally valid, at least within the democratic world, I am well aware that academic structures around the world, even within the democratic world, do differ (Wæver 1998; Tickner and Wæver 2009). The same holds true for relations between academia and the state and society and the structural conditions of and for these relations. These differences may bisect all three analytical levels, but I suspect they are especially relevant in the third level, of society. These differences influence the problems and opportunities facing academia and the way academics can discharge their responsibilities toward the wider public and engage. Admittedly, I am familiar mostly with Israeli and American academia, although I have knowledge of universities in different countries. My analysis may therefore be a little biased and tailored to these two national contexts in particular. But as academic environments around the world (mostly democratic) do have a lot in common, I think that the arguments presented here—certainly their general thrust—are universally applicable (at least within the democratic world). At most, certain minor modifications will be needed in specific national contexts.

The Principles

As explored extensively in feminist epistemology and elsewhere (see, for example, Engelstad and Gerrard 2005, 6; Harding 1986, 137–38; 1991, 163; 1998, 188; Potter 2006, 140; Smith 1987, 92; Tickner 2005; see also Baert 2005, 136, 153–54; du Preez 2008; Mannheim 1952, 148; in IR see Adler-Nissen 2013; Amoureux and Steele 2015; Hamati-Ataya 2011, 2013; Rosenau 2003), reflexivity, or strong reflexivity, means being critically aware of the normative and ideological assumptions and social and cultural commitments that constitute the standpoint from which each theoretician studies and analyzes the social world. Self-reflexivity involves looking inward at all those extratheoretical mechanisms that confine theorizing but also enable it. Critical awareness of the normative and ideological assumptions operative in theorizing ensures an awareness of the essential contestedness of our definitions. In essence, therefore, self-reflexivity critically engages the strategy of fixating or emptying meanings of concepts and definitions and of trying to decontest what is essentially contested. Self-reflexivity is accordingly a vital component for studying and using conceptual politics.

But there is a problem with self-reflexivity. As committed as feminist epistemology is to self-reflexivity, its adherents also recognize the obstacles before it. Mary Hawkesworth justly argues, "The notion of transparency, the belief that the individual knower can identify all his/her prejudices and purge them in order to greet an unobstructed reality has been rendered suspect" (1996, 92). She also explains that "the perspective of each knower contains blind spots, tacit presuppositions, and prejudgments of which the individual is unaware" (1996, 96). Despite the demands of both the feminist standpoint epistemology project and critical constructivism, self-reflexivity may prove impossible. It may remain unachievable because of the blind spots concealing the normative and ideological assumptions from theoreticians (and others) and the social and cultural commitments that form their standpoint. If that is indeed so, then how are we to achieve the desired self-reflexivity?

The answer is in placing research in a communal setting. It is indeed difficult for individuals to identify and overcome their own blind spots and be conscious of the assumptions and commitments that are essential in their theorizing. But overcoming blind spots can be possible within the community of researchers working *as* a community. Research is communally embedded and also largely communally conducted (Engelstad and Gerrard 2005; Weldon 2006). We do not necessarily conduct our research jointly, but even those who research and write alone rely on the community of researchers. We study and train in academic intuitions with experienced professors until it becomes our turn to teach the next generation of researchers. And we constantly engage with our colleagues' research. This is the path of research: We circulate our work in progress to colleagues, expecting their useful comments, then comment on their work when asked. On another level we peer-review articles and research proposals, and we ourselves are peer reviewed. We hope and expect that this peer-review process is done in good faith. The idea of peers itself suggests a communal setting. These and other practices all help to embed our research communally. Acknowledging this communality resolves the difficulty of blind spots. Though indeed we may be blind to the content and specificities of our own assumptions and commitments, we can and should be aware of their existence and constitutive role, aware of their function in generating the essential and irresolvable contestedness of the concepts we study and use in our research.

There are therefore two levels of self-reflexivity (Ish-Shalom 2011c). The first is a general awareness of the existence in theorizing of assumptions and social and cultural commitments and their crucial and constitutive function in conceptual politics. The second is mindfulness of the exact content of those assumptions and commitments and the complex ways they produce contestedness. The first and more general level of self-reflexivity is available to the individual theoretician, and each theoretician can be critically aware of the existence and importance of assumptions and commitments in theorizing. The second and more specific level of self-reflexivity is available to the community of researchers as a community. This second level of self-reflexivity is actually quite common. Theoreticians usually examine their colleagues' theories critically and point out any assumptions and commitments embedded in them. Part of the almost daily practice of theoreticians (at least critical theoreticians) involves disclosing the normative and ideological assumptions implicit in other scholars' theories. Thus, we can safely argue that the community of theoreticians is capable of employing self-reflexivity as an epistemological principle for studying conceptual politics.

Pluralism, or more accurately political pluralism, is associated with liberalism. John Rawls (1993) called it reasonable pluralism and championed pluralism as constitutive of his political liberalism. He argued that political liberalism acknowledges that values and virtues are always politically contested and that reasonable pluralism allows political liberalism to function as a political scheme for attaining a just, fair, and cooperative coexistence between different reasonable doctrines. Rawls thought that reasonable pluralism enables democracy to be regulated and guided by what he terms the "Fact of Democratic Unity in Diversity," arguing "that in a constitutional democratic society, political and social unity does not require that its citizens be unified by one comprehensive doctrine, religious or nonreligious" (Rawls 1999b, 124). For Rawls, tolerance within the reasonable pluralism framework means acknowledging and respecting the moral worthiness of other stands or doctrines (1999b, 59), or at least the reasonable ones, because they themselves embrace reasonable pluralism.

According to Rawls, reasonable pluralism strives for "a fair and stable system of cooperation between free and equal citizens who are deeply divided by the reasonable comprehensive doctrines they affirm" (1993, 44). And the same is true for cooperation between theoreticians with different (reasonable) sets of belief systems. As an organizing principle of the diverse community of theoreticians, pluralism will facilitate precisely that, a fair and stable system of cooperation. It will also allow this community to function in enriching, productive way to overcome and even use the disagreements stemming from the contestedness of the concepts we study in order to advance research (see also Jackson 2011; Levine 2012). In an arena like academia, where diversity is a fact, pluralism is a necessity (Nowotny 2003, 155). But more so, and echoing John Williams's reformulation of pluralism, pluralism is not merely derived from the empirical fact of diversity, it is also justified by the welcome fact of human diversity (in academia and elsewhere). Following Arendt and adhering to the tradition of the English school, Williams (2015, 20) argues for "a refocusing upon what ought to be at the heart of any pluralist case—the normative value of the diversity of human communities." In this reformulation of pluralism Williams fittingly links community and pluralism, interweaving the two normatively and inherently.[1]

But for pluralism to operate, another principle must be upheld, namely the commitment to transparency, as the mechanism for disclosing and acknowledging the moral commitments upon which theorizing rests. Understood thus, a commitment to transparency is a prerequisite for truthful deliberation between theoreticians, either in the form of John Rawls's original position or Habermas's ideal speech situations (Dryzek and List 2003, 26), and as such it can help to clarify the agreements and disagreements and their sources, that is, the moral groundwork of the contestedness of the concepts that are studied and employed in theoretical studies. Without a commitment to transparency, which is achievable through an individual and communal self-reflexivity, there cannot be a sound basis for fruitful and enriching deliberation. Self-reflexivity alone will not suffice. It centers too much on the self (even the communal self). Therefore. in order to create bridges between reasonable yet contesting theories, reflectors must disclose what they discover through self-reflexivity. In this way transparency makes the private public and in making it public allows the desired truthful deliberation to arise. Transparency transforms theoreticians into interlocutors, and the commitment to transparency forces our theoretical reflections into an academic, communal, public sphere where we can truthfully and honestly strive to elucidate the phenomenon of contestedness together with its sources and implications. A commitment to transparency founded on self-reflexivity and community organized around pluralism would therefore make theoreticians acknowledge the contestedness of the concepts they study and deal with it fruitfully, fruitfully both for their research and for their wider society.

T. M. Scanlon writes about "substantive responsibility" (1998) that it involves things people are required to do for each other. Theoreticians are not above substantive responsibility, and just as substantive responsibility binds other people, so it binds theoreticians to their wider society. Substantive responsibility dictates that theoreticians should use their competencies and advantageous resources for the benefits of society. This includes increasing the public's understanding of the essential contestedness of political concepts and the conduct of conceptual politics. As we saw, this understanding, especially within politically attuned constructivism addressing conceptual politics, has the benefit of escaping the political manipulation of fixating or emptying meanings and facilitates public Habermasian deliberation that helps to breed pluralism and the construction of reasonable and democratic agreements. Given that scholars enjoy this beneficial capacity, they are bound by the principle of substantive responsibility to engage and share this capacity with their wider society.

Yet there is one point that needs addressing before we embrace this normative conclusion. The analysis so far may have conveyed that there is an inherent and essential difference between theoreticians and wider society. It might imply an elitist conceptualization of democracy where theoreticians should join hands with the political elites in managing their polities, almost like Plato's philosopher-kings who know what is best for the common good and how to secure it, without the destabilizing, ignorant, devastating meddling of the common people. This reading not only bestows on theoreticians substantive responsibility, it also assigns them symbolic and material privileges associated with membership in a powerful elite. This interpretation is linked to the normative debates surrounding the understanding of society and democracy. In other words, this interpretation is itself part of the conceptual politics surrounding the unsolvable disagreements regarding the conceptualization of democracy: is democracy elitist and structural, or is it participatory and deliberative? There is thus a different reading of the role and status of theoreticians and the sources for that role; this reading does not depict theoreticians as an inherently privileged elite but as having vocational competences and advantageous resources that may be useful in the services of the polity and society, but only when used in a participatory and deliberative manner.

As we shall see, the elitist and structural conceptualization of democracy presents the interests of the powerful and risks co-opting academia to the service of such sectorial interests. An elitist reading of democracy and academia's role within it also betrays the respect due to the humanity, sociability, reasonable judgment, and political faculties that all people possess (at least potentially). As Avner de-Shalit argues, while justifying participatory and deliberative democracy "We value participation itself, not simply as a means of reaching decisions" (1997, 74). Participation and deliberation are the political apparatus that give due respect to the human traits and faculties mentioned above and help to actualize them by nourishing an awareness of the essential contestedness of concepts and the political mechanisms for addressing that contestedness. In other words, they are the democratic traits and practices that make academia truly engaged.

According to this reading, theoreticians' ability to understand and address the contestedness of concepts does not stem from any special characteristic not shared by the rest of society. Instead, it is the product of working in an academic-research setting and the theoretical competence developed through the theoretician's training. It can therefore be shared with society in general, although this is no small challenge. It is not something essentially secluded in academia and naturally possessed by theoreticians but a social privilege acquired thanks to public resources, among other things. As a result, theoreticians should strive toward civic engagement. As theoretician-citizens (Ish-Shalom 2013) they should seek to cultivate the principles of self-reflexivity, communal setting and dialogue, pluralism, transparency, and civic (and conceptual) engagement in the wider public. Privilege carries weighty responsibilities, and theoreticians should labor to raise public awareness of the contestedness of concepts. They should also raise awareness of the contribution that having competence in commanding Habermasian modes of openly and dynamically reasoning and attaching meaning to political concepts makes to public deliberation. That is the aim of the dual analytical gaze: to cultivate a Gramscian sensitivity to how conceptual politics is practiced, along with a Habermasian-inspired responsibility toward changing the present practices in conceptual politics. And that's what it means to understand the workings of the "Quisisana clinic," identify its weak points, and help bring down its walls.

The next chapters will develop this argument further and propose measures to concretize these principles and help academia engage in the proper sense, with the appropriate approach.

5 ✦ The Individual Level

Zooming In, Zooming Out

Concepts, those essentially contested political entities, form the building blocks of our theories. I use the word "our" because they belong to each of us as theoreticians, as individuals working in the demanding environment of academia. The fact that concepts are essentially contested and are essential components of theorizing is the entry point for the first measure of engaged academia, which focuses on the individual theoretician. Later chapters deal with the level of the collective and level of academia and the nonacademic world.[1]

We find that an epistemological and methodological strategy emerges when we focus on the centrality and importance of concepts as the building blocks of theoretical constructs and their morally and politically contested character. The strategy can be useful for theoreticians in facing their normative dilemmas and discharging their responsibilities to the wider public. This strategy, *zooming in, zooming out*, involves a two-step strategy in which theoreticians zoom in on the internal components of their theoretical constructs, namely the concepts, and zoom out in the sense of defining and conceptualizing them normatively with moral sensitivity and an eye to their effect on society outside academia.

Zooming In

The first step focuses on building the concepts (zooming in) and is not particularly novel in itself. We are expected to take our concepts seriously and accordingly train methodologically to define them. Definitions function academically in the same way that tagging, naming, and labeling function publicly. Definitions are the academic practice of bounding. We bound concepts by definitions in order to ascribe meanings that make concepts unique and specific. Definitions should provide an optimally accurate description of concepts. Definitions are distinguished from their public equivalents by the precision and rigor of the methodology that qualifies them academically. By bounding concepts, definitions offer an optimally accurate description that allows clear identification of social objects that fall within the scope of our study while filtering out those that do not. A definition must therefore be exhaustive in the sense of including all social objects supposedly captured by the concept, while being exclusive in the sense of ruling out all those that fall outside the concept's domain. Another fundamental criterion of theory construction is operationalization. This means ensuring that a definition is testable, refutable, and, if possible, helpful in measuring the phenomenon investigated. Jointly, exhaustiveness, exclusiveness, and operationalization provide us, or at least so goes the conventional wisdom, with a razor-sharp scientific apparatus for developing and testing our hypotheses. Moreover, since the definitions are supposedly transparent and neutral, they are disposed to rational and objective concurrence among theoreticians, a concurrence that is supposedly free of all moral commitment and normative bias.

But if this depiction of how we define our concepts is true and accurate, then why are those very concepts contested, moreover with the same contestedness that plagues our studies and embeds our theories in the moral commitments and normative groundwork from which they should be liberated? The first step in justifying my proposed zooming in, zooming out strategy is to answer this puzzling question.

In the social world, definition involves rounding and bounding what is unrounded and unbounded. In the social world, things do not fall neatly into human-made concepts (see also Onuf 1989, 24–25). At best, boundaries are fuzzy. Social objects are linked by comparable features and set apart by distinctive features. Hence, defining involves an arbitrary delineation between social objects, be they phenomena, processes, or otherwise. Perceptive as he so often was, Friedrich Nietzsche captured this succinctly, "Every concept originates through our equating what is unequal" (1968, 46). Defining is the inflation of the importance of some differences, setting apart some phenomena and processes (rounding). It also involves undermining and even ignoring the relevancy of other differences in order to draw various other phenomena and processes (bounding) together. This is the only way definitions are possible in the social world. As Sheldon Wolin argues, political concepts are not "written into the nature of things but are the legacy accruing from the historical activity of political philosophers" (2004, 6). William Connolly similarly observes that "to adopt without revision the concepts prevailing in a polity is to accept terms of discourse loaded in favor of established practices" (1974, 2). Accordingly, similar to naming, labeling, and tagging, defining is an act of social construction of social categories; to define is to participate actively in the social construction of social reality.

Take war. We already saw in a previous chapter how it can be labeled and named in a fuzzy way while still carrying political implications. But in IR it is first and foremost one of the main phenomena and concepts in security studies and the central phenomenon and concept for mainstream international security scholars (Walt 1991, 212). This being the case, it tends to be defined using the three criteria of exhaustiveness, exclusiveness, and operationalization. The use of the well-known operationalizable figure of 1,000 deaths, used in the Correlates of War project, is an arbitrary heuristic boundary[2] differentiating between events with 1,000 dead, which are classed as war, and events with a mere 999 deaths, which are not (as if one death can make all the difference between war and not war!). Note, though, that this arbitrary definition serves the moral purpose of studying war. The intent is to understand the causes of war and find a cure for that particular human malady. This research strategy follows a Weberian distinction between selecting and executing research: between morally vetting a particular research agenda based on considerations of pressing social problems and executing the research using objective scientific criteria (Weber 1949, 21–22, 61; for IR writings that follow Weberian lines and recommend bridging theory and relevant policy issues, see Lepgold 1998; Walt 2005).

I should immediately add, however, that the distinction between selecting and conducting research is only one part of Max Weber's sophisticated and nuanced understanding of the relations between science and ethics, facts and values. Weber argued relatedly that although science (including social science) is concerned with empirical facts and not evaluative judgments, scientific research is not devoid of values. For Weber, scientific research is inescapably value committed. As Patrick Jackson explains regarding Weber,

> The fact that we have a perspective—that our results were produced by application of concepts and procedures derived from a specific set of values—is philosophically and epistemologically important, but it has little or no

bearing on the question of whether a piece of work is "scientific" or not. Instead the decisive issue is *internal validity*: whether, given our assumptions, our conclusions follow rigorously from the evidence and logical argumentation that we provide. (2011, 22)

Thus, it can be said that Weber was acutely sensitive to the ethical underpinning of our academic work and might have been sympathetic to my proposition that academics should be more aware of what is being done with their concepts in the world outside academia.

The Correlates of War researchers had the more simple version of Weberian strategy in mind when they proposed their operationalizable yet arbitrary definition of war. The definition's arbitrariness is indeed heuristic, and as such it is helpful. But it also has problems and limitations. First, the arbitrariness obfuscates the original moral intent, discarding morality by the scientific wayside. Second, the arbitrary definition intervenes in the social world. It does this not only through the Weberian strategy of helping practitioners to formulate cause-driven solutions to the pressing social problem of war, but also, and more fundamentally, by delineating the category of war and carving a new phenomenon from it represented by a novel concept: "new war." Put differently, defining war as "new" involves formulating new understandings of social reality and hence actively participating in the social construction of social reality. Think of the definitional disputes in the new war literature and ask yourself: Is it war at all? Is there anything new about it? And while many methodological, ontological, and epistemological issues have been raised when answering these two new-war questions (Newman 2004; Malesevic 2008), our conception of this hellish phenomenon also raises political and moral issues. For example, what normative importance should be attached to the requirement of wars being fought between regular armies under the accepted definition of "old war"? Or why is it so morally important for conflicts to be (almost) symmetrical, as implicitly required by the "old war" criterion of combat between regular armies?

There is nothing exogenously obvious about these conceptual (and sometimes measurable) boundaries, and this conclusion supplies further backing for the argument defended here regarding the contestedness of political concepts. Boundaries between concepts and categories are not objective; they are embedded within normative groundworks. Defining is not a neutral and objective bounding practice. It is a moral and political act, though not necessarily a conscious one. And both politically and morally there is a lot at stake in definitions, for example, of security and war.[3] Now, more than ever, we are finding moral and legal questions concerning just war theory and its applicability to contemporary asymmetrical conflicts. The stakes are high for those involved in contemporary conflicts: Who is eligible for protection under the war conventions? How should we calculate the proportional and necessity criteria in combat situations? Should we revise the war conventions, who should undertake this, and how should it be done? (Akkerman 2009; Gross 2010; Davidovic 2016). The answer to these questions is fundamentally linked to the definitional issues of war. These concepts contain significant moral and political substance that is perceived as neutral all too often. The supposed basis for rational, objective concurrence and scientific repeatability is in fact very much contested.

Yet the contestedness of the concepts and their moral and political contents are hidden from the public eye and by and large also from the scholarly eye; among other things, they are hidden by the operationalization of the definition. Operationalization entrusts research with the language of scientific objectivity. It hides the moral commitments and normative groundwork of the concepts forming the building blocks of theoretical constructs. These moral commitments are involved whenever researchers define the concepts they are working with (e.g., security, war, and democracy) and theoretically construct the social categories later they shape into rigorous research programs. So operationalization obfuscates the normative underpinnings of theories.

The fact that researchers define and participate in the social (or sociopolitical) construction of social reality carries several epistemic and moral implications. First, their engagement in these activities raises questions regarding the claim of objectivity and neutrality. And it does this on two fronts: claims of objectivity and neutrality fail in terms of both the alleged value-fact distinction and the dichotomous separation between theoreticians and the subject matter they theorize about. Regarding the fact-value distinction (see also Frost 1996, 2–23; Hamati-Ataya 2011), I demonstrated above that fact and value are closely linked in theoretical practice and that different conceptualizations of the facticity of security are founded on different normative groundworks. This is not a contingent effect (nor is it restricted to theorizing security). Facts do not order themselves objectively into parsimonious theory (Hawkesworth 1996, 90–92; Guzzini 2005, 498). Hence theorizing requires an extratheoretical mechanism to sort and filter data and construct parsimonious theory from the complex intricacy of social reality. This extratheoretical mechanism consists of a priori normative, ontological, and epistemological assumptions that necessarily precede theory. These a priori assumptions enable the construction of theory through "affect[ing] the process of determining which data are relevant, which are less so, and which have no relevance at all" (Ish-Shalom 2006b, 441). In other words, there can be no theory without a normative groundwork and moral commitments. Theoretical knowledge is indeed about facts, but it is about facts in a value-laden way.

In addition, the alleged separation between theoreticians and their subject matter appears to be fallacious. Theoreticians are not just external observers of the social reality they study. By defining the concepts in their theories, they are involved in constructing categories and participate in forming, shaping, and constructing political events and social processes. Habermas's communicative action framework highlights this point: "In the model of communicative action, social actors are themselves outfitted with the same interpretive capacities as social-scientific interpreters; thus the latter cannot claim for themselves the status of neutral, extramundane observers in their definitions of actors' situations" (1984, xiii). Anthony Giddens asserts the same thing with his double hermeneutics, defined as "a mutual interpretative interplay between social science and those whose activities compose its subject matter" (1984, xxxii). This means that theoreticians are (and should be) part of society as producers of valuable knowledge that is both value laden and has the potential to be translated into actual policies.

It should be stressed that this is not just an abstract, jargonistic, theoretical argument about the potential of theoretical constructs to affect reality. At times, the theoretical definitions that theoreticians propose are indeed translated into policies and therefore affect social reality. This is what happened with the democratic peace (Ish-Shalom 2013; Büger and Trine Villumsen 2007), and this is what happened with conceptualizations and theories about security. During the "golden era of security studies," security scholars and experts placed their expertise at the service of different states and administrations, and as Bruce Kuklick aptly phrased it, acted as blind oracles (2006). Scholars like Bernard Brodie, Albert Wohlstetter, McGeorge Bundy, Walt Rostow, Thomas Schelling, and Henry Kissinger introduced policymakers and policy executives to their theoretical knowledge and abstract definitions and had an immense impact on the rise of the Cold War.[4] Concepts are in fact political as well as theoretical and have a dual importance for the political and the academic fields. Third, as a consequence of the last two implications, and as discussed above in depth, theoreticians bear various responsibilities to the societies and social reality they study and actively participate in shaping. As soon as the mask of objectivity and neutrality is torn away, the ivory tower cliché no longer shields theoreticians from their social, political, and moral responsibilities to the societies they study, theorize, and actively shape. Those who act are accountable for the results of their actions, and those with moral commitments are accountable for those commitments. And because theoreticians both act and act with moral commitments, they are accountable for their acts; namely they bear responsibilities to their societies for their acts and the ramifications of their acts. As I analyze elsewhere, theoreticians have several kinds of responsibility, including social, political, and moral responsibilities (Ish-Shalom 2013). Several measures ought to be taken to discharge these responsibilities, which involve three levels: the level of the individual, the level of the community (or the community of communities), and the level of society. *Zooming in, zooming out* suggests a measure to discharge these responsibilities on the individual level. This is true especially of the second part of the strategy, which involves zooming out. Zooming out is the epistemological and methodological step that ensures that theoreticians will stand up for their responsibilities, affirm their own moral commitments, and convey those moral commitments to other members of their scholarly community and other citizens of their polity. I now turn to this second and more novel move, zooming out.

Zooming Out

As we saw, the concepts our theoretical constructs consist of are political and contested; they have several possible meanings, each informed and justified by different normative groundworks. Besides the normative groundwork of the concepts and the theoretical constructs in which they are embedded, there is the set of responsibilities that theoreticians ought to adopt. These two attributes, the first of which relates to the concepts and the second of which relates to the conceptualizers, oblige zooming out. Notwithstanding the operationalization of the concepts and language of scientific objectivity that theoreticians (mostly positivists) use, the choice of one meaning actually means embracing one normative framework. As we saw, when the theoretical discourse and its decontested concepts migrate outside academia, this choice sometimes takes on real-world ramifications. That is why zooming in should be accompanied and supplemented by zooming out. Zooming in asks us to focus our theoretical rigor on reaching a better definition of our concepts. Zooming out affirms the inadequacy of exhaustiveness, exclusiveness, and operationalization as stand-alone criteria for defining. Zooming out burdens theoreticians with the obligation of defining their concepts morally, requiring they will be willing to morally justify the definitions they use to operationalize the political concepts they theorize by. And to do this, they must self-reflexively and critically engage with the moral commitments that inform (sometimes unconsciously) their theoretical definitions. It also obliges them to judge the possible real-world ramifications of their theoretical definitions in moral terms. It is not that all possible ramifications are foreseeable, but theoreticians should do their reasonable utmost to foresee the possible real-world ramifications of their theories and evaluate them morally.

Though at first glance this strategy may seem quite modest, it has fundamental implications and outcomes for social research. One obvious outcome of the zooming in, zooming out strategy is improved interactions between social and political sciences and moral and political philosophy (Onuf 1989; Adler 2005; Kahn-Nisser 2011; Wiener 2014; Williams 2015, 18). While some social and political scientists may see this as a devastating blow to scientific integrity and the soundness of their work, moral and political philosophers will not see it this way. Perceptive philosophers usually pay attention to the realities of the world and the theories that try to explain them (Enoch 2004, 240–43; Chernoff 2009, 161). This is obviously so with consequentialism, which is supposed to judge the outcome of actions (or rules) and cannot proceed without somehow forecasting these outcomes using causal mechanisms that link acts (or rules) to outcomes. This causal mechanism is sought in social and political science theories (see, for example, Singer 1972, 241).

The same tendency to use social and political science theories to understand real-world processes also exists in deontological moral theories. Deontologists also rely on causal mechanisms borrowed from social and political sciences. As C. A. J. Coady argues from the deontological standpoint that "even those of us who think that truth, in some substantial sense, does apply to moral discourse need to acknowledge that moral truths are supported by practical reason and are dependent in complex ways on issues of practicality" (2004, 788). The complex relations between moral and practical reasoning, or, in the terms employed here, between moral and political philosophy and social and political sciences, are relevant across the different security issues and problems addressed by both these disciplines (each with its own methodology and aims). We find it in just war theory, which is based on the security reasoning that "if there is no probability of achieving the just causes, the war's destructiveness will be to no purpose" (Hurka 2005, 35) and the war will be deemed unjust. We also find it in attempts to justify conscientious objection that also focus on the prospective outcomes of this act and whether it would "have a devastating effect on the integrity and continued capacity for efficient functioning of the military" (McMahan 2006, 387; see similar reflections by John Rawls on civil disobedience, 1999a, 328). If they are expected to have such a devastating effect, moral judgment may sway against conscientious objection. The ability to forecast those outcomes does call for reliance on and familiarity with relevant social and political science theories.

So philosophers are well aware of the work going on in the social and political sciences. Moral and political philosophers perceptively rely on causal mechanisms to establish their justificatory schemes. In other words, they need to keep social science theories in mind in order to set up their moral and political theories. Zooming in, zooming out calls for the philosopher's awareness and reliance to be backed by a complementary awareness and reliance on the part of social and political scientists. To this end, social and political scientists must be aware of the moral and analytical work of moral and political philosophers. They don't need to invent the moral wheel. They just need to be able to use the moral definitions that support their moral commitments in a self-reflexive fashion.

As we saw, theoreticians' moral commitments are operative in the acts of defining and the theorization that follows. Quite often, however, theoreticians are unaware of the inherent moral aspects of defining and theorizing and hence do not acknowledge them. Operating in the dark and being unaware also means that their moral commitments are not fully developed, and this can cause internal weakness and problems with the operationalization requirements and epistemological position of research (McSweeney 1999, 43). An example of this is Stephen Walt and John Mearsheimer's attempt to influence American foreign policy. Rodger Paine writes that through their realist theoretical insights Walt and Mearsheimer acted as critical theoreticians arguing against the war in Iraq (Payne 2007). Yet, as both Paine and Ido Oren (Payne 2007; Oren 2009) point out, Walt and

Mearsheimer's experience with changing the reality they study was counter to their positivism and its commitment to a separation between research and researched.

Zooming out, then, endorses critical theory praxis and tries to find a more conscious, reflexive, and acknowledged attitude toward the workings and implications of the theoretician's moral commitment (for recent examples, see Geis and Wagner 2011, 1577; Hobson 2011, 1918; Levine 2011, 5; 2012). Zooming out calls for moral commitments and their implications to be made explicit and transparent to both theoreticians and theorized (Nowotny 2003, 153; Jasanoff 2003, 240; 2007). This strategy encourages theoreticians to be able to morally justify the definition they choose when theorizing and be willing to engage critically with their own moral commitments. Their doing so could contribute significantly to the moral and analytical improvement and enrichment of the definitions of their concepts. And regarding security, the different theoretical approaches explored in the first part of the book should explicate the role of theoreticians' normative groundwork in defining and theorizing security—and encourage their use it as a justificatory apparatus that is not merely a neutral, operationalizable method. Thus, realists should use their consequentialism to justify conceptualizing security narrowly as militarized international security; and the same is true regarding critical security studies, which should use a critically oriented deontology to justify security as emancipation. Human security studies should use the capability approach to justify security as freedom from poverty. Feminist security studies should use care ethics to justify security as safeguarding against the actual and daily persecution of the marginalized, and poststructuralists should use their ambivalent relativism to avoid foundational conceptualization and definition.

All this will improve theorizing, its products, and its theoretical constructs. I do not pretend this will be an easy task. It is daunting but doable, and the social, political, and moral responsibilities of theoreticians require it. Moreover, zooming in, zooming out serves as the basis for all the other measures of engaged academia, as we shall see below.

Truth

But before considering these measures, another nagging question should be addressed, the question of truth (see also C.A.S.E. Collective 2006, 475).

Shouldn't the definitions and theories that we expect to be precise also be faithful to truth? Shouldn't they just be true? And while the answer of course is yes, there is still nothing simple about being true. There are several theories of truth. They include correspondence, coherence, pragmatic, and consensual theories, each with its own criteria for deciding truth (see, for example, Booth 2007, 231–32). But which theoretical criteria should we use to determine what truth is? How do we decide which theory is valid and which is true? This is bearing in mind that these theories are theories of truth and that we must pick out one that gives us a set of criteria that lets us decide which theory is true and what truth is. But we need these criteria to choose one of these theories. So here is the problem with truth: we need truth criteria to choose truth theory, and we need truth theory to choose truth criteria. We are locked in circularity in such a way that truth remains impenetrable.

But that does not mean we should abandon the notion of truth, since true and false do exist. For example, it is true, dear reader, that you are reading this sentence now. It is also true that Descartes had hands and that their existence helped him to cope with radical doubt (Descartes 1988, 76–77). And it is also true that security, war, and other related concepts and phenomena exist. War exists and causes real suffering and insecurities. This is a true fact. Insecurities also arise for other reasons, for example, hunger or lack of political freedoms. This is also a fact and as true as a fact can be.[5] I do not question the reality of the phenomenon of security. Nor do I question, as Jean Baudrillard did in a poststructural fashion, the beyond-the-text reality of war (1995). All I do is raise questions about the appropriate attributes of defining the concept that represents these phenomena. What I ask is how theoreticians should approach defining and suggest that they should supplement their usual definitional approach with normativity. I argue that within the act of defining, within the practice of bounding, fact and value truly join metaphorical hands to produce truth as a living entity that should be treated as such (Ish-Shalom 2011d, 839). It is in the definitions we use that value encircles and generates fact and where fact derives value and circumscribes it. And this is a truth that we should cherish. We should cherish it not by abandoning academic rigor, but by joining different academic disciplines and methodologies in order to produce exhaustive, exclusive, operationalizable, *and* normative definitions. Theoreticians must strive reflexively and dialogically to explicate the normative groundwork that is inherent in their acts of defining the concepts they use in constructing theories. Theoreticians must explicate the normative groundwork of their theories, be ready to justify that groundwork truthfully, and convey those moral commitments to other members of their scholarly community and other citizens of their polity. We will in what follows see the proper way to convey these moral commitments.

6 ✦ The Second Level

The Community of Communities

There is a tremendous multiplicity of views and theories in IR, but not enough pluralism in either the Rawlsian sense of respecting other reasonable views and theories or in the sense of meriting, valuing, and nurturing this multiplicity. On the contrary, all too often IR finds itself in interparadigmatic wars (and "big debates") in which many of us dogmatically shut our ears to other arguments (Sylvester 2013). This tendency impedes our capacity to establish truth as the living entity proposed at the end of the previous chapter and to constitute academia as an engaged entity. Instead of dismantling the walls of the "Quisisana clinic," academia is involved in the politics that reconstitute the clinic within academia. The prospects for a truly engaged academia and establishing truth depend on the willingness to participate in open, sincere dialogue founded on mutuality and openness of mind. This is especially true when we embrace the opening move of the book, recognizing that the concepts we analyze and mobilize for our theories are essentially contested. When multiple legitimate definitions exists that are all founded on different sets of normative commitments, then the conceptual world we occupy and study guarantees the multifaceted being of truth: no single theoretical perspective holds the one absolute key to a monolithic truth. This explains the importance of acting as a community of dialogue and the ethical and no less important epistemic significance of pluralism and dialogue. To this end, I wish to offer certain normative principles that should guide us in our efforts to establish academia as a scholarly community that offers its members a forum for engaging in and through dialogue and the opportunity to produce meaningful and truthful knowledge.

My normative proposal for organizing the scholarly community has three foundations, each of them more communally driven than the last.

Together the three will justify my call for an engaged academia as a community of communities. The first foundation is John Rawls's pluralism, the second is Kymlicka's multiculturalism, and the third is Martin Buber's dialogical philosophy. Rawls's pluralism (or political pluralism) establishes the need to respect other (reasonable) theoretical perspectives, multiculturalism provides added moral force to the need for toleration, and dialogical philosophy affirms the merit and duty of open-hearted listening. Each of these foundations adds normative and epistemic force to a pluralistic and dialogic community that can be conceptualized as a community of communities.

Pluralism is anchored, among other things, in the understanding that the basic units of our shared political lives, be they concepts and categories, values, norms, rights, or virtues, are essentially contested. This is an understanding that defies both dogmatic universalism and moral relativism (see also Galeotti 2007; Kratochwil 2007, 506; Seymour 2010, 204) and supports a middle ground that respects diversity without approving an attitude of everything goes. With this in mind, John Rawls (1993) championed reasonable pluralism as constitutive of his political liberalism. For Rawls, democratic society is governed by the "Fact of Democratic Unity in Diversity." This diversity is comparable to the aforementioned IR multiplicity of theoretical perspectives, a multiplicity that in fact upholds respectful cooperation and does not deteriorate into interparadigmatic war. Reasonable pluralism is what enables political liberalism to function as a political scheme for achieving a just, fair, and cooperative coexistence between different reasonable doctrines (Rawls 1999b, 124). The same also holds true for cooperation between theoreticians with different (reasonable) sets of belief systems. Pluralism as an organizing principle of the IR theoreticians' community will facilitate exactly that, a fair and stable system of theoretical discussions benefiting all theoretical parties. Accordingly, it can facilitate the functioning of this academic IR community or community of communities in fruitful and enriching ways, normatively overcoming and epistemologically utilizing the disagreements and diversity reflected in the contestedness of the categories and concepts we study. In the academic arena, pluralism, where multiplicity and diversity is not just a fact but a welcome fact, is a necessity (Williams 2015, 20).

The respectful and just cooperation between different theoretical perspectives (or the communities that advocate these theoretical perspectives) can also help in overcoming the problem of the blind spots that lower the chances of successful self-reflexivity at the level of the individual scholar. The problem of blind spots and their effect on self-reflexivity has already been analyzed and likewise the way that blind spots prevent scholars as individuals from recognizing and identifying their assumptions, convictions, and commitments. But the community of researchers *as* a community can help us overcome the problem of individual blind spots. In the communal setting of theoretical research, theoreticians are already committed to critically scrutinizing colleagues' theories and exposing the assumptions, convictions, and commitments embedded in them. It is part of the almost daily practice of theoreticians (at least of critical theoreticians) to identify the normative convictions and ideological inclinations implicit in other scholars' theories. Thus, scholars are equipped to mutually and reciprocally unravel blind spots and hidden assumptions. They counterbalance blind spots and show that the reciprocal and mutual benefit in their practice lends epistemic force to organizing academia as a community committed to fulfilling this potential.

But what do I mean by community? I certainly do not mean community in the sense of a homogenous group that shares a total belief system. I do not mean community as a monolithic imposition on its members. When I discuss community, I mean academia as a group of people who share certain core beliefs that loosely unite them, while diverging on many other important beliefs. They are united by the broader academic values of public truth-seeking, openly, methodologically, rigorously, and with a sense of healthy skepticism. Yet it is a community of theoreticians who are divided along numerous axes and by numerous a priori assumptions such as how to establish truth (epistemology and methodology), the content of that truth (ontology), and what to do with that truth once it is established (ethics). It is a community comparable with Rawls' democratic unity in diversity in the sense that it is constituted by multiplicity and values, merits, and upholds this multiplicity using the principles of pluralism, multiculturalism, and dialogue. It is indeed a loose community and nothing like Ferdinand Tönnies's gemeinschaft or gesellschaft; but it is a community nonetheless by any moral sense.

Furthermore, the unity in diversity continues to work and loosen the community itself as a priori assumptions coalesce into different and (again loosely) distinct theoretical communities consisting of realism, liberalism, critical theory, feminism, constructivism, poststructuralism, and many more. These are the basic paradigmatic building blocks of our discipline.

But to even speak of the community as those who share a specific paradigm, such as the realist community, and liberal, Marxist, constructivist, English school is too constraining and misleading. These communities can all be further subdivided. Thus, realism can encompass the loose communities of classical realism, structural neorealism, neoclassical realism, and let us not forget offensive and defensive realisms, each communally organized around its total, shared belief-systems. The same internal subdivision can also be applied within the liberal, Marxist, constructivist, English school, and other communities, and the communities can be organized around subject matter rather than theoretical assumptions. It is sensible to talk about the communities of theoreticians who study and theorize international political economy, conflict resolution, human rights, transitions to peace, transitions to war, globalization, global justice, integration, identity formation, civic-military relations, and so on. And the same holds true for the criterion of methodology, say the communities of quantitative, qualitative, and formal modelers, comparatists, historicists, discourse analyzers, and more. Each of these criteria is robust enough to legitimize a section in the International Studies Association, and indeed many do constitute such sections. Each can be seen as a community, but note too that none can be totally delineated from the other communities. A community, say, structural neorealists, can be distinct from the community of neoliberal institutionalists, yet some of its members can, for example, be jointly united in the community of formal modeling. It may even be seen by critical outsiders as one community, the "neo-neo" community (Wæver 1996). Scholarly communities, like all the other categories studied earlier in the book, have fuzzy borders, and delineating them firmly requires bounding (and rounding) practices. Enter multiculturalism as the second foundation for organizing academia as a community and as the normative perspective that translates pluralism from an individualistic orientation into a communal one and an attitude of respect to the guarantee of liberty within and between communities.

The normative thrust of multiculturalism has two movements. The first movement involves the sheltering of minority groups within the wider society, enabling them to conserve and cultivate their own culture. The second, which is especially valid with nonliberal communities, is to protect the members of minority communities from oppression by their own groups and guarantee them liberty, most importantly the liberty to leave their group if they wish. In the words of Kymlicka, the leading normative theoretician of multiculturalism, "Liberals can and should endorse certain external protections, where they promote fairness between groups, but should reject internal restrictions which limit the right of group members to question and revise traditional authorities and practices" (1995, 37).[1] The risks facing IR theoreticians, whether members of mainstream positivistic communities or more marginal communities of the postpositivistic and critical ilk, are not as stark and dramatic as those usually discussed in multiculturalism. IR scholars do not face genital mutilation or schooling prevention. The stakes are different and may involve overcoming structural and personal obstacles to getting published and receiving research grants as well as overall marginalization in academic settings. Worst-case scenarios involve difficulties in getting promoted, a grave risk indeed, especially when trying to surmount the tenure hurdle. In departments overpopulated with positivists, critical theoreticians (assuming they were hired in the first place) may face higher obstacles to promotion than those facing their positivist colleagues. And the same may hold true for the junior positivist scholars in a postpositivistic department (albeit a rarer sight). These paradigmatic obstacles can function like the oppressive internal obstacles of nonliberal groups that prevent their members from quitting the group and force young scholars to join paradigmatic communities based on disciplinary constraints rather than scholarly considerations. More common problems are domineering doctoral advisers who abuse their power to enforce a particular theoretical perspective on their advisees (regrettably, other forms of abusive relations, such as sexual harassment, also exist). A commitment to multiculturalism works against such obstacles to promotion and career development (where these obstacles are not founded on genuine considerations of academic excellence). And it sits well with the academic ethos of academic freedom, the goal of which is to enable us all to write and teach without bowing to the sociological and political considerations of disciplinary power imbalances—without fearing censorship or retaliation either from within or from outside academia.

The disparity of power within the IR community of communities also carries the opposite risk, namely the voluntary ghettoization of the communities, especially the more disempowered and marginal postpositivists. And it is understandable on the human level that we would prefer discoursing with like-minded people rather than struggling with resentment, disagreement, and misunderstanding outside our own theoretical party (Sylvester 2013, 615). The fact is that ghettoization defends integrity against disciplinary pressures by offering communal warmth, a preferable alternative, surely, to confronting censorship or retaliation and conforming to more dominant methods and perspectives. Nevertheless, regardless of how understandable and convenient it is to converse exclusively with like-minded people, the result is the lack of the type of true and fruitful interchange that enriches theoretical discussions and is at the heart of the academic vocation.

We therefore need multiculturalism as a normative model for addressing dogmatism, interparadigmatic deafness, and interparadigmatic wars. The aim of this model should be to get the broader IR community to want to listen or at least be willing to listen, and for critical theoreticians not to be overwhelmed by the urge to seek safety in a warm postpositivist ghetto. In our context, then, the normative thrust of multiculturalism should be to facilitate bridge building and dialogue within and between the different constituent academic communities of the community of communities. Consequently, the normative principles derived from multiculturalism that should guide us in constructing an academia that is a community of communities are the same normative principles that we keep meeting in this book—namely pluralism, transparency, self-reflexivity, and dialogue. Together, these four principles can guarantee "*freedom within* the minority group, and *equality between* the minority and majorities groups" (Kymlicka 1995, 152). We discussed the first three principles—pluralism, transparency, and self-reflexivity—earlier, and I now wish to explore the principle of dialogue.

Theoretical interchange can be conceptualized as deliberation. Deliberation is a democratic virtue that, as I have argued, can also be epistemically useful by helping to clarify theoretical agreement and disagreement. But if we take theoretical conversation and deliberation a step further, we arrive at Buber's notion of dialogue. Buber focused on the possibility of entering into a genuine dialogue in what he called the *I-Thou* relationship. For Buber, an I-Thou relationship establishes an interpersonal sphere that enables a true community to be constructed. Buber's philosophy is immensely rich, multilayered, and very wide in scope. He was one of those Renaissance individuals whose writing expands on diverse topics such as theology, biblical studies, political and social philosophy, epistemology, sociology, education, and Zionism. Buber (1878–1965) was born in Vienna, and his academic and intellectual career took him to Germany. In 1938, the rise of Nazism and persecution of Jews drove him to Palestine, where he was appointed the first chair of the sociology department in the newly established Hebrew University of Jerusalem. Although he had an interest in sociology from an early stage and studied under Wilhelm Dilthey and Georg Simmel (Avnon 1998, 24), the horrors of World War I and later of the Holocaust heightened his interest in the human studies and social and political philosophy. Buber's interest in the possibility that genuine human relationships could help in curing the alienation he saw in modern society (Silberstein 1989) were sparked by the maladies of modern society.

The core theme of Buber's philosophy is dialogue as an authentic human phenomenon which involves a meeting between persons fostered by a mutual and intentional opening of hearts. It is dialogue that acts as the thread that gives Buber's mature philosophy unity.[2] It is fleshed out in his anthropological philosophy, his social and political philosophy, and his understandings of epistemology and ethics.

Buber maintained that despite living in a state of social alienation, man can heal society by entering into interpersonal dialogue conditioned on presence, true intention, and mutual opening of hearts. These three traits can lead to genuine dialogue which constitutes the I-Thou relationship as a relationship of unmediated listening and unity of existence. Constituting the I-Thou relationship establishes the interpersonal sphere that Buber calls the *Between*, which allows a community to be constructed as a We. Community is characterized by the quality of its constituent I-Thou relationships, which gravitate toward a common *Center* where several I's are bound into a We, which Buber envisioned as a form of ethical human and social existence. The Center is the shared facet of human society that reduces alienation and allows dialogue to take place. The obverse kind of relationship is the *I-It* relationship, which instrumentalizes society's members and distances them from each other. I-It relations maintain the alienated conditions of human society, preventing the constitution of the dialogical community as We.

According to Buber, I-Thou and I-It relations not only exist between persons but between persons and nature and persons and intellectual essences such as theory (Vermes 1988). It is here, in the relationship between persons and nature and between people and theory, that Buber's phenomenology is most pronounced, and where his philosophy is best suited to understanding the qualities and functioning of science, theory, and the communal nature of academia. Buber understands science and theory as relating to nature in the I-It mode, which is characterized by distance and instrumentalization. Admittedly, this way of doing science and social science furthers material progress. However, Buber emphasizes that relating to nature this way may hinder greater human progress. Accordingly, we should strive for a more balanced and humanized science that relates to nature and social reality in an I-Thou mode as well.

Alexander Kohanski describes the essence of the Buberian dialogue as follows, "In the act of speaking *I-Thou* one must be willing to step into relation with the other without holding himself back, without putting the other in doubt, without reservation whatsoever. This is the true state of dialogue" (1982, 22). And this is how Dan Avnon described the I-It relation, which is the obverse kind of relation involving no real dialogue: "In an *I-It* attitude to being, the person tends to distance himself from the other, to create in the interpersonal a quality of relationship characterized by the person's desire to distinguish him- or herself by accentuating differences, by emphasizing the uniqueness of 'I' in contrast to the other" (1998, 39). These two quotations capture the essence of true dialogue. In an encounter between two humans, they can open their hearts with mutuality and reciprocity and establish a genuine understanding and unmediated relationship conducive to the construction of truth as a plural and living entity.

Buber's dialogue goes further than deliberation because it not only facilitates sincere and democratic conversation within an existing group, but also facilitates community. True dialogue in an *I-Thou* relation is a fundamental precondition for establishing human community,

> The special character of the *We* is shown in the essential relation existing, or arising temporarily, between its members; that is, in the holding sway within the *We* of an ontic directness which is the decisive presupposition of the *I-Thou* relation. The *We* includes the *Thou* potentiality. Only men who are capable of truly saying *Thou* to one another can truly say *We* with one another. (Buber 1947, 213; see also Arnett 1986)

And it is this community, freed from alienation, that will enable and even ensure ethical relations between all its members and later on also between members across communities. A community that can withstand its disempowered minority status will prosper against external pressure and produce meaningful and resilient theoretical knowledge.

Moreover, dialogue advances external theoretical conversation and interchange. It helps in overcoming the common and problematic academic practices mentioned above, such as dogmatism, turning a blind eye to the insights of other theoretical frameworks, and a tendency toward all-out interparadigmatic wars with gatekeepers who do all they can to prevent the publication and promotion of theoreticians who do not adhere strictly enough to the theoretical creeds they advocate. These practices become semi-institutionalized in journals that seem like theoretical bastions closed to other theoretical perspectives and departments that recruit like-minded researchers and churn out acquiescing students in a kind of academic cloning facility. Sadly, these departments are common in universities, including the most prestigious ones. In our academic world, it is sometimes enough to label scholars constructivist, postmodernist, or for that matter realist in order to shut their colleagues' minds to their ideas, depriving them of a chance to benefit from their writings. As argued above, this predisposition is especially harmful to scholars whose ideas place them in marginalized theoretical parties, parties that lack resources and positions of power. For such scholars, enforced closure encourages self-imposed ghettoization and marginalization. And marginalization not only harms the marginalized individuals but also the broader IR community by depriving it of true and fruitful interchange. Buber's dialogue joins pluralism and multiculturalism here in delivering multiculturalism's promised good of "*freedom within* the minority group, and *equality between* the minority and majorities groups" (Kymlicka 1995, 152). And this promised good is what fosters the building of fair and productive bridges between theoretical parties.

These fair and productive bridges are founded first and foremost on a healthy sense of self-reflexivity with its awareness of vocational and individual limitations. This takes us back to the issue of self-reflexivity that is reaffirmed by the Buberian dialogue. Self-reflexivity, that is, goes hand with hand with dialogue and community. Buber argued that there can be no true knowledge of the world and human society and community without self-knowledge, or as we call it today, self-reflexivity. "Philosophical knowledge of man is essentially man's self-reflection, and man can reflect about himself only when the cognizing person, that is, the philosopher pursuing anthropology, first of all reflects about himself as a person" (Buber 1947, 154–55). In order to know reality, one must know one's own assumptions that act as filters and distort the true encounter with reality. Buber conceived theoretical knowledge very similarly to feminist standpoint epistemology, the claim that all knowledge—theoretical knowledge included—is situated both socially and politically; that is, all knowledge is determined by the position of the knower in the social hierarchy and his ensuing social and political commitments. As Lawrence Silberstein clearly explains, for Buber, "The sociologist lacks an Olympian perch from which to look down and see things independent of his or her own perspective" (1989, 170). The same understanding drives feminist epistemologists to call for self-reflexivity or, according to Sandra Harding's conceptualization, strong reflexivity, which she characterized as requiring that the objects of inquiry be conceptualized as gazing back in all their cultural particularity. According to this view, the researcher, through theory and methods, stand behind them, gazing back at his own socially situated research project in all its cultural particularity and relationships with other projects of his culture—many of which (policy development in international relations, for example, or industrial expansion) can only be seen from locations far away from the scientist's actual daily work (Harding 1991, 163). Put differently, it is important for researchers to be critically aware of their own idealist assumptions and social and cultural commitments that affect their research and theoretical framework. Expressed in phenomenological terminology, being aware allows bracketing,[3] which mean that in the encounter with social reality, theory and any other unintended biases and filters must be put on hold to achieve a direct and unfiltered encounter with social reality. There can be no theory without assumptions and commitments that "affect the process of determining which data are relevant, which are less so, and which have no relevance at all" (Ish-Shalom 2006b, 441). It is important for scholars to identify a priori assumptions and social and cultural commitments in their theories and understand how these function as filters and biases that interfere with a genuine encounter with reality. Communally practiced dialogue facilitates this personal competency and practice of self-knowledge or self-reflexivity.

It is noteworthy that Buber does not ignore the importance of science, including social science, and theory, which he considers a crucial aspect of human activity. Through science we can address the complexity of the world, making it is essential for progress (Silberstein 1989, 120). By distinguishing, measuring, and comparing different phenomena, people can achieve some control over their environment and produce artifacts leading to material progress. Buber evaluates science positively and highly esteems its output (Silberstein 1989, 120). This ties in with the following chapters, which analyze the public merits of theory. However, the essence of relations that are characterized by controlling nature and using it to produce artifacts for material progress is the essence of instrumentalization and alienation. The scientific approach works on the basis of I-It relations that are detached from reality and social reality (Friedman 1976, 172) and from fellow citizens and scholars. Accordingly, while respecting science and certainly not rejecting its utility, Buber allocates it its proper place. Science is crucial for material progress but we should not mistake material progress for human progress, and we should not let the I-It scientific approach imperialize our relationship with nature, reality, and social reality (Friedman 1976, 172; Silberstein 1989, 174). Besides this instrumentalized I-It scientific approach, it is also important to cultivate a direct relationship with nature, reality, our fellow citizens and scholars, and social reality writ large. These direct relations must be unhindered by theory or any other systematic assumptions that we use in engaging our surroundings. We can achieve this phenomenological understanding once we engage ourselves in dialogue, and it is this type of understanding that legitimizes the strategy of zooming in, zooming out explored in the previous chapter.

To approach the same understanding differently, reality is complex, and to get a hold of it we equip ourselves with theory and systematic thinking. Theory, that is, is a competent tool for organizing reality heuristically and helping us to cope with it, for example by shaping plans and policies that navigate the complexity and produce what Buber calls material progress. But I hasten to add that complexity also entails richness and that richness is not something to be "coped" with, but something to enjoy. And to enjoy the richness of reality and social reality, we must be willing to bracket theory and other systematic thinking that prevent us from having a direct and phenomenological relationship with reality and social reality. In Buber's words, "Each of us is encased in an armor whose task is to ward off signs" (1947, 27). Bracketing theory allows human progress that is not just limited to the material but includes the ideal, intellectual, and cultural aspects of our humanity. It was this human progress that Buber urged us to seek in the belief that it would help liberate modernity from alienation. Bracketing enables theoreticians to identify and understand their theories' weaknesses and limitations; it contests dogmatism and allows the construction of a true, pluralistic academic community of communities capable of engaging with society; it advances thinking about social and political problems and participation in deliberating better policies; it helps achieve a flexible and effective execution of those policies. This perspective assigns theory an important though confined social role. Drawing on Richard Rorty's terminology of the ironic liberal (1989), we can characterize Buber as an ironic theoretician. Rorty tried to reconcile his own relativist undercurrents with a political commitment to liberalism in a perspective he called ironic liberalism. Buber too tried to reconcile his commitment to science with an equally forceful understanding of its narrowness; hence, ironic theoretician. I agree with Buber's perspective and maintain that this should be the nature of our commitment to the role of theory and theoreticians alike.[4] Heuristically speaking, theory is indispensable to confronting reality's complexity, yet this complexity is irreducible, which means we should be aware that by heuristically theorizing complex reality we are losing some of its richness. Additionally, theorizing reduces the complexity of reality and inevitably distorts it. A lack of awareness of the distortions and a priori assumptions guiding our theoretical quests and generating distortions may sabotage our encounter with reality and affect the quality of any policies derived from the theories. Therefore, it is important to complement our awareness and ironic theorization with pragmatism, modesty, and flexibility when constructing our theories and executing any derived policies. This all leads us to experience a sense of community where theoreticians participate in *I-Thou* relationships and listen to each other truly and sincerely without imposing their theories on either colleagues or fellow citizens. It is a true dialogic community that fosters pluralism and multiculturalism and acts to register the truth.

What does it mean in practical terms to organize academia as a dialogical community of communities? There are various measures that can help us to achieve this, including measures relating to conference design, advising graduate students, editing scholarly journals, policy on faculty recruitment, and showing more solidarity with and respect for our part-time colleagues. First, I suggest that workshops are the right venue for scholarly meetings and genuine, face-to-face meetings. Instead of streaming toward mammoth associational conferences which (let us admit) are mostly performances practiced among huge publics (but rarely in front of them), our emphasis should be on intimate and recurring workshops where a small number of scholars can meet, having read each other's papers, with ample time to present and take part in constructive discussion. Rather than channel considerable resources into major annual conferences, our focus should be on these smaller venues, which should be organized on a recurring basis and where possible produce cooperative special issues and edited volumes. We should also try to gather scholars from different paradigmatic parties (or communities) as well as different cohorts and career stages at each workshop. This will ensure a plurality of theoretical voices, genuine discussion, and the development of a healthy irony toward theory. The field should also be opened via journals and departments, whose practice should reflect their commitment to a plurality of theoretical perspectives. This should be the responsibility of the editors (as well as the editorial boards and reviewers). We need editors to send manuscripts to fair reviewers, those who are not likely to reject our ideas because we have different theoretical affiliations but will genuinely judge the quality of our argumentation. The same holds true for department chairs and faculty. We need them to show a commitment to pluralism in their recruitment policies, promotion procedures, and teaching and student advisory practices and culture. And true dialogue is indeed possible within the framework of advising graduate students. Genuine advising has two non-mutually exclusive forms: first, long lasting, I-Thou relations between adviser and advisee, including one-on-one meetings, and, second, creating groups of graduate students that can act as a We dedicated to scholarly cooperation. Those two forms can ensure close presence and listening. Moreover, advising should not be understood as a form of cloning or indoctrinating students to subscribe to a particular theoretical party, but as helping them become scholars who fulfill their potential and educating them in the ways of true pluralism.

And then we have the thorny issue of part-time and adjunct faculty who do not enjoy tenure with the academic freedom, work stability, working conditions, and social benefits that come with it. The number of part-time lecturers is on the rise and so is their percentage among American university and college teachers, where their number is 50 percent and in community colleges where they are 70 percent of faculty (Eagan, Jaeger, and Grantham 2015, 452). Budgetary constraints, growing student populations, and neoliberal management practices are increasingly causing academic administrators to recruit this way (National Center for Education Statistics 2001; Schuster and Finkelstein 2006; Gappa, Austin, and Trice 2007; Coalition on the Academic Workforce 2012). Thus, more and more PhD graduates are locked into insecure, unsatisfactory jobs without any real academic future, few social benefits, and no protection of academic freedom. Tenured (and tenured-track) faculty tend to ignore them, making the part-timers feel alienated from their academic institutions as second-class citizens who disrespected by permanent faculty (Eagan, Jaeger, and

Grantham 2015). This is wrong and harmful for the part-time academics and detrimental to creating a true community as it should be constituted and practiced. All this has far-reaching implications. Evidence shows that the reliance on part-timers and adjunct faculty prevents the dialogical commitment to students that I suggested is part of the communal setting of research. For part-timers are less available to students (Umbach 2007) and less able to enter into I-Thou relationships with them (and their colleagues). Thus, the spreading practice of hiring part-timers is destructive to the part-timers themselves, to students (many of them will find themselves part-timers), and to academia as a community (of communities).

Academics should struggle against the spreading and abusive phenomenon of part-timers not only for the usual moral and justice reasons but also for the sense of community that should guide us. A number of intermediate measures have also been suggested in the struggle to end this abusive working practice. Tenured staff should seek to improve the working conditions of part-timers and strive to integrate them into the academic community. Eagan, Jaeger, and Grantham (2015) have studied the satisfaction levels of part-timers, focusing on involuntary part-timers (those who unsuccessfully aspire to a tenured-track position). They suggest several modest measures that can help part-timers. These include making the part-timers legitimate participants in departmental and institutional decision-making, providing them with office space and career development options, and recognizing their achievements with awards. These modest measures are all aspects of showing respect, which the part-timers are entitled to, and helps create a sense of community.

Part-timers and adjutants are the outcome of processes that are not all controlled by academia. Shrinking budgets, rising student populations, and neoliberal management norms and practices also affect academia's relations with the administrative staff without which no university worthy of its name can function and with which some university executive managements, constrained with budgetary difficulties, succeed through divide and rule to break any sense of communal solidarity. This is even worse with other populations who are responsible for tasks that are outsourced to external contractors such as cleaning staff and in some countries security personnel. Academia as a community (of communities) must not ignore these staff and leave them by the wayside. They, like part-timers, students, and faculty members, are essential to the running of institutional academia, and we need to start thinking of them as part of our community. Whatever is internally essential to the structure of academia (in contrast to, say, farmers who grow the food we need to eat to do our academic job) should be part of academia as a community, as a We constructed on a set of I-Thou relations. Acting thus, academia may become the moral model it should be. It will also be morally better positioned to reach outside and engage polity and society.

IR should be organized as a community of communities in which communities are understood loosely and along several axes, including the theoretical, normative, methodological, and organizational, and subject matters. In this community of communities there is not only multiplicity but also self-reflexivity, pluralism, multiculturalism, and dialogue. These four principles, which fit in so nicely with the principle of academic freedom, can guarantee that academia as a community of communities will be equipped to academically pursue truth as a plural and live entity. The IR community of communities will also be prepared to act as engaged academia in an environment of essentially contested concepts. We now turn to this aspect of engaged academia as I suggest how to engage the public and, no less important, how not to engage the state.

7 ✦ The Third Level

Structural Problems

The first two levels are internal to academia and academics. The third level, engaging with state and public, is external and hinges also on entities and institutions external to academia. It depends on the structural conditions of academia but also on those of state and society, the structural relations between academia and state and society, normative dilemmas arising from those structural conditions and relations, and decisions taken not only by academia but also by state and society. The first section explores some of the tensions stemming from structural conditions that arise between academia and the state and the dilemmas they create. The section suggests that because of these tensions, relations between academia and the state are confrontational and, from the perspective of academia at least, also problematic. The upshot of this analysis is that (1) academia should focus its engagement efforts on society and not the state, and (2) think tanks may be more appropriate state agentials for applying academic ideas to state interests. They may thus function as academia-state intermediaries. The next two chapters will concretize the proposals for engaged academia in two common academic practices: forecasting and consultation. The chapters analyze the concrete risks of academia-state relations and how forecasting and consultation should be better performed when they arise through engagement with society.

Structural Conditions of Potential Tensions

Let us consider the different rationales of university and state. Both are institutions. Both are generally expected to be managed and administered by rules and regulations that are transparent, fair, legal, and rational. Both fairly regularly fail these expectations. Among other things, both operate to benefit their members. But it would be safe to say that this short list in fact exhausts the similarities between these two institutions. The list of differences is longer and more substantial than the list of similarities. The principal mandate of states is to provide primary and public goods, such as welfare and security. States are committed to providing these goods for their members, namely their citizens. In this crucial respect states are sectarian and partial, committed to their citizens often at the expense of other people. Universities, as their name implies, are committed to a more universal constituency that they supply with a universal good, namely knowledge, which they can produce and distribute generally and impartially. That is not to say that academics necessarily lack partial interests and preferences. As the next chapter on academic forecasting and democracy explains, it is possible that academia may be invested in particular and sectorial interests, which could be the interests of academics as a distinct and interested professional group, or academics belonging to and representing a certain socioeconomic class (if so, then it is probably the middle to upper middle class).

Here my theoretical framework parts ways with Karl Mannheim's sociology of knowledge. Mannheim relates to what he terms the intelligentsia, a broader category than my own reference to academic theoreticians, which he sees as socially unattached and outside any particular class. Thus, as a group, the intelligentsia has no class interests, and intellectuals can distance themselves sufficiently from any perspective to achieve a total perspective on politics. Mannheim therefore had great expectations from the intelligentsia and assigned it an important unifying role in politics (see especially 1936; see also Jackson 2011, 172). Perhaps it was his mistaken claim of social nonattachment that led Mannheim to his later disillusionment with the intelligentsia and to his abandoning hopes for their ability to play a positive political role. John Heeren (1971) analyzes the evolution that Mannheim's expectations about the intelligentsia underwent. I have a different starting point and see academic theoreticians as socially grounded and attached and hence quite possibly interested. But, I suggest, academic theoreticians have assets and capabilities that, alongside the modesty and caution I call for, can equip them for the role of theoretician-citizens.

But be that as it may, academia is not (necessarily) bound by statist interests. So, although it might be partial to some extent, it is not (necessarily) partial in the statist sense. Also, whatever academia's possible sectorial interests, they probably tend toward the cosmopolitan, especially if those interests represent academia as a distinct professional group (rather than as part of the middle class). After all, academia operates on the global level and in the international domain and the professional networks that academics develop are transnational. But even the middle to upper middle class is more global in reach and perspective than other classes. At least in that sense, universities can and should be committed to the universal and aspire to be so committed.

These structural differences project an attitudes toward research. While states are certainly interested in the production and distribution of knowledge, their main interest is and should be applied research for the welfare and security of their citizens. Universities are chiefly interested in basic research, in knowledge for its own sake. This distinction imperfectly echoes Robert Cox's (1981) famous distinction between problem-solving and critical theory. The applied research that interests states is the kind produced by problem-solving theory. And while most theoreticians do not define themselves as critical theoreticians, critical theory, which is critical in the sense of theorizing the rise and fall of systems, including the system of states or universities, is the territory of university-based research. While states may try to harness university-based research for their own agendas (sometimes against the agendas and interests of other states), universities try to maintain their research autonomy, admittedly while being financed by states.[1]

In IR, and especially in conflict and security studies, states and universities could be on a collision course. There are several reasons for this. First, this is where universities' interest in basic research might conflict with states' needs for applied research. IR scholars seek to understand war and conflict: their origins, nature, unfolding, and ending. States wish to use this research, among other things, to overcome their adversaries in war and conflict. This collision course is set despite the not necessarily dichotomous difference between basic research and applied research. University-based scholars would like to apply their basic research especially in the areas of security, war, and conflict. They do wonder about the best way to apply their knowledge gained from basic research. But, whereas university-based scholars would like to use knowledge *to overcome war and conflict*, the state organs want to use that knowledge *to overcome in* war and conflict. That is one crucial difference that should not be ignored: although there is no dichotomous delineation between basic and applied research, the thrust of university-based war and conflict scholars is toward the universal and (conditionally) impartial application of knowledge, whereas the thrust of state-employed experts is toward sectarian and partial application. Put differently, and to return to Cox's distinction, although the aim of both academia and the state is problem-solving, the two may have different problems in mind. For academia and its experts, the problem is war and conflict. For state and its experts, it is defeat. Academia may aim to overcome war, while states aim to overcome *in* war.

This is not to argue that states seek war or that all scholars are committed to the pursuit of peace. I only note that as *institutions* the operative rationales of states and academia have different directions. Notwithstanding their probable commitment to stability and peace, states, or at least most of them, must take the possibility of war into account and must plan for this scenario. On the day of reckoning, states and their security organs will be expected to lead a successful war (overcome *in* war). Academia is mostly free of such reasoning. True, universities in conflict zones need emergency procedures for what to do and how to close down in the event of crises and violent conflicts. For example, Israeli universities organize emergencies drills, and Palestinian universities operate daily under military supervision and intervention from Israel or local Palestinian militants. But these are the exception rather than the rule, and academia as institution is free to pursue peace and must be normatively committed to this cause (overcome war).

Besides the difference in aims, there is a second difference: the state organs involved in war and conflict are mostly the security sectors, which are committed to secretiveness. Universities are committed to transparency, of course, which leads to striking disparities in the ethos and operating procedures of university-based scholars compared with the security sectors. However, the security sectors do have an interest in recruiting university-based experts and utilizing their skills, knowledge, and capabilities. Thus there is always a risk of university experts being co-opted to serve sectarian state interests secretively instead of acting transparently on behalf of universal interests: of becoming agents of overcoming *in* war rather than agents *of* overcoming war.

And there is another difference, and an acute one, especially in terms of security, war, and conflict. The state and the university have different timelines. The state's interest in war and conflict peaks at times of war and conflict; it thus is shaped in and by crisis. States look for consultation and expertise in situations of conflict. And then their expectations and demands take on new urgency. The university's treatment of war and conflict is a lot more tranquil. It is shaped by the same structural features that shape basic research, and these features are time consuming. When a crisis erupts and the state needs its experts most of all, the academics may not promise to be there. The structural differences between state and university are quite stark, and in terms of security, conflict, and war they are fundamental.

The three tensions that we noted above are significant. They highlight considerable risks for academia in cooperating with and serving the interests of the state. The most serious risk is co-option and betraying academia's universal commitment. And the risks are such that they should caution academics against cooperating with the state. But there is another important point to note: Academia still can and should benefit the world outside it. However, it should not do so through the state and state organs (or not principally). The benefit to the world outside academia should be provided especially for and through society, through the principles of engagement that are outlined in the book's conclusions.

Cooperation with state should not be categorically banned (even if academia could have imposed such a ban). But when such cooperation is being carried out, it must be handled with the utmost caution, while bearing in mind the risk of co-option. Additionally, think tank experts might be those who are optimally placed for meeting state requirements for research-based knowledge, expertise, and advice. They can operate within the time frame of the state in crisis and are mostly interested in applied research. In the collision course of state and academia, think tanks can be mediators; not only in the sense of a 'transmission belt" (Lepgold 1998), but also as shock absorbers. They can translate academic universal and basic research into something that the state needs and can cope with. Likewise, by providing the much-needed expert information, think tanks help the university-based experts in withstanding the heavy pressure from the state that may result in co-option, making university-based experts serve sectarian state interests instead of the interests of universality. There is also some sense in maintaining a good flow of knowledge from university to state practitioners, including security agents, because knowledge can help moderate state objectives and behavior. Hence, there is a need to strike a balance between maintaining the autonomy of universities and making sure university knowledge does not remain secluded in academia. A kind of delicate balance must thus be found between seclusion against co-option and cooperation for the common good. Think tanks might play a crucial role in striking this important and delicate balance.

Basic Research versus Applied Research

Take the scenario of the mad political scientist, who following decades of careful research, induces that the state is the cause of war and conflict. The mad political scientist approaches senior statespersons and presents them with the results of this meticulous study, expecting their applause and maybe even a juicy state grant to study how we might peacefully disassemble the state. Perhaps like the mad political scientist we should expect the statespersons to mobilize resources and disassemble the state, hence increasing the life prospects of the state's citizens and lots of others around the world: a somewhat naive expectation, but not devoid of some internal reasoning. If the mad political scientist seeks a universal act of disassembling all states, the costs and benefits could be distributed equally and no state would be affected more or less than any other state. The recommendation even combines the realist reasoning of relative gains with the liberal reasoning of absolute gains. All else being equal (which it never is), state and universal interests are not in conflict, which may motivate cooperation between states to disassemble themselves.

But what if that same mad political scientist's meticulous study leads to a somewhat different conclusion? What if it concludes that the cause of conflict and war is not the state per se but the power disparities within the state system? And what if it concludes that the way to overcome conflict and war is by redistributing power resources between all states, by taking away from the most powerful and giving to the weakest, with the aim of leveling all states? Now, imagine a plausible scenario, that the mad political scientist is the citizen of the most powerful state. And after all wasn't IR declared an American discipline (Hoffman 1977)? Now would you share the expectation that statespersons should finance a follow-up study on how to subtract from their own state in order to give to other states so that everyone is level? Note that this time, certain (though not necessarily all) fundamental interests of the mad political scientist' state and the other states diverge and even conflict. Well, in this scenario the chances of the mad political scientist gaining the ear of the statespersons are close to nil. Enter Coburn's amendment.

Coburn's amendment (first round in 2009) and the heated public discussion around it reveals the deep-seated or potential animosity between state and university, especially in the field of political science, between those who study politics and those who practice it. In 2013, after years of failing to push forward radical bans on financing research proposals in political science, Senator Tom Coburn adopted a new tactic of moderating his demands and using procedural circumstances to help pass his revised amendment, which states that if a proposal is not recognized as "promoting national security or the economic interests of the United States" the National Science Foundation would not be allowed to finance it. Though the immediate target of the Republican senator from Oklahoma was American election studies, his wrath made no discrimination between social sciences as a whole. Social sciences are presumed guilty unless proven otherwise: they work against US interests or at least fail to promote them and thus do not deserve state funding.² But there is another insight to be drawn from the Coburn amendment and the imaginary mad political scientist—that the distinction between basic and applied research is not so stark (Jasanoff 2003, 229). Obviously basic research is applicable and generates applied research (which in turn generates more basic research). But sometimes basic research is itself applied research. Yet the process of projecting basic into applied research can take many forms. Among other things it is grounded in the interests, ethos, and motivations of the institutions where the projecting occurs. Think of war and conflict, which are among the most salient phenomena and concepts in the field of security. The sectarian interests of the state may lead state-based experts to try to project basic research about war into strategic guidelines on how to overcome others in war, how to win the war over the state's specific enemy. University-based conflict and security scholars are meant to be guided by the universality of academia and apply the basic research of war and conflict to critical reflections on how to win over war, how to end the phenomenon itself. This is a major distinction that is greater than the distinction between basic and applied research, a distinction that is actually a continuum.

This distinction also dictates a cautious attitude by academia when asked to advise state institutions on conflict and war. On the one hand, academia should be keen to establish channels for influencing state conduct. Establishing these channels may help academia benefit society, for example by providing alternatives to war and by moderating state violence. Think of harnessing state agents by giving them information about just war stipulations or widening and broadening their understanding of the notion of security: how security can be understood and practiced not just in terms of safeguarding it when there is fear of a military threat, but also when there is fear of lack of food, sexual harassment, or dictatorial domination. These are all legitimate fears that can cause insecurity in both individuals and collectives. Hence they are all legitimate concerns for security agents—or at least they could be if these agents' understanding of the essentially contested concept of security is widened and broadened (for example, by university-based security experts). Although academia has a commitment to basic research and knowledge for its own sake, its responsibilities need to include benefiting society as well. And nothing in the discussion so far indicates that basic research necessarily conflicts with benefiting society, at least not when society is conceptualized universally as humanity as a whole. But basic research can certainly clash with benefiting society when seen along particular and partial lines, when society is bounded within the state. Thus when asked to advise state organs on conflict and war-related issues, university-based conflict experts should be cautious about cooperating with state, as cooperation can lead to co-option in the sense of succumbing to state sectarian objectives.

Transparent Academia and Secretive Security Sectors

There is yet another consideration to be noted that is especially relevant to war and conflict studies. Militarized conflict is the business of security agents that are committed to secrecy, whereas their university counterparts are and should be committed to transparency. This theme is explored further in a later chapter, but since it is relevant here as well, I will touch on it briefly.

Transparency is the commitment to disclosure and openness. Secrecy and secretiveness are a commitment to confidentiality and concealment. Transparency is for academic security experts what secretiveness is for security agencies and agents: it is the key to success and thus an occupational ethos and vocational ethics. Notwithstanding certain caveats (explored below), we do expect and are accustomed to secretiveness in military conduct, and we expect transparency from academia. Academia is bounded and constituted by transparency. Transparent disclosure is an ethical and epistemological precondition for accessing truth and objectivity. Many academic approaches, ranging from positivism to radical feminism, have argued for transparency and complete openness; for positivists, full transparency allows replication of experiments and studies in order to confirm or refute results and theories: we need to know the data set, analysis procedures, experimental manipulations, definitions, and assumptions underlying the study structure. When we know all these things, we can proceed to replicate the study and see if we get similar results. The political scientist might be mad, but his research procedures are all open so his colleagues can scrutinize them. Transparency, then, is a sort of insurance policy guaranteeing the soundness of research, whoever conducts it. Transparency is a basic epistemological and methodological requirement for mainstream positivism.

And the same is true beyond positivism at the other end of the academic spectrum. Standpoint feminist epistemologists, for example, argue for transparency as a way to achieve strong objectivity. In combination self-reflexivity and transparency provide a fuller understanding of a person's cognitive and emotional processing when thinking about and theorizing the world. If we disclose to ourselves and others the biases that distort our theories, we facilitate the understanding of how such biases function and affect our theorizing process. Combined with transparency, self-reflexivity allows us to understand the origins of those biases and how they are created in the social setting where we live and experience life and which forms our social standpoints. And it is these social standpoints that allow us to conduct research, though they also limit our ability to gain outlooks broader than our own narrow perspective. According to standpoint theory, it is important who conducts research, since our personalities, identities, values, and interests are all embedded in the process of research and thus influence our theoretical outcomes. This proposition produces two more arguments. The first, somewhat like positivism, is that transparency helps the research community to highlight the personal traits that shape research biases and help correct them in the name of better, less biased research. The second argument is more radical, as feminist standpoint theoreticians argue that strong objectivity is directly correlated with the theoretician's marginality. What they mean is that as a cautionary measure, the disempowered and marginalized adopt also the perspectives of the powerful who are their potential victimizers. The disempowered and marginalized thus have a broader view of the world and hence a wider theoretical perspective. In other words, they have an objectivity that grows increasingly strong. Transparency is both a personal and communal resource that helps us understand strong objectivity and identify those with the potential for it. Learning from them may help all of us improve our research so that transparency is a precondition for good research. We may find that the mad political scientist who is marginalized as a madman does have strong objectivity, and we should seriously discuss his findings regardless of state pressure and the Coburn amendment.

In transparency terms, security sectors and agents are diametrically opposed to academia and academic experts. Security sectors and agents are defined by secretiveness. We need secretiveness to surprise on the battlefield, and surprise is one of the main means to achieve victory in war. Indeed, the art of concealment (and deceit) has been perfected by militaries and other security services. The state, with the public, mobilizes for this concealment through censorship laws, counterintelligence services, and antitreason laws targeting betrayers of national secrets. Thus, another structural distinction between state and university is their diametrically opposed positions on the secretiveness-transparency axis: Secretiveness is a constitutive and definitional feature of the security sectors just as transparency is a constitutive and definitional feature of academia.

Time

The difference between basic and applied research is reflected in another structural feature of academia: the timeline of university life, research, and publication. Consider how long it takes to produce the kind of research our universities merit. Certain time elements are substantial, like the planning and conduct of research. But the process is also influenced by the pace at which one completes the preliminary stages, for example, the stage of raising funds before the research begins. Quite often this requires significant effort, energy, and time in writing and submitting proposals that then go through the review process, which may delay the research a year or two. And only then, once the funds are gathered, can one recruit research assistants to help gather the data. The researcher then analyzes the data amid all the myriad assignments of university life (such as reviewing other researchers' proposals); thus the research can substantially be prolonged. Now comes phase three of the research, the race to publish. Without publication, no research is really over. We are now talking about several more months for reviewing, rejections, reviewing, revising, resubmitting, and acceptance. The acceptance verdict marks the fourth phase, when the research joins the infamous publication backlog that languishes in the CV under the heading of "forthcoming." Even with the welcome innovation of prepublication (Online First, Advanced Articles, FirstView, etc.), matters still drag on for another few months. A year or two then passes before final publication. After that comes the nail-biting, as researchers wait for articles to refer to their published research (a lot of time for nail-biting). The cycle is now fully complete and the researcher can start pushing for promotion, which takes another eternity (it could be during this eternity that our colleague, the mad political scientist, lost his sanity ages ago). The university has all the time in the world.

Academic life proceeds at its own languid pace, on which it thrives. This pace also structures academia's time expectations, which enables the structure of the academic publication industry to endure and the publication backlog to reach its present monster levels. We no longer expect to produce relevant pieces of research, relevant in the sense of providing useful information in a timely manner. By the time our research is published, it is already out of sync with the world. Our perspective is the academic perspective. Arguably, the added value of academic research is not immediacy, but retrospectivity. An open question is whether immediacy and retrospectivity can be combined. Perhaps the added value of retrospectivity is just a self-justificatory mechanism. Relevancy and retrospect are certainly combined in the exact and medical sciences with novel publication models. So maybe it is not impossible to combine the two. Maybe we got used to this lingering on the part of academia and accept it as a force majeure.

But we are also hostages of this timeline, as we are evaluated and merited on its basis. If we wish to be recognized in our circles and gain promotion, we must submit our work to this sluggish process and structure our research to its demands. This is a quasi enslavement. And even now in the era of tweets and personal blogs, the focus of most of us is on this traditional publication venue, and so is our research. No wonder. Universities credit faculty members mostly, in fact almost exclusively, for traditional peer-review publications. Many universities declare their commitment to good citizenship both inside and outside the academic halls. Academics are encouraged to accept administrative tasks and contribute to society. But when push comes to shove, when evaluating our performance in the crucial hiring phases and more so in getting tenured and promoted, the universities' declarations are exposed as nothing but cheap talk. We are not seriously credited for our good citizenship, especially not those of us conforming to the practices, principles, and measures I call engagement, namely the deliberating interaction with the broader society. This university policy of crediting creates a structure of incentives that influences academics' decisions on investing their limited resources. Too often good citizenship is set aside. Publications are only merited and credited when they are peer reviewed and follow the well-trodden paths dictated by traditional, old-fashioned, time-consuming academia. There is really not much time left to write op-eds, commentaries, and what have you. Academic research is strong as retrospect and in retrospect. It is weak on relevancy.

Unfortunately, even if we have grown used to it, the world has no time for this kind of dragged-out timeline (and publication priorities), especially not during conflicts that tend to unfold as crises. A crisis is a state of instability that requires immediate decisions (Hermann 1972). That immediacy clashes with the lingering pace of university. Executive decisions, especially in a crisis, call for data and information in a timely and relevant fashion (Nowotny 2003, 152). Executives need the products of research in exactly that fashion which university-based scholars have forsaken. This is another structural schism that divides university and state and can heighten the tensions between the two institutions. The state expects timely research and can blame university-based scholars for failing to deliver the goods they were supposed and expected to deliver, especially if they are state funded. That makes university-based conflict scholars vulnerable to accusations of detachment from the urgent needs of citizens, that is, of not contributing helpful ideas when crisis and conflict erupt.

Combining the Three Sets of Contrasts

Going back to our friend the mad political scientist: his commitment to transparently pursued, universally impartial knowledge brings him into conflict with his state and its security sectors with their interest in secret, timely, and sectorially applied knowledge. University-based conflict scholars and state agents may inhabit two unbridgeable worlds, and our mad political scientist and his saner colleagues could find themselves torn between obverse interests, pressures, and institutional ethea. Moreover, the mad political scientist not only faces external pressures to cooperate but perhaps also an internal dilemma over the question of cooperation. Despite such obverse interests and ethea, there are also good reasons for the sides to seek communication and for the mad political scientist to find a middle ground or mediator to help lessen the pressure on him and his colleagues to cooperate with the state.

And there are good reasons to cooperate. Academia is often state funded and expected to repay the state, for example with advice. Public-funded bodies owe the public something in return for taxpayers' funding, and the public can reasonably and legitimately expect access to beneficial knowledge. Second, and aside from public expectations, consultation can also supply a public good, and a responsible academia should try to contribute toward the public good. In the field of conflict, academia could contribute by proposing alternatives to violence along with ideas for moderating state and security sector behaviors. In the broader field of security, academia might suggest an alternative conceptualization of security and reach out to the public through the wider and broader conceptions of security among the various schools of security, such as the critical and feminist schools. The newer conceptions and understandings of security can change public expectations of the state—especially regarding its commitment to citizens and the behavior of its agents in war time. Broader and wider conceptions of security can also widen public expectations and lead citizens to expect the state to provide more than just national security. Citizens could expect the state to provide and equip them with capabilities that would enable them to prosper and gain agential standing. Regarding state agents' behavior, broadening and widening the concept of security might be the best educational mechanism for the state to address women's fears of sexual harassment and rape in wartime and show respect for their autonomy. Note, though, that much of the educating role of academia and (critical) university-based experts is effected through public deliberation and citizens, not necessarily through official state organs. Note too that academia's educational role produces strong public coherence as defined sectorially by the state and universally by academia. No longer does there seem to be a disconnection between the public as defined by state borders and the public as defined globally by humanity. Their interests may be shared. Divergences in publics' understandings could cohere around universal interests in moderation and prudence regarding resort to war, conduct of war, and postwar routine. With their ability to make positive contributions, university-based conflict scholars should not stand idly by. They should try to play a proactive role in promoting public goods, like moderation.

University-based conflict scholars can also benefit themselves from cooperative relations between academia and state. Sometimes the only way for experts to gain access to essential data is by cooperating with the security services. Committed as they are to secrecy, security services are habitually tightfisted about sharing information. They might consider sharing their information if they recognized a potential gain and would probably condition access to knowledge on a commitment to secrecy. The bargain would be clear: information in return for an agreement to secrecy and for valuable consultation. This is a heavy price for the mad political scientist and his colleagues who are committed to basic research and transparency. But without that wealth of confidential data, scholars can hardly practice their expertise, which depends largely on knowledge. And of course there are more mundane and human considerations linked to working with the security services, such as the tempting prospect of privilege and power associated with being part of the club, among those who advise the powers-that-be (but more on that later).

Thus, there are quite a few benefits selfish and otherwise to be gained from intimate cooperation with state and its security practitioners. But the benefits come with the heavy price tag of surrendering academia's commitments to basic research, universality, and transparency. Cooperation may end up being co-option. The mad political scientist may find himself serving the powers-that-be and working against all he is committed to and believes in, including universal interests. On the other hand, if scientists do not wish to lose the benefits of cooperation, namely the flow of beneficial knowledge, there are the following options. First, they can work with society through the channels of deliberative and participatory democracy and attempt to widen and broaden the public's understanding of security by presenting novel and critical conceptions. Society, not state, must be the aim of any truly engaged academia committed to the struggle to ensure that citizens do not experience the Quisisana clinic and to combining security and democracy in one proper semantic field. Second, we should look for an institution that can bridge these worlds and through its in-betweenness network literature ease the flow of information, reduce the price tag of rapprochement between academia and state, and relieve the pressure on the mad political scientist and his colleagues. It should be an institution whose nature, functioning, incentive structure, and rationale is "in between."

Think tanks are the answer to this in-between world, as they are an institutional arena with the goals and function of applied research and a vocational culture of expertise that respects basic research and methodology, perhaps not always rigorously. Another caveat is in order here, much like the earlier one regarding academia. The analysis offered here of think tanks may be biased due to my acquaintance with the Israeli and American worlds of think tanks. Some differences may exist between think tanks from different states as well as in their positioning between academia and state. Again I suspect, however, that the commonalities are more substantive than the differences, so that the general thrust of my argument should hold, at least across the democratic and developed world: think tanks should be assigned a role as "in between" academia and state.

Think tanks genuinely credit their researchers for interaction with the world and motivate researchers to expend resources and energy on this interaction. Obviously think tanks are not homogenous. Some are in universities and are part of the university's institutional world, while others have no university affiliation; some belong to political parties and serve political and ideological platforms (Mirowski and Nik-Khah 2013), while others are politically neutral; some have general interests, while others are very narrowly focused. More importantly, though some think tanks are universally oriented, far more are statist and oriented to their state. They are particularistic in the statist sense of acting as translators of universal basic knowledge into state-driven applied research. Another thing that qualifies think tanks as go-betweens is that they include representatives from both worlds. This refers to both university-educated experts and sometime even university-*based* experts who double their university affiliation with a think tank association, along with former security agents who joined the research world as a second career. This mix is another institutional feature that gives think tanks the bridging capacity we seek. And, of course, think tanks often develop their own widely accessible, fast-tracked publication media venues. They publish commentaries, blogs, working papers, executive summaries, and so on, and credit their researchers with these publications, which are widely circulated across numerous channels and diverse audiences, including the executive, the public, and academia. This means think tanks are well equipped to produce applied and relevant research and circulate and facilitate the application of immediate knowledge in peacetime and conflict. They often also achieve public respectability as knowledge producers and gain the trust of state and security organs whose language they speak. Thus they have the ears of the security establishment they routinely advise.

Note too that think tanks operate in different institutional environments than universities. They have no right to exist unless they are policy-oriented and problem-solving and have a full commitment to applied research. Their whole raison d'être is to influence the political system and security establishment directly (Smith 1991; Stone 1996; McGann and Weaver 2002; Rich 2004; McGann 2007). Therefore, in the case of think tanks, co-option is a lesser issue since they are potentially part of the establishment and have a vested interest in cooperating with it. They are a true intermediary between academia and state. So it stands to reason that labor should be divided between university-based conflict experts and think tank-based conflict experts. Being policy oriented, think tanks are the transmission belt (Lepgold 1998) and responsible for translating basic academic research and theoretical knowledge into applied research, producing policy guidelines and practice.[3] Moreover, by providing the state and its security organs with these translation and transmission services, think tanks can also act as shock absorbers and reduce possible pressure on university-based conflict scholars.

The mad political scientist can now press on with his research, thinking perhaps that in a conflict, when immediate and relevant knowledge is required, his knowledge can and sometimes will be translated into immediate use. He is now subject to less pressure and may move ahead in his tranquil research mode, transparently and universally producing basic research, aware of having the institutional option of doubling his affiliation and becoming involved in the think tank world and contributing directly to the immediate distribution of relevant knowledge. By doubling his affiliation and using think tank communication channels and writing styles, he can directly contribute to the public good and, as analyzed, use his academic scholarship to combine the sectorial statist understanding of public with the universal one. That way the mad political scientist can ensure that winning in war and conflict means winning over war and conflict, if not today, maybe tomorrow.

With this in mind, we can now turn to two concrete activities academia sometimes provides state and society, forecasting and consulting, and analyze how they should and should not be performed. Applying the dual analytical gaze, we take another stride forward and focus on the

Habermas-inspired facet of the dual gaze, namely academia's responsibility for changing how present-day politics is practiced. This is addressed in the next two chapters. The first examines the issue of forecasting through the concept of democracy, and the second examines consulting in the context of security. Each chapter will add moral force to the proposal for an engaged academia and together help to triangulate security, democracy, and academic scholarship.

8 ✦ Traveling Forward in Time

Forecasting and Realizing the Spread of Democracy

The grandfather paradox describes the logical problem (or even impossibility) of time travel. Suppose you travel back through time to the day when your grandfather was young, well before he parented your mother. In a violent feud you stab him to death. What then? Is your own existence still possible? Since your mother has not been born, you yourself can't possibly be born. By traveling back in time could you have you annulled your own existence? This thought experiment gets even more paradoxical if we try to take it a step further. If you were not born, you could not travel backward in time, nor could you kill your grandfather. Time has returned to its "natural" course. Your grandfather parented his daughter, your mother, and she gave birth to you. You are now alive again, a time traveler, and slayer of your own grandfather. And so on and so forth. Your grandfather, mother, and you are locked in an unending cycle of appearing and disappearing, Like a dying electric bulb that flashes on and off, but without fading to black. It can go on forever, if "forever" has any meaning in this type of time-traveling scenario. Note that the event that locks all the participants in the paradox need not be on the epic scale of slaying an ancestor. Any minor event during your time travel can change the course of events and prevent your birth.

What is the link between the grandfather paradox and the academic's role in an environment of contested concepts? What does the paradox teach us about engaged academia? The original purpose of the paradox was quite different from my aim here. The grandfather paradox was generally used to prove the logical impossibility of time travel though there have been philosophical attempts to salvage time travel from the paradox's claws. I have another reason for mentioning the paradox, which is morally oriented. The paradox tries to show the logical obstacles to the present interacting with the past—the logically impossible consequence of an extraneous agent who starts a process, extraneous in the sense of not belonging in time. I wish to analyze the moral and democratic dilemmas involved in the present interacting with the future; the possible negative moral and democratic consequences of an extraneous agent starting a process, where this time extraneous is in the sense of not necessarily belonging democratically, or at least in the sense of involving agents whose legitimacy to intervene in democratic processes can give rise to normative issues and thus be questionable.

The argument is based on the following reasoning. Forecasting, including academic forecasting, commences processes that interact with social reality and affect its course of evolvement. Academic forecasting is founded on theoretical research that, as argued and demonstrated above, is grounded in normative commitments and assumptions. Hence, academic forecasting may introduce the moral commitments embedded in the forecast into the evolution of social reality. Hence, judged from a democratic perspective, forecasting can involve prioritizing and empowering certain interests, preferences, and values compared to others, and could end up distorting democratic processes. Problems and distortions especially arise when the forecasting theoretician comes from outside the democratic or democratizing community subjected to forecasting. So we need to consider if and how democratically appropriate forecasting is possible, especially on the subject of democracy and the spread of democracy and democratic norms.

My proposal is to forecast as theoretician-citizens, that is, as members of an engaged academia that acts in a participatory and deliberative way in and through the public sphere and through civil society. And it is here where the grandfather paradox becomes relevant by changing its function from proving the logical impossibility of time travel to grounding the normative proposals of an engaged academia whose dual analytical gaze can intervene in public and political discussion, open space for criticism, and strengthen democratic agency rather than elitist structures of dominations.

Forecasting in the Social Sciences

Prognostication is inbuilt in theorizing. We prognosticate regularly on the basis of theory, and with good reason. First, theorizing involves finding patterns (and explaining them). If there are patterns, they can supposedly be projected into the future. So it makes sense to prognosticate based on theory. Second, we prognosticate using the methodological tools of hypotheses to test the validity of our theories (de Sola Pool 1978, 29). If a theory finds patterns, then its prognosis should come true. If it does not, there may be something wrong with the theory; if the prognosis fails, prima facie, the theory is refuted. Hypothesis-based prognostication is therefore a powerful methodological tool. Of course, it is not as simple as it looks. Patterns in the social world that are covered by social science theories are mostly probabilistic. So we cannot expect prognostication to be totally accurate. Deviant cases are almost always the rule in social sciences, and the question of how many cases we need to refute or validate a theory remains open. Karl Popper made a point of this question, raising the problem of induction to establish his own principle of falsifiability (1963). And it is not always clear exactly when the prognostications should come to pass and testify to a theory's validity. Sometimes the time frame is part of the prognostication. For example, take the cycle genre, such as the Kondratiev wave, Kuznets cycle, or Modelski's long-cycle theory (Modelski 1987). They usually come with a time tag, specifying how long it should take to validate the forecasts. Mostly, though, this issue is not so clear, and there is a question about the time allocated for verifying the hypothesis. Notwithstanding these two difficulties, prognostication is used to test theories and is especially achievable due to the patterned nature of the processes that theories cover and discover.

A third reason to prognosticate based on theory is that doing so might be socially useful (Mearsheimer and Walt 2013, 436). Prognostication involves applying the beneficial potentiality of theory as an intellectual accomplishment that is rich in informative and analytically processed knowledge regarding the causes of complex processes and multifaceted dynamics of their evolvement. Accordingly, theoretically grounded prognostication can be very helpful in shaping policies, which are public tools for coping with the complexities of the social world and the multifaceted nature of social processes.

Although the tendency to prognosticate when theorizing is inbuilt there are at least two things that reduce our ability to prognosticate processes and events in international politics. The first is ontological. International relations are an open system (Bhaskar 2008; in IR see Wight 2006, 51–52) and as such influenced by too many variables to be reliably predicted.[1] That is, the same thing that makes theory a potentially beneficial tool, namely, the complexity of the social world, also limits our ability to theorize. This is a point worth stressing because it gives rise to an irresolvable tension between potentiality and our real ability to actualize that potentiality that we should be aware of. The second challenge to prognostication is epistemological and concerns the nature of theory. The prognostications discussed here are grounded in theory, and by nature theory is to some extent grounded in personal standpoints and moral commitments (more on that below). Thus, our prognostications are partial in that they advance a specific set of values and interests (albeit not in any statist fashion), usually at the expense of other values and interests. And just as there can be several theoretical explanations for any events and processes that we study, so they can have multiple prognostications. As argued above, a plausible explanation for having several possible explanations is that the concepts that form the building blocks of theories are essentially contested. Contestedness necessarily invites the moral into the theoretical. The normative commitments of theoreticians are necessarily implicated in the process of constructing theories. Thus, prognostication in the social sciences feeds on the tension between potentiality and the actualization we just mentioned.

While it might not be a precise scientifically based prediction that "dispenses with probabilistic interpretations" (Choucri 1978, 4) and tries to offer accurate foretelling, social science theory-based prognostication is far from being a subjective prophecy, as it follows strict methodological and epistemological rules. I will therefore designate the practice of prognostication based on social science theories: "Forecasting," Nazli Choucri explains, "is made in terms of alternatives . . . [and] involves contingencies" (1978, 4; see also Freeman and Job 1979; Gaddis 1992–93, 6). Prognostication in the social sciences is therefore an intermediate creature, as it is partly scientific and partly not so scientific, and it offers some beneficial potentiality for society by helping it shape effective policies and confront the complexities of the social world.

The Transformational Powers of Forecasting

Forecasting has the potential to shape behavior. Think of the impact of weather forecasting on our daily habits: the way we dress, what we say, our plans for our annual vacation (and don't we just love criticizing forecasters when the weather proves them wrong). Prognostication about international relations and the spread of democracy may be less reliable than the weather forecast, and it is certainly less reliable than other types of scientific prediction. But it too can shape the course of events by influencing the expectations and behavior of social actors. And in contrast to self-chastisement, which is practiced in IR so very often (for a recent example, see Walt 2012), forecasts influence expectations and promote forward-looking rational planning and in doing so engender processes of social change.

The translation of forecasts into actual behavior involves several mechanisms. For example, forecasts can become self-fulfilling prophecies if policymakers mobilize them when devising policies. They can also become self-refuting prophecies. By publishing politically laden prognostications, political actors use forecasts as tools to struggle against what they consider unwarranted sociopolitical processes. And then we have cases when theories are misused by politicians and ideologues to advance their own agendas (de Sola Pool 1978, 31). We find this first option, that is, when politicians consciously mobilize forecasting to devise policies, quite commonly. One example, from the domain of trying to spread democracy in the world, was Walt Rostow's recruitment by the Kennedy administration in the early 1960s to translate his modernization theory into a policy blueprint (see Ish-Shalom 2006a). Rostow's forecast that modernization would lead to the most modern and positive political institution of all, democracy, was followed by the translation of his theory into a policy blueprint. This was the forecast that modernization with its attendant growth and prosperity would establish the foundation for a modern, democratic society by pursuing education, which in turn would promote social and political skills. Rostow's forecast was that modernization would also engender a sense of agency and community in the citizens and a feeling of responsibility regarding active participation in shaping the common life, responsibility that lies at the heart of democracy as a political culture and set of norms (1988, 111–19). Rostow did not stop at abstract theory; he used his theoretically grounded forecasts to develop concrete foreign policy recommendations, arguing that the United States should supply the investment needed by developing countries to overcome the obstacles besetting their development. A second point Rostow stressed was the importance of social justice. He believed that states could only prevent large gaps from growing between different sectors of society by providing social justice; gaps could impede the social cooperation necessary for national growth, development, modernization, and democracy. Rostow also highlighted that while the United States could help facilitate to growth in developing countries, the majority of the burden and the main work and responsibility lay with the developing states and their societies. Rostow saw modernization as synonymous with democracy and active political participation, neither of which could be imposed from outside or by applying paternalistic pressure (Millikan and Rostow 1957, 55–78; Rostow 1961, 48–49; 1964, 142–43). This is a point we shall come back to from a different angle.

By means of his various posts during the Kennedy administration, Rostow helped to reason and establish the Alliance for Progress. The Alliance's goals were formulated in the summer of 1961 and included economic growth and greater equity in the distribution of public resources such as education and health. Rostow's theory-grounded forecasts became reality (albeit short lived). Essentially, his theoretically grounded forecasts became self-fulfilling prophecies.

Conversely, the most notable historical example of self-refuting forecasting is Karl Marx's sociopolitical predictions and Otto Von Bismarck's introduction of social policies. When Marx presented his economic theory and forecast that unavoidable economic processes would lead to the rise of the proletariat and to the collapse of the capitalist economy and bourgeoisie order, the conservative Bismarck took it as a warning and introduced the first set of modern welfare laws. He thus alleviated the social tensions of the era and in doing so may have contributed to refuting Marx's economic theory (Riedel 2007). Another example of self-refuting forecasting more directly related to democracy is Robert Putnam's theory of social capital and his own involvement in the American public sphere to counter the worrying patterns he saw and theorized about. As explored at length by Oren (2006), Putnam's theory of social capital and its importance to the vitality of civil society and democratic norms led him to forecast, especially in his celebrated *Bowling Alone* (2000), the decline of the American polity. But, as a concerned citizen, Putnam refused to surrender to the pessimism of his own theoretically grounded forecasts. He became a civic activist and spearheaded the social and political initiative of the Saguaro Seminar and its offshoot BetterTogether. Putnam used these vehicles to head the struggle against his theory's forecast and try to revitalize American social capital and polity. If Putnam's civic efforts are successful, Putnam the forecaster will be proved wrong and the theoretical indicators Putnam believed were a harbinger of the decline of social capital in the United States will not forecast the future of the American polity (which is not to say that his theory will be refuted, only his theory-grounded forecasts). Political will may win the day and Putnam's forecasts will ultimately refute themselves. As Oren's writes,

> If Putnam's social reform campaign continues to gain momentum, he will have created a new social fact—growing public awareness of his thesis and the human volitions and decisions informed by this awareness. This fact will constitute a new antecedent condition for a new correlation between, on the one hand, postwar generations and an attitude of disinterest in television and, on the other hand, a high level of civic engagement. This new correlation will transcend and remove from actual operation, if not invalidate, the old correlation between (a) the postwar generations and television and (b) lack of civic engagement. (2006, 97–98)

Putnam tries energetically to refute his own forecasts. Morally concerned and democratically engaged as he is, he uses his forecasts for political impact and to change the course of sociopolitical American processes. Thus, forecasts can be mobilized to refute themselves in the service of a sociopolitical agenda.

And then there are cases where the theories may be mobilized but the practice is detached from the intent and even the content of the theory. Basically, the theories are mobilized after the theoretical concepts have been emptied of meanings or fixated with meanings that are expedient to some political agenda. This was partly true with the democratic peace theories that forecast that "if enough states become stably democratic—as may be happening in the 1990s—then the possibility emerges of reconstructing the norms and rules of the international system to reflect those of democracies" (Maoz and Russett 1993, 637). This policy-oriented (conditioned) forecast, which appears toward the end of Zeev Maoz and Bruce Russett's seminal article, encapsulates the prescriptive logic of the democratic peace theories. If democracies do not fight each other, or if they hardly fight each other, then the more democracies there are in the world, the more peaceful the world will be. Note how cautious and conditioned Maoz and Russett are in their forecasting (which uses a theoretical explanatory vernacular), but also how important it is for them to add this hopeful note. They wish the relevance of their theory to be clear. But they are also cautious because they know how probabilistic their theory of democratic peace is and how dependent it is on circumstances external to the theory itself (as in the case of Rostow). Yet by the time ideologues and politicians adopted their theory and made political use of it, arguably to advance a zone of democratic peace, the cautiousness had evaporated (see Ish-Shalom 2013). We thus find the neoconservative pundit Joshua Muravchik forecasting in 1991, "The more democratic the world, the more peaceful it is likely to be. Various researchers have shown that war between democracies has almost never occurred in the modern world" (Muravchik 1991, 8). This forecast, which was still probabilistic, was the first major step toward politicizing the theory and basing forecasts on it. Another prominent neoconservative pundit, Charles Krauthammer, learned from the democratic peace "to extend the peace by spreading democracy and free institutions. This is an unassailable goal and probably the most enduring method of promoting peace.... The zone of democracy is almost invariably a zone of peace" (2001). Forecasting assertions like these led the way to the US National Security Strategy promulgated on September 17, 2002, which institutionalized promoting democracy as the main strategy in fighting global terrorism, aiming "to create a balance of power that favors human freedom" (White House 2002). The politicization process culminated in the Iraq War, which was explained and legitimized among other things with reference to the pacification effects of democratization that would supposedly lead to a peaceful Iraq and peace in the Middle East. Democratic peace implied that, if it can be made to happen, democratization might eliminate war (Huber 2015, 35). The irony here is that theoretically grounded forecasting about the pacifying powers of democracy were twisted into an engine for war and politically fixated theories grounded in liberal conceptions of democracy with conservative conceptions.

The Normative Groundwork of Theoretically Grounded Forecasts

Yet twisted and distorted as this process of politicizing democratic peace theories was, it still very much involves the transformational powers of theoretically grounded forecasts. Thus, like the weather experts, IR theoreticians acquire a role in our lives through their forecasting. But IR theoreticians are different from weather forecasters in at least one crucial sense: their theories and derived forecasts are based on their standpoints and moral perspectives. And as Robert Cox asserted and we already quoted above, "Theory is always *for* someone and *for* some purpose" (1981, 128). A critical reading of theory reveals the normative foundations that always inform theory by defining the essentially contested concepts that are its building blocks. And we need this normative foundation in order to define concepts and engage in parsimonious intellectual processing about the complexity of the social world: to engage in the act of theorizing. Facts do not order themselves objectively into parsimonious theory. And as we saw earlier, social scientists need extratheoretical mechanisms in order to bound and round, sort and filter data, devise categories and definitions out of fuzzy social phenomena and be able to construct parsimonious theory from the abundant data and complexity of the social world. This extratheoretical mechanism for bounding practices and theory-making calls for making a priori assumptions, including normative ones, which necessarily precede theory.

We find these normative foundations in the theories examined above, for example, in Rostow's theory of modernization, which was one of many that existed in the 1950s and 1960s, the golden era of development studies. Some theoreticians offered a conservative and elitist interpretation of development and democracy. David E. Apter, Lucian W. Pye, Robert L. Heilbroner, and others conceived development in terms of economic or political efficacy (Heilbroner 1963; Apter 1965; Pye 1966). Since they saw democracy as an unnecessary side effect of development or even a hindrance to progress, it is hardly surprising that Heilbroner believed that a centralist, almost authoritarian, administration was needed to promote development and address social tensions (1963, 22–30, 145–64, 167–83). Other scholars suggested Marxist-leaning interpretations of development that were adopted by the United Nations Economic Commission for Latin America (ECLA) for a while. This commission, chaired by the prominent Argentine economist Raúl Prebisch, had another theory of the factors that inhibit economic development and thence political development. Whereas opposing theories considered these obstacles part of the domestic arena, the ECLA ascribed them to global structure and the terms and conditions of world trade and world production. It blamed world trade for exploiting underdeveloped countries, concluding that liberalization would not solve the problems. The solution lay in the opposite direction: in focusing on import substitution industrialization (ISI) and social reform, particularly the agrarian kind (ECLA 1971, xl–xlviii). The idea for this solution involved conditioned forecasting: if states focused on import substitution industrialization, they would boost their likelihood of developing successfully. The theory yielded a forecast that produced a policy blueprint. This policy blueprint was adopted with varying success by many Latin America countries, among them Argentine, Brazil, Chile, and Uruguay.

Alongside the conservative and Marxist theories we also find liberal theories of modernization and liberal or progressive understandings of democracy, including Rostow's theory of modernization. Rostow based his theory on a belief that humans can apply rationality to control the environment and, to an extent, human fate (1961, 4–12). For Rostow, this capacity and its usefulness were the crucial conditions for modernization. In a kind of homage to the mechanistic and optimistic materialism from which post-seventeenth-century liberalism sprang, he termed them a Newtonian conception. His optimistic materialism is evident throughout his theory. Contrary to the Marxist approach to development, whose stress is on the conflictual relations in society, Rostow focused on cooperation between different groups and elites, even suggesting the possibility of social harmony, which he believed would lead to economic growth and political development, that is, modernization and democratization (1988, 77). He likewise argued that at the heart of the problem of underdevelopment lay not the gap between developed and developing countries, but the gaps within the developing countries themselves. The way to address these gaps, he suggested, was by introducing parameters of social justice and better-balanced development policies (1964, 134–35; 1988, 110). In a forecast-like approach, Rostow argued that different societal sectors and elites could collaborate on distributing resources to communities and advance the development of the society in general, not just the prosperity of a few. This in turn would create opportunities for the rise and mobilization of a new and young leadership and chances for social mobility; it would eradicate gaps between city and village and give rise to opportunities for empowering local communities (Millikan and Rostow 1957, 28–34). We can see, then, that at the heart of Rostow's modernization theory and forecasting lies the liberal expectation of a spillover from economic elites to society in general following the expansion of the market economy based on principles of justice and welfare.

In some important aspects, Putnam's faith in social capital reminds us of Rostow's modernization theory. Central to both these theories are social networks that enable people to live prosperous, democratic lives. That means democratic lives, according to the progressive and liberal conceptualizations of democracy, where the everycitizen participates in an ongoing manner in the deliberations that shape the community's reason, behavior, organization, and policies. If the social network loosens, so does the democracy of the polity. Note, first, that these theoretical assertions produce forecasts and, second, that they are morally grounded. We also see Putnam's liberal mindedness in his more strictly IR theory, his seminal two-level games model (1988), where he takes IR theory to the level of domestic politics, interest groups, and the interplay between internal political maneuverings and state foreign policy. The progressive conceptualization of democracy is an outgrowth of liberal optimism, which regards humans as rational beings. This view accepts that people have emotions, desires, and communal traditions and attachments that influence their lives, identities, and communal behavior. However, those emotions and desires are governed to a large extent by rationality and by rational calculations. Moreover, the rational individual is seen as the locus of indivisible civic rights. Thus, this progressive and normative conceptualization of democracy centers on the concepts of participation, deliberation, and rights, seeking to enlarge the scope of citizens' political participation. Political participation and deliberation are viewed as evolving from rationality and resulting in individual and public reasonableness. The forecasting quality of Putnam's theorizing and the fact that it is grounded in a liberal worldview and morality brought President Clinton to meet Putnam and embrace his prescriptions. It also drove Putnam to take on the role of civic activist and set himself the task of refuting his own theoretically grounded forecasts.

The progressive nature of this conceptualization of democracy is especially apparent when we compare it to more minimalist and structural conceptualizations of democracy, which are embedded in a conservative skepticism regarding human potentiality and faculties. According to the conservative conceptualization of democracy, it is not rationality that drives human action but a mix of perennial desires, instincts, and communal traditions and attachments, a mix deeper than rationality that compels humans to strive for power. For Morgenthau, man is compelled by animus dominandi, an animal driven by its nature to seek domination over others (1946, 191–96). For Samuel Huntington, as result of this, mixed civilizations are the driving force of conflictual international politics (1996).

Earlier we discussed how conservative skepticism is based on ontological and epistemological assumptions that constitute normative commitments and conceptualize democracy as an elitist project and how two fears dominate the conservative conceptualization of democracy. The first fear is the fear of the human pursuit of power, which makes societies arenas for combative competition and destabilized social and political order. The second is the obverse fear, the fear of a dictatorial monopolization of power by those who seize power. Conservatives found their cure for these two dangers in Schumpeter's faith in ruling elites and in having minimal structural democracy. On the one hand by holding regular elections, democracy guarantees that no power will lasts forever. This prevents the dictatorial monopolization of power and controls those in government through checks and balances. On the other hand, by confining citizens' political participation to elections it blocks their excess involvement and checks the potential for social destabilization and political chaos.

If Rostow and Putnam represent the more progressive conceptualization of democracy, then the elitist and minimalist model can be found in Bruce Bueno de Mesquita and his coauthors' formal modeling of winning coalitions and selectorates (1999). For Bueno de Mesquita et al., democratic accountability is a very restricted and structured notion, constrained by the incumbents' calculations of the efficiency of tactics for buying their political seats. According to this conceptualization of democracy, no holds are barred, and the single notable difference between democracy and autocracy is the size of the winning coalition as a proportion of the selectorate. As Bueno de Mesquita and colleagues are keen to emphasize, "Our model explains these diverse phenomena without attributing superior motives or greater civic mindedness to one kind of leader over another. The explanation is driven purely by self-interested leaders who seek to retain office and face alternative institutional arrangements" (1999, 805). This is very much the elitist Schumpeterian conceptualization of democracy described above where democracy is the competition between members of the elite over governance and effectively over the heads of the public.

The next theoretical move by Bueno de Mesquita and his coauthors, which also involves forecasting, is to argue that due to their inability to buy their seats with private good and their consequential need to succeed in their policies, especially in fighting wars, democratic incumbents do not attack other states if they do not anticipate victory and they also try harder to win the wars they do fight (1999, 799). Hence, "Because autocrats do not try as hard in war, they make attractive targets for democracies" (1999, 799), and democracies will tend not to attack each other. But as this is the reason for (a very limited version of) the democratic peace phenomenon and not some sort of normative commitment or democratic communal bonding, the peace between democracies is indeed merely the probabilistic and temporal absence of war. There is no guarantee of peace, in fact, far from it:

> Our theory does not state that a war between democracies is impossible. Rather, we show that the conditions under which a democrat will attack another democrat are more restrictive than the conditions under which a democrat will attack an autocrat. . . . Autocrats always are the more attractive targets, but when two democratic leaders have unsuccessful domestic policies, war between democracies is most likely. (1999, 804)

Note again the forecasting quality of the last move of Bueno de Mesquita et al., how entangled theory is with the drive to forecast, whether for methodological and epistemological reasons or to discharge the social responsibility that some theoreticians feel they are ascribed with. And note too how deeply grounded concept and theory and their derived forecasting are in normative commitments and groundwork. One cannot understand Bueno de Mesquita's theory if it is detached from his normative commitments as manifested in his understanding of democracy.

Democratic Dilemmas

Theory-grounded forecasting has the potentiality to influence reality, and at times that potentiality materializes. When a theory-grounded forecast does indeed influence reality, that forecast can inject the normative commitments that inherently and inevitably exist within theory itself into the democratic process of shaping policies. Or when manipulated by ideologues and politicians, forecasting can distort the original intentions of the theoreticians and hence inject countering normative commitments. Whichever is the case, three democratic dilemmas arise: (1) Is it legitimate to inject hidden moral commitments into the process of policymaking, especially when forecasters are outsiders? (2) Unequal access to democratically grounded forecasters may have the potentiality to empower the powers that be and help them gain additional power resources. (3) Forecasting can be hijacked by skillful politicians, which not only serves the powers that be, but serves them by advancing agendas that oppose those the theoreticians-turned-forecasters support. These dilemmas will all be addressed and examined in turn. But first let us return to the essentially contested concept of democracy and offer some preliminary definitional remarks. Note that I take a normative stand over the conceptual and definitional debate on democracy, namely over which definition of democracy is more appropriate, and to justify my definitional choice.

Democracy, among other things, is a mechanism for peacefully organizing and distributing different and conflicting values and interests. I stress "among other things" because this is one of the contested issues in defining democracies. Some theoreticians understand democracy procedurally, as value neutral, as necessitating neutrality between conflicting values (Dahl 1971). According to this understanding, politics is competition over the distribution of interests and values, and democracy's almost sole purpose is to guarantee that the competition will be bounded, to avoid violence and gain procedural fairness. Other theoreticians understand democracy to be more substantive, as encompassing and being grounded in a set of values and principles. As such, and by definition, democracy cannot be value neutral; it itself is a system of values and principled norms. Arguing value neutrality merely masks the true values and principles that form part and parcel of what democracy is and is for. Being democratic already shapes the competition not only as bounded competition but as competition that sanctions some values and advocates others. The fairness in question is more than merely procedural, it is also about the content of values and interests represented in the public sphere. Not all the values and interests should carry equal weight. Rawls found a middle course between these two views in his *Political Liberalism* (1993), which advocated liberal democracy as the system that organizes the relations between the comprehensive doctrines that are decent in the sense of being tolerant toward other decent comprehensive doctrines. By that he consciously understood value neutrality as a moral commitment to tolerance and pluralism, as being in itself a value and a democratic norm. Following Rawls, there seems to be no escape from values and norms in democracy, but they can be interpreted and implemented broadly enough to encompass a wide range of moral commitments and idea systems. Some fundamental democratic norms and principles as we discuss below are thus openness, sincerity, inclusiveness, sovereignty, and political equality. Within this broad normative scope, democracy can indeed function as a procedural mechanism for organizing decent politics fairly and distributing values and interests across the polity.

The question that now arises is how in this context can fairness be maintained that is at once procedural and more than merely procedural (in the sense discussed above); how can it be founded on and yet also advocate the aforementioned principled norms? How can this fairness be maintained when making theoretically grounded forecasts that serve society but also involve democratic dilemmas and problems? I will open this discussion by examining one of the most fundamental democratic principles—political equality. Political equality is the principle that each citizen has one voice and one voice only. But, like many of the definitions we discussed earlier, including security, it is only true formally and partially. For example, in most democratic countries voting in elections is not compulsory.[2] No one is forced to elect. Some, that is, do not express their voice, or, put more accurately, they use their voice by not voicing it. This is a legitimate act although it might be linked to alienation from democracy and abstention from public life. Other citizens demonstrate the opposite predisposition, namely a powerful commitment to democratic participation or a specific value/interest. It is a commitment expressed as a willingness to invest considerable resources to secure their values/interests. Some do this through lobbying, others through persistent, tireless campaigning for their cause; others are prepared to take stronger action in demonstrations or civic disobedience (or, moving outside the scope of democracy, engagement in political violence or other illegal and illegitimate acts). We do not need to discuss these alternatives separately, just to point out that in reality there is not and cannot be full political equality because some individuals and parties are more enthusiastic or more forceful and effective than others. All else being equal and within the bounds of reasonableness, this inequality may still conform with the essential formal political equality and hence be democratically legitimate.[3]

But what happens when theoreticians turned forecasters enter into the public sphere and inject certain values through their forecasts (Christensen 1978, 62), especially when those values are hidden by the ethos of scientific objectivity and neutrality, and doubly so when the theoreticians themselves are not member of the democratic/democratizing polity (which is not a rarity)? I argue that this can pose real problems for the fairness of democratic procedures and the principle of democratic equality. There are three reasons for these problems: theoreticians are not supposed to form a particularistic lobbying party in the sense of having and advancing partisan interests and values. According to G. W. F. Hegel's terminology

(1942, 197–98; see also Avineri 1972, 155–61) and Marx (1994, 243–57; see also Avineri 1968, 41–64), academia has the potentiality to be a universal class that transcends particularism and advances universal interests. This, after all, is the purpose and end of generating academic knowledge. Think "university," think "universal." And this universal purpose and academic end may conflict with the injection of values through the act of forecasting, values that may be partisan and promote one ideological framework over others. Note that this dilemma stems from an inherent tension between academia's ethos and end as a universal apparatus serving universal values, and how theory (and derived forecasts) is implicated with particular values that may be ideologically derived and class-based. How can we reconcile the universal aspirations that appear in the theories of Rostow and Putnam with their particular participatory understanding of democracy and the particular liberal outlook that sustains that understanding? How can we reconcile the universal aspiration in Bueno de Mesquita's theorizing with the conservative foundation of his theory and its derived Schumpeterian elitist conceptualization of democracy? It may well be that the tension is intractable and that life is full of such unsolvable tensions. Sometimes the best we can do is be aware and help make these tensions transparent. But this awareness is difficult to achieve given the scientific ethos of objectivity and neutrality that stops theoreticians from engaging in real and thorough self-reflexivity and committing themselves to transparency.

When the injected values are hidden, when they lie beyond the veil of transparency, arguably they are even more detrimental to democracy. Only when values and interests are publicly and openly discussed can they be truly evaluated, scrutinized, checked, and balanced; only then can they meet the democratic standards and principles of openness and sincerity, and only then can theoreticians turned forecasters engage the public and open up the sought-after space for criticism. If this does not happen, there will not be much difference between the theoreticians turned forecasters and the politicians who help create the Quisisana clinic and stifle real democratic deliberation by turning concepts into doxa and fixating them with, or emptying them of, meanings. But in reality the injected values *are* often hidden by the ethea of universality, objectivity, and neutrality ascribed to theories. As we saw above, the values on which theories and theory-grounded forecasts are grounded are usually unacknowledged, which means that democratic discussion is marred by (at least) partial and perhaps unintended concealment. Now this concealment, which is unacceptable in any true and thriving democracy, actually hinders critical scrutiny and evaluation and weakens democratic deliberation, openness, and sincerity. Therefore, concealment essentially harms the quality of democracy (and violates the commitment to transparency, which as the next chapter shows, should be a constitutive ethos of academia) at least when not conceptualized minimally and structurally.

Furthermore, if these theoreticians turned forecasters are from a different polity, they will distort the democratic process even further since their forecasting injects the values and interests of noncitizens who should not generally be represented. If, among other things, democracy was understood above to be a mechanism for peacefully organizing and fairly distributing different and sometimes conflicting values/interests, it is generally understood that the values and interests referred to are those of the citizens of the polity that the democracy represents and compromises for. Theoreticians may rightly see themselves as cosmopolitans, and they can surely free themselves from the tight embrace of the state and its interests. Yet in a world of states, it is still the interests and preferences of the citizens that should count most. Also, the attempt to inject preferences that can be conceived as foreign into the mechanism of democratic representation is often considered illegitimate and carries the odor of illegitimate imperialism infringing on the principle of sovereignty as self-government. Therefore, injecting values by means of theory-grounded forecasts could manipulate democratic representation by introducing the values/interests of noncitizens or influencing deliberation through the participation of agents who do not legitimately belong to the polity. Think of Rostow and all the other theoreticians from developed countries who forecast about other states, influencing democratization in the developing world (or retreated from it) while injecting their own liberal (or other) set of values. Think of Rostow shaping the Alliance for Progress and advancing his own preferred model of democracy over alternative models such as the socialist-inclined model preferred by Prebisch, Parekh's communitarian model, or the Kerala/DAWN model with its sensitivity to the gendered aspects of development. Rostow himself saw the need for caution when helping to advance democratization from the outside. But unknowingly and unintentionally, he became involved in this exact process, without the requisite cautious approach.

To summarize, it seems that by injecting values and interests through theory-grounded forecasts, theoreticians betray their universal aspirations and can end up distorting the democratic process of openly evaluating transparent values and interests. Sometime they may even illegitimately inject the values and interests of noncitizen theoreticians that should remain external to the sovereignty of democratic processes.

A second and related problem is that citizens do not always have equal access to forecasts. The politically empowered and the educated sectors have greater access to theoretically grounded forecasts, and the more educated sectors have a greater chance of networking with academics, sharing a common academic background, or inhabiting the same social milieu. The politically empowered, decision-makers, and policy elites may have more resources and staff to help them access and analyze forecasts and more opportunities to use them. Hence, theoreticians may be helping to erode the principles of inclusiveness and political equality still further. Note that theoreticians may want to contribute to the quality of the democratic process (by deliberating alternative policies) and outcomes (by facilitating better chosen and executed policies). Theoreticians' understanding the potential benefits of theoretically grounded forecasts in coping with complexity may well be the reason they provide their forecasts to the polity. But by providing their theoretically grounded forecasts, they may favor those who are already favored and better positioned. This, of course, severely harms the democratic principle of political equality and institutionalizes the elitist model of democracy further.

On the other hand, it could be argued that the harm is compensated by an improved decision-making process and policy outcomes, which both outweigh the significant harm to political equality. However, there is reason to doubt that. If the powerful are the ones empowered by the theoretically grounded forecasts, then it will be their values and plausibly their interests that are served by the forecasts. This is no recipe for better policies, just a recipe for biased ones. This recipe is for policies that serve the powerful and those with assets and resources. For example, the powerful could favor an elite-driven democracy. The wealthy could favor a free-market capitalist democracy. Men could favor a patriarchal model of democracy based on a strict distinction between private and public. The powerful could use forecasts to legitimize and advance their preferred models of democracy over other models such as participatory, welfare, or gender-sensitive models of democracy. Thus, the powerful can gain further over the weaker sectors of society.

And then there is the third dilemma that arises from the possibility of politicians manipulating theories and forecasts. In that scenario, and as happened with the democratic peace theories that were used to justify and legitimize war, if politicians manipulate democratic theories and forecasts, the true intentions and values of the theoreticians can become distorted to advance different values, sometimes opposing the theoreticians' own. The resulting harm to democracy is twofold: First, there is a misrepresentation of values and preferences where the values and preferences of some, even if very few, theoreticians turned forecasters are misrepresented and hence not truly presented in the policies arising from the negotiations (which are the process in which bounded democratic competition operates). Thus, the policy outcome is not fully democratic in the sense of being a true representation of the real preferences of the citizenship. Second, the theory-grounded forecasts actually facilitate the manipulation and degradation of the democratic quality and deliberation, which are founded on and conditioned by openness and sincerity. Manipulation is the opposite of openness and sincerity and of democracy. Of course, this is not unique to theory-grounded forecasts. Politicians can excel in manipulating whatever comes their way to serve their needs. As framers of the forecasts that allow manipulation, theoreticians should try to protect their forecasts from this negative political fortune as much as possible.

The Theoretician-Citizen as Forecaster

Now that we have examined these three dilemmas and problems, the question is, how should theoreticians approach theory-grounded forecasting if they still want to engage in it? Given that there are several benefits to theory-grounded forecasting, including benefits to society, they should not abandon forecasting. But theory-grounded forecasting should address the three dilemmas as much as it possibly can. We will recall the dilemmas are (1) injecting values, sometimes by foreign forecasters, (2) unequal access to theoretically grounded forecasts, which is very harmful to political equality, (3) serving the powers that be by advancing the agendas they support and not the agendas supported by the theoreticians turned forecasters.

To address these three dilemmas, the forecasts of theoreticians turned forecasters should be offered in the spirit of theoretician-citizens working within the parameters of engaged academia. Theoretician-citizens are those theoreticians who consider themselves to have social and political responsibilities that they discharge in the public sphere and through civil society. They assume these responsibilities after recognizing the virtues and merits of theory for providing helpful insights into dealing with the social world, with all its complexities and difficulties. They morally understand that both as human beings and citizens their duty is to share the virtues and merits of theory with society in a participatory and deliberative manner—through civil society and not through the elitist networks and closed institutional arrangements of the executive establishment. Their role is the important one of acting as citizens who are trained to be circumspect and self-reflexive theoreticians rather than imperious, Platonic, know-all philosophers acting in a sort of kingship.

Forecasting as theoretician-citizen means offering forecasts while considering the sensitivities, preferences, and interests of the public, not just the closed circles of decision-makers and their networked elites (see also Nowotny 2003, 152). It means considering how forecasting serves those sensitivities, preferences, and interests or fails to serve them. Note that there are several ways to serve them. They include helping to realize them and acting to legitimize them politically vis-à-vis the sensitivities, preferences, and interests of the powerful elites. Alternatively, serving the sensitivities, preferences, and interests of the public can mean critically examining them and finding them to be impractical or improbable. All of which implies that serving the public does not mean bending academic rigor, integrity, and freedom, and surely not twisting theories and their derived forecasts to comply with any public expectations.

Additionally, to forecast as theoretician-citizens is to explain the theorizing process and its resultant theory and theory-grounded forecast as much as possible. Theoreticians turned forecasters are required to explain how their forecasts were derived from theories and the roles that moral values played (and played necessarily) in bounding and devising concepts and shaping the forecasts. It is to understand and explain that, inasmuch as a prognostication is theoretically grounded and contains features of scientific prediction, because it is an intermediate step it also contains some of the characteristics of subjective and unreliable prophecies. That is due both to the ontological complexity of the social world and to the morally founded nature of the epistemological standpoint of the theory and theory-grounded forecasting. Since subjectivity is involved, theoreticians must show modesty and caution when evaluating forecasts' relevance and practical application and when presenting their forecasts to the public. Sheila Jasanoff argues similarly for

> "technologies of humility." These are methods, or better yet institutionalized habits of thought, that try to come to grips with the ragged fringes of human understanding—the unknown, the uncertain, the ambiguous, and the uncontrollable. Acknowledging the limits of prediction and control, technologies of humility confront "head-on" the normative implications of our lack of perfect foresight. (2003, 227)

Accordingly, in the public sphere the forecasts should not be treated with finality but seen as helpful raw material, one among many relevant data sets that the public can consult and weigh as part of the policy-shaping process. This is, after all, what democratic deliberation means. The importance of factors external to the scope of the theory and theory-derived forecasts adds force to this last point. Rostow came up with forceful theory from which he derived forecasts and a policy blueprint. However, notwithstanding their theoretical forcefulness, the forecasts in fact failed the test of real-world, long-run implementation. John F. Kennedy's assassination, his succession by Lyndon B. Johnson, and Johnson's increased military involvement in Vietnam weakened the White House's political commitment to Rostow's policy, so that the Alliance for Progress and its promise of spreading democracy and democratic norms faltered and failed. The Alliance's failure again highlights the irresolvable tension between the complexity of the social world and the expected simplicity and parsimony of theory. Many variables remain outside the scope of theory that might be justified heuristically and by the epistemological call for parsimony. Yet the heuristic advantages can be a two-edged sword when theories and their derived forecasts are implemented as a policy blueprint in the real world, with all its complexity and richness, because when they are implemented, the variables that were excluded from the theory for the sake of parsimony and simplicity could become crucial for making it workable, thus hindering effective implementation. This happened with a host of variables regarding political will that were excluded from modernization theory and ultimately thwarted efforts to employ it as a policy blueprint. The lesson from this irresolvable tension is not to see forecasting as an accurate prediction of future scenarios but to weigh and specify sets of conditions that can increase the chances of achieving a desired outcome if those conditions are fulfilled. This is a modest and conditioned mode of forecasting that recognizes the force of theory as well as its limits.[4] In this way, theory-grounded forecasts are not offered as conclusive know-all elitist forecasts, but as helpful, relevant raw material that is treated as such and consulted by the public.

Modest conditioned forecasts of this type can be circulated by theoretician-citizens within the public sphere, where arguments, including the normative groundwork of theories and their derived forecasts can be scrutinized sincerely and valued openly. Circulation of forecasts by theoretician-citizens also reduces the problem of influence by foreign theoreticians since the forecasts along with their constitutive values will be disclosed to the citizens who can then scrutinize and evaluate them. Thus, the problem of foreign influence from foreign theoreticians' forecasts will be less acute. All theoreticians whether foreigners or local citizens should offer their forecasts transparently as raw material. Citizens can then decide what to accept and adopt based on their own understandings of their values, preferences, and interests. Thus, they can be what they need to be—their own best judges. Thus the democratic principles of openness, sincerity, inclusiveness, sovereignty, and political equality are kept intact, or at least the damage to them is minimized, while the benefits produced by theoretically grounded forecasts to the process of policymaking are provided.

Theoreticians can also protect their forecasts from political misuse and abuse and guarantee that they are used sincerely and as intended. They can achieve this through participation as theoretician-citizens and active engagement in the political fortunes of their forecasts. Furthermore, participation as theoretician-citizens requires theoreticians turned forecasters to practice self-reflexivity and reflect on their own moral commitments and values. It also requires them to ensure that their normative groundwork is not only transparent to themselves and other theoreticians but also to the general public. No values should remain hidden and thereby taint democratic deliberation. The presentation of forecasts openly in the public sphere also minimizes their degrading impact on political equality and prevents inequality and elitism, as the public sphere is the participatory arena where access to information is universal and fairly free.

By pursuing this participatory path and deliberating on their own functioning, theoreticians turned forecasters can avoid the grandfather paradox turned forward. They can prevent slaying processes of democratization by not weakening core democratic principles such as openness, sincerity, inclusiveness, sovereignty, and political equality. Only by truly participating in democratic deliberations as theoretician-citizens can they guarantee through their theory-grounded forecasts the opening of space for criticism and the nourishment of democracy rather than its obstruction in the Quisisana clinic. Only thus they can discharge their political and social responsibilities toward democratic and democratizing polities as part of an engaged academia.

9 Moving Away from the Heart of Darkness

Advising the Security Sectors

> The reaches opened before us and closed behind, as if the forest had stepped leisurely across the water to bar the way for our return. We penetrated deeper and deeper into the heart of darkness. It was very quiet there. (Conrad 1989, 50)

As the Copenhagen school convincingly demonstrated, security is (at least partially) the result of speech acts and processes of securitization that are performed by speech acts. But security is not alone in being enacted this way. It is not the only speech-actable phenomenon. We can learn this from an email addressed to me:

> On June 16–17, 2011 we will be hosting a two-day workshop on security expertise in Copenhagen, Denmark. The workshop explores the relation between science and politics in the field of (international) security through the concept of expertise, and has the explicit goal of strengthening the dialogue between Science Studies and Security Studies. On this occasion we would like to invite you to participate.
>
> Given your recent articles on the relation of international relations scholars to policy practice, and your outline of criteria for practicing transparency and reflexivity in social science, we would be delighted if you could contribute to the workshop in summarizing your thoughts in addressing the specific problems faced in security studies/policy.

This email is a speech act that enacts me as expert and bestows on me the aura and authority of expertise. It is not immediately obvious what my expertise is, but the message indeed speech-acts me into the role of expert. And it is in this capacity and with the authority of expert that I was invited to reflect on the normative aspects of regulating academic expertise on security. What this reveals is a banal yet fundamental truth about experts and expertise: they are enacted, affirmed, and reaffirmed by speech acts (at times by none other than the experts themselves) and acknowledged by relevant audiences. Or as Ole Jacob Sending (2015) adds in a Bourdieuian reading, expertise is about the dynamics of recognition of authority (6). The recognition of authority is drawn from material and symbolic resources (21) and granted according to evaluative criteria specific to various fields (24); it establishes relations of subordination (12). In other words, expertise is an authoritative status granted by a given audience, an attributional mark (Berling and Bueger 2015).[1]

But if that is the case, there is a problem. If both security and expertise are speech-actable and (at least partially) stem from speech acts, then there is no Archimedean point from which to leverage their relationship. What complicates matters further is that security and expertise (at least partially) constitute each other. The people who define security by enacting this or that domain as a security issue are experts, which includes academic scholars. This is the crux of the bounding practices discussed in the first part of the book, where I described defining as the academic variant of bounding practices. Security can also help define particular people as experts, or at least relevant experts. For example, if the environment is considered a security issue, then people with environmental knowledge can be enacted as having expertise. Thus, even those who have acquired knowledge do not become security experts until that knowledge has been perceived as relevant.

So there are two constructed phenomena that sometimes construct and constitute each other. The question now is how to regulate relations between them safely and consistently with engaged academia. It is here that transparency kicks in and becomes a normative help. The axis around which the argument in this chapter will be constructed is transparency and its opposite, secrecy. I will argue that transparency is and has to be a constitutive and definitional characteristic of academic expertise and scholarship, while secrecy is, and to some extent should be, a constitutive and definitional characteristic of the security sectors. I also argue that this core distinction should guide our thinking on regulating the power of academic security expertise. It will help us see how security experts can relate to the security sectors without being co-opted by them and serving the manipulative dynamics of securitization—in other words, without helping to maintain the Quisisana clinic, which is so detrimental to democracy and democratic agency.² Hence, I will argue, academic security experts should resist the temptations presented to them by a close relationship with the security sectors. Instead of forming an alliance with security agencies and practitioners, a fairly common practice among security experts, they should act as theoretician-citizens and fellows of engaged academia and be active in the public and civil sphere with the aim of enriching the public and civic deliberations over security. In the spirit of the dual analytical gaze, academic security experts can help to transform the speech acts of securitization to approximate ideal speech acts and thus democratize both security and securitization.³

Transparent Academia and Secretive Security Sectors

Transparency is a commitment to disclosure and openness. Secrecy and secretiveness are a commitment to confidentiality and concealment. Transparency is to academic security experts what secretiveness is to security agencies and practitioners. But let us start with some caveats, and there are several. First, ascribing secrecy to security sectors and transparency to academia is an exercise in archetypes. It is about how we see these sectors and the set of rules that should constitute their modus operandi; it is not necessarily how they operate. We know that reality is messier than a set of archetypes and rules even if those rules are constitutive. The security sectors are infested with leaks. Sergeant Manning's leak of classified documents to WikiLeaks may be one of the most striking cases, but it is certainly not alone. Academia is infested with concealment, for example, the concealment of incremental progress before a scientific breakthrough that can be proudly announced and personally accredited. But note that common as they are, these practices are considered illegitimate deviations from the ideal expected from practitioners in security and academia. Second, the rules also legitimize exceptions: Academic peer-review occurs behind the veil of double anonymity, and most referee letters for dissertations, promotions, grants, and so on, practice single-blind anonymity. Moreover, we cherish this anonymity, claiming that it guarantees honest evaluation and academic quality control. This anonymity is simply a form of accepted and justified secrecy. In the security sectors, even the kind discussed here, namely security agencies in established democracies, the caveats have an obverse nature. We usually know the identities of high-ranking officers who head our militaries and intelligence agencies, and in the democratic world we largely know the extent of public spending on security. These are manifestations of expected transparency. Yet the caveats are the exceptions to the rules and reveal our true expectations of these two institutions—the security apparatus and academia. We expect and are accustomed to military secrecy, and we expect transparency from academia. We would be concerned if the military revealed its operational plans and would be dumbfounded if academia decided one day to keep quiet about its methodological procedures. Transparency is a constitutive feature of academia inasmuch as secretiveness is a constitutive feature of the security sectors. And there are very good reasons for this.

Academia is bounded and constituted by transparency. I will argue below that it has an ethical obligation to act transparently, but there are also arguments of a different kind for transparency in academia. Foremost of these are the epistemological arguments. It has long been argued that transparency is a necessary epistemological requirement for gaining access to truth (or in other arguments, access to objectivity). Epistemologically speaking, many academic approaches ranging from positivism to radical feminism have argued for transparency and complete openness. Positivists call for transparency as it allows the replication of experiments and studies to confirm or refute results. To ensure this, no less than full transparency is needed: we need to know what data set was used, the analysis procedures, experimental manipulations, definitions, and the assumptions of the study structure. Once we know all these, we can try to replicate the study and see if we get similar results. Thus, transparency is a basic epistemological and methodological requirement for mainstream positivism.

But the same is true for other approaches at the other end of the academic and epistemological spectrums. For example, standpoint feminist epistemologists argue for transparency in the name of strong objectivity. Theoreticians such as Sandra Harding and Donna Haraway provide a host of supporting arguments for self-reflexivity and transparency. When conjoined, self-reflexivity and transparency offer a more complete understanding of the cognitive and emotional processing that occurs when we think about and theorize the world. When we disclose the biases that distort our own theories to ourselves and others, it helps our understanding of how these biases affect the process of theorizing. Remember zooming in, zooming out. In combination, self-reflexivity and transparency help us to understand the origins of biases and how they are created in the social setting we inhabit and which forms our social standpoint (on standpoint epistemology see Harding 1991, 163; 1993; Haraway 1988; Hawkesworth 1989; Laslett et al. 1996; Potter 2006, 131–32; Smith 1987; Tickner 1992, 21; 2005). These social standpoints are what enable us to conduct research. But they also limit our competency in gaining outlooks broader than our own narrow perspective.

Social standpoints are especially limiting for the socially and economically privileged or politically powerful. Generally, being privileged and powerful means seeing the world through a restricted perspective while lacking any incentive to broaden it. People who are marginalized, oppressed, and deprived in society have an incentive to acquire a broad perspective. Because of their less well-off position, deprived people must think about the wishes of the powerful. To avoid trouble and secure what they need, the deprived must form an understanding of how the powerful conceive the world. In other words, they need to access the social standpoints of the powerful and integrate that perspective into their own. Moreover, there is a political incentive for the marginalized, oppressed, and deprived sectors of society to align their own perspectives with other marginalized people to form workable coalitions. Consequently, marginalized sectors can achieve an inclusive perspective based on their social standpoint: they can achieve Harding's strong objectivity (Harding 1993, 54; see also Mohanty 2003, 511; Tickner 1992, 16).

This general observation is also true for academic scholars and experts: inferior socioeconomic or political positioning in academia is translatable into a superior intellectual and scholarly outlook. Put succinctly, being academically excluded enables being theoretically inclusive, which accounts for the assumed potentiality of feminist scholars and experts to surpass mainstream and malestream scholarship in their theorizing and attain strong objectivity. For this potentiality to be actualized, feminist scholars must engage in self-reflexivity combined with full transparency, and should act to broaden the perspectives in academia through true pluralism backed not only by ethical considerations but also by epistemological ones.

Take security, for example. Feminist standpoint theoreticians argue critically that traditional and mainstream security understandings and conceptualizations are confined by statist, militaristic, and masculine standpoints and reflect privileged social positioning (Tickner 1988, 430; Hutchings 2008, 99). Because mainstream (and malestream) theoreticians have never experienced the daily routines and incidents that women experience, their understanding of security cannot encompass women's understanding of security and risks (Tickner 1992, 14; Hoogensen and Rottem 2004, 156; Blanchard 2003, 1298). According to the feminist standpoint, it is only by including the experiences and standpoints of marginalized women that the theoretical study of security can expand its understanding and be more inclusive and more universal, that is, more strongly objective in its conceptualization and theorizing of security (Tickner 1992, 5). Such strong objectivity would consider both the particular risks and violence that women experience daily and the harms that women experience in times of war (Hoogensen and Rottem 2004, 165; Tickner 1992, 134–35). Feminist theoreticians argue that security theory must account for such widespread practices as sexual harassment, the sex trade, poverty, and (in some places and cultures also) honor killing, female genital mutilation, and other patriarchal and power-inflicted practices (Hansen 2000). Security theorizing must also broaden its perspective and account for wartime phenomena such as mass rape (Blanchard 2003, 1300).[4]

The broader and wider understandings of the threats to and security of marginalized people including women, the differential impact of war on women, and the common exclusion of women from conflict resolution and peace processes have in fact fueled the global campaign that resulted in Security Council Resolution 1325, passed on October 31, 2000. The resolution, which "calls on all parties to conflict to take special measures to protect women and girls from gender-based violence, particularly rape and other forms of sexual abuse, in situations of armed conflict" also mandates a greater role for women in postconflict reconstruction and peace-building, stressing "the importance of their equal participation and full involvement in all efforts for the maintenance and promotion of peace and security" and urging "all actors to increase the participation of women and incorporate gender perspectives in all United Nations peace and security efforts" (United Nations 2000). Note the resolution's emphasis on perspectives. Different life experiences generate different perspectives and understandings of security, and for security to really matter, it must be inclusive and resonate nothing less than Harding's strong objectivity.

Hence, standpoint theory, which highlights the importance of experience and the need to reflect transparently on one's own sensitivities, experiences, and biases, argues for the need for transparent theorizing to achieve strong objectivity, in other words, a more inclusive and universal outlook and theories.

Besides the epistemological argument, in being encompassing and including previously ignored perspectives, the feminist outlook also carries moral weight and raises normative considerations. These considerations bring us to the ethical arguments for academic transparency, the foremost of which is grounded on reciprocity as a forceful moral principle that regulates duties, obligations, and rights in social settings. Reciprocity is defined as the "practice of making an appropriate return for a benefit or harm received from another" (Blackburn 2005, 310). As a moral principle, reciprocity echoes Immanuel Kant's categorical imperative, that is, being willing to enact upon yourself that which you enact on others. And it is through this categorical imperative that the power of reciprocity kicks in and burdens theoreticians with the moral obligation of transparency.[5]

Reciprocity burdens theoreticians with transparency because of the special way we theorize the social world. In studying human society, social scientists expose human desires and beliefs, linking them causally (or constitutively) to social mechanisms: for example, how human risk-aversion shapes consumer behavior; how identification with one's group produces solidarity; and how rational calculations shape the balance of threats and mutual deterrence between states. This last example, which is obviously linked to security studies and securitization theory, is an excellent example of how desires and beliefs are engaged in security. Security is linked to the objective and material status of being secured or unsecured. But perhaps to an even greater degree, security is related to such powerful feelings as hope and fear, the expectations and hopes of security and the fears associated with not having it.[6]

As these examples show, inner states of mind are important for explaining social phenomena, including security. This does not mean that inner states of mind are the only means to explaining them, or even that causal or constitutive relations function only in one direction, from states of mind to social structures. On the contrary, social structures and social processes, including fears and hopeful expectations for a better and more secure world, also shape inner states of mind. Nevertheless, inner states of mind are an important part of the workings of social sciences. Moreover, by exposing otherwise hidden and unknown social mechanisms, theories can generate social dynamics that would never have emerged without theoretical knowledge. Earlier we discussed these possibilities and dynamics, so I will be brief now. For example, theory can become a self-refuting prediction. That is how Oren understands the civic process aimed at revitalizing American social capital that Putnam initiated in an effort to prevent the fulfillment of his own theory-based pessimistic prediction of the demise of American social life and political future (Oren 2006). Alternatively, theory can be mobilized by policymakers and become a self-fulfilling prophecy. When Kennedy took office in 1961, he was alarmed by the United States' deteriorating relations with Latin America. He approached academia and appointed Rostow as the deputy special assistant to the president for security affairs (under Bundy, another academic). Later, in December 1961, Rostow was made chairman of the Policy Planning Council at the State Department, which deals with longer-term policy planning for the United States.[7] Kennedy hoped that applying Rostow's modernization theory would generate democratic changes in Latin America and foster positive, secure relations in the region. For a while, then, Rostow and his theory were agents of change in the Americas. The administration believed that his economic expertise also meant security expertise and expected that implementing Rostow's modernization theory would improve hemispheric stability and security. Security studies were also used during the Cold War, when they "contributed to the development of operations research and logistical techniques. In other words, security studies helped in constructing the language of nuclear politics and define its universe of the thinkable" (Villumsen and Büger 2010, 2; see also Klein 1994).

These two aspects—making inner states of mind transparent and the sociopolitical effects of making them transparent—should prompt public interest in holding social scientists to the rules of transparency. Furthermore, these aspects ought to produce a commitment to the moral principle of reciprocity among scholars and experts themselves—to conduct themselves as they demand of others. In terms of our present discussion, this means a commitment to uphold transparency and disclose and acknowledge experts' moral and normative commitments: commitments that shape their conceptions and theories and give them an ideological and normative bent.[8] Normative arguments are thus added to the epistemological arguments for transparency. Since theory can be a powerful agent of change, the public has a vested interest in committing it to the rules and practices of transparency. Furthermore, the ethical force of reciprocity binds theoreticians and experts morally to subordinate themselves, or more accurately subordinate theory and theorizing, to the requirement of transparency and to try to disclose the standpoints, normative commitments, and ideological bent of the theories. In transparency terms, the security sectors are diametrically opposed to the academic sector since they are constituted and defined by secretiveness. And in order to secure security according to the conventional statist and militarist conceptualizations of the term, security sectors have been equipped to the teeth. They are also careful not to overly disclose their capabilities and intentions since secrecy guarantees surprise on the battlefield and surprise is one of the most efficient weapons in wars. That having been said, it is also true especially for deterrence that under special circumstances and for specific reasons overt threats and the explicit signaling of intentions and capabilities can be an important military tactic. This was a lesson effectively taught during the Cold War by Schelling, following his theoretical work on deterrence (1960). Signaling is supposedly a transparency-based practice. However, this is not always the case, since there may be advantages to signaling partly false intentions and capabilities, and in order for false signals to be credible, true intentions and capabilities must remain concealed or at least ambiguous. Hence, signaling-based deterrence is not fully based on complete transparency either, but rather is a tactical policy based on a mixture of transparency and secrecy. The same is true for relations with friendly allies. Security sectors tend to cooperate and share knowledge, intelligence, and even operational plans with friendly foreign security services. But even then, they usually hide certain core components of the information from both their allied security sectors and their own publics. And naturally they try to keep any concealed components a secret. This was skillfully captured by Andrew Barry: "Transparency potentially generates a further set of secrets concerning the production of information which has been made public" (2006, 25). Accordingly, cooperation between allied security services will never be truly transparent (and at times not even cooperation between different security agencies within the same state). The not infrequent cases of espionage between friendly states, such as the case of Jonathan Pollard, who was caught spying on the United States for Israel, is testimony to this.

In general then, secrecy is essential for security services and agencies, since a military that wishes to be able to win wars must conceal its trumps from its enemies. Indeed, the art of concealment has been perfected by military and other security services and the state, with the public assistance in this concealment via censorship laws,[9] counterintelligence, and laws against treason targeting those who disclose national secrets. Thus, the aforementioned caveats indeed create important and democratic enclaves of transparency in the security sectors. But democracy notwithstanding, these caveats are only enclaves in cultures where secretiveness is recognized as necessary and publicly and democratically defensible. Accordingly, and as argued earlier, secretiveness is a constitutive and definitional feature of security sectors just as transparency is a constitutive and definitional feature of academia.

Regulating Security Experts and Security Sectors

Although both the security sector and the academic sector are, among other things, constructed by speech acts, in terms of regulating security experts and security sectors there is one constitutive and definitional feature where the two sectors diverge. Academia with its security experts is (and should be) committed to transparency; the security sector for its part, with its practitioners and agencies, should be committed to secretiveness (within the reasonable limits of democratic norms and procedures). This fundamental difference should be a guiding principle when regulating the relations between the two spheres, their principal institutions, and their agents.[10] In a nutshell, my proposal is that academic security experts should resist the temptation that forms an inherent part of the close, intimate relationship with the powers- and security-that-be, and start acting like theoretician-citizens in the public and civil sphere. This proposal might carry some radical implications and will perhaps seem counterintuitive to some. We know that academic security experts and security practitioners do in fact cooperate to the extent that the two fields can merge into one (dys)functional field (Büger and Villumsen 2007). There could also be powerful incentives for this type of close cooperation. First, academic centers may be government funded and as a result expected to advise governmental agencies, including security agencies. Second, academic security experts can also benefit from the quantity and quality of harvestable data that such cooperation will produce. Without cooperation, academic security experts will be left outside the circle of knowledge, strangers to that exclusive club and its access to secrets. And if they are excluded, it will be difficult to function as experts, who thrive on informative data. Third, security practices are linked to special privileges. As Hugh Gusterson argues, rites of secrecy can constitute communities or secret societies that are bounded by the bonds of secrets and the feeling they are privileged elites (1996, 88). Fourth, there is the temptation of power, a temptation to gain access to the corridors of power, an all too human attraction to which academics are not immune. But the desire for close cooperation with the security sector is not only a result of self-centered drives. It appears reasonable enough that if experts want to influence and enrich policymaking, they will seek to whisper into the ears of the powerful from a position of being privileged with intimate knowledge they have gained through a close relationship with the security and intelligence sectors. In other words, there is a strong incentive to try to become part of the political and security establishment that sets priorities and plans the policies to achieve them.

Thus there are quite a few benefits, both selfish and nonselfish, to be gained from cooperating intimately with security practitioners and security agencies. But there are also costs, and they are quite heavy. The main cost is that cooperation may lead to co-option. For one thing, the data gathered while in the intimate circle of secrecy may be restricted by the commitment to secrecy that comes with joining the club (Gusterson 1996, 88). And how can academics uphold the academic principles of transparency and universal spread of knowledge if the information they obtain is classified? How should they deal with this dilemma? If they honor their commitments on entering the closed circle, they will betray their academic vocation and basic academic instincts. If they remain loyal to their academic vocation and instincts and make public their academic and theoretic use of classified information acquired through cooperation with the security sectors, their commitment to secrecy might be breached, and they could be charged with treason. I suggest that this painful dilemma might lead to co-option into the security sectors' rules of secrecy.

Even more problematic from the critical standpoint is that the academic security expert's ability to scrutinize the working assumptions, guiding principles, and official conceptualizations of the security sectors and other sectors of the political system would be compromised. We very much need to be outside this circle in order to examine these assumptions, principles, and conceptualizations critically and speak the truth to the powers that be. Remember standpoint epistemology. A critical attitude is a perspective nourished and maintained by being outside the circles of power.[11] If the connection to the powers that be (including the security sectors) is too close, it could compromise the broad perspective needed to develop a critical stance. Think again of Rostow and his roles within the Kennedy and Johnson administrations, for example, his appointment as special assistant to the president for security affairs. Rostow worked closely (and at times secretively) with the security sectors and security agencies in this capacity in various theaters, such as Latin America and Vietnam. With Vietnam, his views were hawkish and militaristic, contrasting sharply with his general views and policy perspectives on Latin America, except Cuba (Ish-Shalom 2006a, 302). His close cooperation with the security sectors and agencies within the parameters of secretiveness might have contributed to those hawkish and militaristic views on Vietnam and Cuba. He thus may have been co-opted by the security sectors and consequently lost that characteristically broad perspective of his theoretical writings. Adler noted similarly about American scholars during the Cold War that their access to government secrets made them feel "insiders" (1992, 115). Gil Eyal has commented about Israeli scholars of the Middle East and their heavy involvement in Israeli military intelligence in the early decades of the State of Israel that they made a Faustian bargain (2002, 687).

The controversy over the US Army's Human Terrain System (HTS), which was deployed in Afghanistan and Iraq from 2006 to 2014, is another paradigmatic case of the social sciences co-option by security sectors. The program goal was to provide the army and its commanders with information about the local populations and region in which it fought and governed. Social scientists from a variety of disciplines, especially anthropology and sociology, along with political scientists and regionalists, were deployed alongside fighting units and collected data using various methodologies, including interviewing locals. HTS drew strong criticism from academia, and the American Anthropological Association, being sensitive to the role of anthropologists in the program, was especially vocal. A report commissioned by the AAA, released in December 2009 by the Commission on Engagement of Anthropology with the US Security and Intelligence Services (CEAUSSIC), condemned HTS for infringing the ethical code of the AAA, mainly by risking the lives of researchers and for not enabling "voluntary informed consent" from the interviewees. The report concluded harshly that "when ethnographic investigation is determined by military missions, not subject to external review, where data collection occurs in the context of war, integrated into the goals of counterinsurgency, and in a potentially coercive environment—all characteristic features of the HTS concept and its application—it can no longer be considered a legitimate professional exercise of anthropology" (see also Gusterson 2015). In other words, HTS was considered co-option and criticized precisely as that, for unwittingly serving security considerations.

The scholars' access to confidential information and circles of power thus came with the weighty price tag of co-option and lost academic autonomy. This teaches us to distance ourselves critically from the powers that be and the powers that are to be criticized.[12] If we let ourselves be co-opted by the power centers, we run the risk of losing our critical edge. Bourdieu's distinction between the cynical and the clinical sociologist aptly captures the risk of co-option. As Willem Schinkel puts it, "A cynical sociology makes use of its knowledge in order to make its own strategy more effective, while a clinical sociology uses its knowledge of social laws to challenge them effectively" (2003, 70). And this, I wish to argue in line with Bourdieu, is the main risk to the academic experts' ethos, vocation, and obligation.

Think about all possible conceptualizations of security, with its many traditional descriptors—international, national, and military—in contrast to global, human, social, and environmental. It is not that academia is the driving force behind each of these new and poststatist conceptualizations of security (Blanchard 2003, 1306; Buzan and Hansen 2009, 203), though academia did play an important and critical role in fine tuning and theorizing them and in securing their cognitive and intellectual legitimacy. All things considered, the ability to act in such a critical manner was achieved by experts who remained unaffected by the temptations of power, in other words, those who maintained a healthy distance from the powers that be and also, so to speak, from the security-that-be. This means that in order to retain that critical edge and potentiality, we must avoid being co-opted and drawn into overly intimate relations and cooperation with the powers that be and the security sectors.

Some may argue that I overestimate the risk of co-option and that academic security experts often enter into and withdraw from this kind of intimate cooperation and maintain a critical edge without being co-opted. It is true too that many academic security experts cooperate intimately with the security sectors and genuinely believe they make a positive contribution. I am sure that many of the HTS employees genuinely felt this. Some scholars probably do find ways to benefit their polities through such intimate cooperation while maintaining their critical edge. Others fail in this daunting dual task and fell prey to co-option. Can we determine the rate of success and failure? Can we estimate the overall good and harm of such intimate cooperation? How can we, when the academic community lacks access to information concerning such cooperation of this nature, precisely due to the rules of secrecy that bind the academic security experts who cooperate with the security sectors? Naturally, we can rely on the security experts' responsibility and judgment and leave them to judge whether they are being co-opted and whether they do more harm than good. After all, individual responsibility and judgment are key assets in democratic societies and academic environments, and both democracies and academia need individual responsibility and judgment to prosper. Later, I discuss certain circumstances that necessitate individual responsibility and judgment. But whatever the case, in order for individual responsibility and judgment to function properly, they must be out in the open and subject to scrutiny and checks and balances—even if post factum. If not, individual responsibility and judgment may be corrupted by the effects of absolute power and the problem of blind spots, which can make individuals blind to their own tacit presuppositions and prejudgments (Hawkesworth 1996, 96). This is the reason for the cautionary and critical stance against such cooperation presented here, based on the present analysis of the risks of co-option.

The advice against this type of cooperation does not mean that experts should not try to influence policymaking and contribute to the public discourse. On the contrary, being both academic experts *and* citizens places the burden of responsibility on the experts to try to improve policies and enrich the public discourse. It also gives academia the responsibility to engage as an institution. Theorizing is a rich intellectual accomplishment offering informative and analytically processed knowledge regarding human conduct and social relations. Security conceptions and theories are no exception. They describe the dynamics and processes of security, insecurity, and securitization within social relations and human conduct. Accordingly, theory as a whole and security theories in particular can offer helpful insights that can help shape policies. Because of this beneficial potentiality as conceptualizers of concepts, constructors of theory, and citizens of their polity, theoreticians have social and political responsibilities and a democratic imperative to participate in the political processes of policy-shaping (Ish-Shalom 2013).

It is because of these reasons, responsibilities, and imperatives, which among other things are founded on the principle and outcomes of democracy and transparency, that theoreticians have an obligation to take on the active role of theoretician-citizen (Ish-Shalom 2013). And with this heavy burden in mind, we need to theorize the regulation and organization of relations between academic security experts, the security sectors, and other sectors of the political system. When they are regulated and organized in the right manner, these relations can ensure that the academic commitment to transparency is upheld while offering academic security experts a viable way to engage and shape security policies and enrich public security discourse. It is important for theoreticians to try to influence public policy and enrich democratic deliberation and do this without compromising their commitment to transparency. However, there is one important cautionary caveat. Academics cannot single-handedly change reality, far from it. Nor do they always set the terms of affecting reality, as the example of democratic peace theories has demonstrated. Sometimes, theories created in academia affect reality after being misunderstood and misrepresented in the political sphere. Hence their consequences are not what their theoreticians envisioned. Misrepresentations of democratic peace theories pushed for war and legitimized it (Ish-Shalom 2013). But academics, including academic security experts, do have a responsibility to explore the possibilities of change, should do whatever it takes to help improve reality, and should seek democratic legitimacy for their interventions[13] and cooperate with sectors possessing more resources and possibilities for changing reality. This accounts for the first recommendation for regulating relations between academic security experts and security sectors:[14] These relations should not involve direct close cooperation. Rather, academic security experts should be active in civil society by offering their theoretical insights for public deliberation and enriching public reason. This is worth stressing: the appropriate and democratic way to use theoretical insights is not through the security sectors, not even mainly through the political systems and policy establishments; instead of being obsessed with building bridges with policy elites and security practitioners, academic security experts should be interested in building bridges with the public and civil society. They should be concerned about contributing theoretical insights to the public, transparently within the public sphere, and helping to challenge official conceptualizations of security. If academics adopt that concern, their commitment to transparency will not be overrun by the secretiveness of the security sectors and academic security scholars would not be co-opted.

Academic security experts could then legitimately assume the public role of theoretician-citizens—a role whose very nature and embeddedness in the participatory and deliberative conception and understanding of democracy requires the conduct of democracy in the open, with full transparency.[15] Academic security experts could achieve several objectives in the role of theoretician-citizens. For example, they could expose securitization processes that are detrimental to deliberative and reasoned democracy. Theorizing securitization and publicizing theoretical insights on securitization would help to deactivate securitization as a manipulative political weapon, which, after all, as one of its seminal texts shows, is one of the long-term objectives of the Copenhagen school: "Security should be seen as negative, as a failure to deal with issues as normal politics; desecuritization is the optimal long-range option" (Buzan, Wæver, and de Wilde 1998, 29; see also Lupovici 2014).

Even more importantly, when they function as theoretician-citizens, academic security experts have a legitimate obligation to engage with and enrich people's thinking, stimulate the public's political faculties, and help the public grasp the complex and intricate questions relating to security and securitization. They should not just do this by counseling the public— and they should certainly *not* preach and impose their answers on such issues. They should support people's faculty of asking questions and expressing doubts and incite in them the burdening of responsibilities and democratic agency. This can refine and raise standards of public thinking on security matters by drawing people a little closer to the democratic ideal of citizens who can responsibly reflect on and challenge their leaders and national security agencies. Academic security experts can potentially heighten citizens' sensitivity to what is at stake regarding security as a concept to be bound and a phenomenon to experience: what security stands for, who benefits from it, what it defends against, the entities that supply it, the price tag on security policies, and who pays for them. The democratic ideal academic security experts as theoretician-citizens should work toward is that of citizens who are participants in the intricate art of forming coherent and efficient strategies and security policies.

Then when the above questions are discussed publicly and transparently in a manner approaching the democratic ideal,[16] the dilemma that critical theoreticians face and some feminist scholars have aired can be resolved. Securitization is usually seen, and rightly so, as a manipulative instrument that strengthens the powerful political elites. However, under some circumstances and in the right hands (namely agents with right intentions), securitization can empower marginalized groups by airing their concerns and prioritizing their needs, by portraying them as security issues (Floyd 2011; Hansen 2000; Hoogensen and Rottem 2004). But these same critical theoreticians are aware that securing the positive goal of empowering marginalized groups with the negative instrument of securitization could be detrimental to the long-term cause of an ethical polity with no room for political manipulation. However, if academic security experts operate as theoretician-citizens and are committed to the dual analytical gaze, and if they try to cultivate a public commitment to transparent, reasoned, deliberative discussion on security needs, expectations, and priorities, then the speech acts of securitization can approximate the Habermasian ideal's speech acts, remove securitization's manipulative sting, and ensure its democratization. Transparent and democratic securitization can indeed be performed by speech acts, but they resemble ideal speech acts that can both empower marginalized groups and still sit well with the critical theoreticians' sensitivity to openness, transparency, deliberation, participation, and political sincerity.

It is this educational, not to say enlightening,[17] task that burdens academic security experts when they are committed to transparency and act as theoretician-citizens through a commitment to an engaged academia and democratic norms and values. And this is what will enable them to influence public policy and improve democratic deliberation without compromising their basic and constitutive commitment to transparency.

Relaxing the Strict Prohibitions

But with all due respect to the constitutive importance of transparency, there are other considerations as well. At times and depending on the circumstances, other considerations may override transparency and require (or at least suggest) that security experts (or other experts) give direct advice to security sectors and agencies. For example, we would like ethicians to have direct access to security practitioners and agencies to instruct them on just war theory and the ethics of using force. Under other circumstances, direct consultation with security experts could improve the overall conduct of security sectors and redirect their strategic thinking toward more peaceful and reasoned behavior (think, for example, about planning peace and conflict resolution operations or a state confronting an emergency). Academic security experts could well offer sound advice and improve how these situations are handled. They could try to broaden and widen the conceptualization of security in the security sectors by suggesting conceptions for peace operations and conflict resolution missions, conceptions whose reasoning and normative foundation derive from emancipatory critical security studies, conceptions of human security aimed at agential capability building, or conceptions linked to feminist security studies, with their emphasis on the everyday experiences of the real people who are most exposed to harm from military operations. There are scenarios, that is, where other normative considerations may interact with the normative consideration of transparency and override it, or at least slightly modify it.

These scenarios, and others, point to a possible problem with my rather strict prohibition against direct relationships with the security sectors. But we can think of several solutions to it. First, we could encourage security practitioners to seek academic training that would bring them into direct contact with security experts in an academic institutional environment while exposing them to academic ethics and the commitment to transparency. Security practitioners could acquire knowledge packages for use in their work, which could guide their conduct and obviate any necessity to co-opt academic security experts. If any co-opting occurs, it would be the security practitioners who would be co-opted to some extent by academia's culture of transparency (and other academic values). Second, if the opinion of the academic security experts is that their expertise is needed to improve military conduct, especially for the sake of peace or achieving a conflict resolution, then they may consider cooperating directly with the security sectors. But even then they must insist that this cooperation be conducted thoughtfully, watchfully, and as transparently as possible. Remember HTS and how good intentions (which I am certain guided many social scientists who joined HTS) produced total co-option. Under other circumstances, such as emergencies, academic security experts could be called on to assist the security services and to do so under the strict requirement of secrecy. Under emergency circumstances we can be much more lenient with regard to the secrecy requirement; we can even evaluate the risk of co-option as being overridden by national interests. Problematic as the definition of emergencies can be, and however open to political manipulation (Lev 2004) and to processes of securitization it indeed is, we must concede that there are times when the emergencies are real and when our polity or even humanity as a whole (think of World War II) have real security needs. Under these circumstances, we need to use our practical judgment and decide for ourselves whether they are dire enough to override the academic commitment to transparency. But bear in mind that this dilemma is not unique to transparency or exclusive to academic security experts. There are always situations in democracy where some leeway in democratic principles is needed to defend democratic values. This also applies in the case of cooperation between security experts and security sectors, although, hopefully, the experts' practical judgments and cooperation outcomes can and will be openly securitized post factum to provide checks and balances against possible political manipulations.

Third, as suggested above, a division of labor can be struck with think tank-based security experts. Think tanks work in a different institutional environment than universities. They are policy oriented, and their raison d'être aims at directly influencing the political system and policy establishment.[18] There are incentives for think tanks to commit themselves to transparency, most obviously their political influence. But as a rule their activities differ from those of academics in that they do not produce theoretical work that commits academic theoreticians to transparency. They are policy oriented and thus responsible for translating academic and theoretic knowledge into policy guidelines and practice. They behave like a transmission belt (Lepgold 1998) and cannot achieve their goals without direct and sometimes intimate relations with security agencies and security practitioners. Hence, the division of labor I propose is to let the university-based security experts do the theoretical work and try to change the current state system by working with civil society as critical theoreticians and theoretician-citizens. As for the think tank-based scholars, they can develop problem-solving (Cox 1981, 128–29) policies by working directly with the political and security sectors. That way we can maintain the requirements of secrecy in the security sectors and transparency in the academic sector without abdicating from the two crucial and sometimes conflicting tasks of criticism and problem-solving.

Conclusions

Expertise and security are both speech-actable phenomena and can sometimes speech-act one another into existence. This makes their mutual relations fairly volatile, since they are based on an unstable foundation without Archimedean leverage. I therefore propose that we analyze the two phenomena through the lenses of transparency and secrecy. Academia is and should be defined and constituted by a commitment to transparency; security is and should be defined and constituted by an equivalent commitment to secrecy. Both qualities are important for the successful working of the two institutions and their effective contribution to a functioning and democratic polity.

Accordingly, along with my proposition for an engaged academia, I propose that we regulate the relations between the two sectors by focusing on their foundational features: transparency and secrecy. This has been the underlying premise of the argument in this chapter. Academic security experts are burdened by a democratic imperative to act as theoretician-citizens in the public and civil sphere. And despite a certain leeway, academic security experts must resist the temptation of a close, intimate relationship with the powers and security that be. Generally speaking, they need to counter the security sectors' hegemony over the conceptualization of security and engage and enrich the public and civic deliberation on this issue. Leeway is needed under special circumstances such as emergencies or training for peace and conflict resolution operations. At such times, academic security experts should be able to provide more direct and expedient counseling to the security sectors and perhaps even encouraged to do this. I also argue for some kind of division of labor between university-based security experts and think tank-based security experts. The latter can and should establish direct and regular relations with the security sectors.

By enriching public and civic deliberations regarding security, academic security experts can help to remodel the speech acts of securitization to approximate ideal speech acts. This would democratize securitization so that it also addresses the sensitivities, experiences, and needs of lay citizens and marginalized groups in the security context. That way, academic security experts pledged to a dual analytical gaze could fulfill their critical potential and, by means of engaging, improve security policy while strengthening their constitutive commitment to transparency.

Conclusions • Having an Engaged Academia in a Conceptually Contested Environment

The Gramscian theoretical framework suggested here is that politics is a public effort directed at the allocation of resources—material, ideal, and symbolic. Often, this effort is guided by a conscious effort to gain control over the commonsensical understanding of social reality. It is behind the veil, so to speak, that politics plays a role in the construction of knowledge and political agents wish to hegemonize the public common sense. There is rarely any "social" without "political," and accordingly, constructivism should be the study of the sociopolitical construction of sociopolitical reality. This framework produces several consequences for the constitutive and political role of ideas besides the normative implications for scholars whose professional lives center on the production, evaluation, critique, and circulation of ideas.

Common sense is a reservoir of background knowledge. It frames the human understanding of the environment and so is crucial to the sociopolitical construction of sociopolitical reality. This vital role is what attracts political entrepreneurs to seek control over the common sense, in other words, hegemonize it. The main arena of hegemony is civil society and its educational, cultural, and associational institutions. As explained and demonstrated in the first part of the book, essentially contested political concepts are one of the main vehicles of the hegemonizing effort. The attachment of meaning to essentially contested concepts involves bounding, which frames the common sense. Bounding practices include such acts as defining, naming, tagging, and labeling, and relatedly the uses of analogy and metaphor. In other words, the attachment of meaning to concepts by different bounding practices constructs the understanding of sociopolitical reality. Part of politics involves decontesting essentially contested concepts by fixating them with a single unreflected meaning, or alternatively, keeping concepts fuzzy and meaningless. In both cases, public deliberations ossify into different doxa, and criticism is set aside, weakening democracy. Using the metaphor from the life and death of Gramsci, democracy becomes a kind of "Quisisana clinic" in which democratic citizens are confined and their agency restrained, or to use another metaphor, more familiar from the history of political theory, democratic citizens become lodged in the Platonic cave.

For theoreticians of concepts and contestation, this Gramscian reading of politics speaks of engagement not as a concept in need of analysis (though this is also true) but as a mode of involved academia committed to the dual analytical gaze. Practice of this dual gaze involves cultivating both a Gramscian sensitivity to the practice of politics and a Habermas-inspired responsibility toward changing how present-day politics is practiced. If politics is about the closing of discussion by fixating concepts with one unreflected meaning or emptying them of meaning, then involved academia should be about trying to open the discussion through conceptual engagement. It is through this engagement that the contested nature of concepts, the contestation over them, and the ideological bases and normative significances of those various conceptualizations will be reflected upon and disclosed. Of no less importance, conceptual engagement should be linked to an understanding that the definitions that theoreticians develop are themselves a kind of bounding practice when phenomena are categorized and essentially contested concepts are conceptualized. Hence, academic conceptualizations, that is, definitions, are also normatively grounded. Therefore engagement necessitates both the self-reflexivity of considering one's own conceptualizations and a commitment to pluralism. Theoreticians who are sensitive to conceptual politics and committed to participatory and deliberative democracy should engage as theoretician-citizens; those who do so do not just offer conceptual answers but, no less importantly, also raise conceptual questions, namely questions whose most important social and political function is to continuously open up intellectual space for criticism.

Engaged Academia and Democratic Dilemmas

However, and as explored extensively above, engagement raises a host of questions and democratic dilemmas. Like any theory, IR theories are based on standpoints formed by the life experiences and moral perspectives of the theoreticians who develop them. A theory can also be a political tool. As Cox aptly commented, "Theory is always *for* someone and *for* some purpose" (1981, 128). Thus, (1) normative foundations always inform theory, (2) theoreticians represent or form an interested group (representing a class, say the middle class, or forming a distinct group with its own professional and parochial interests), and (3) the normative foundations of theories may be related to the group of theoreticians insofar as they are interested. And these three stipulations normatively complicate engagement by raising the following three dilemmas: (1) the legitimacy of injecting moral dispositions to the process of policymaking, especially when hidden or when the theoreticians are outsiders, (2) the inequality of access to the involved theoreticians and their advice, hence the potentiality of empowering the powers that be, affording them increasing power resources, and (3) the possibility of being hijacked by skillful politicians, hence not only serving the powers that be but serving them by advancing agendas that clash with those supported by the involved theoreticians.

The second part of the book explored these dilemmas in depth and also the principles that can help academics resolve them, namely engaging without serving the powers (and security agencies) that be and without reifying and helping to institutionalize an elitist model of democracy. Academia, in order to discharge its responsibility, must distance itself from the powers that be and their elitist model of democracy. Notwithstanding the dilemmas, the guiding principle is to engage and be a participatory and deliberative part of democratic life. Academia cannot and should not seclude itself. Though not omnipotent and though success is never guaranteed, academics do have much to offer and have a substantive responsibility to society. They have a responsibility to engage.

Because of this, an irresolvable tension emerges between academia as part of an interested group (whose standpoints shapes all the theories produced by academia) and academia's universal orientation—not just in the sense implied by the word "university"—but as the ideal of pursuing truth as a universal notion. It is an irreconcilable tension between universal and particular. And it is difficult, probably impossible, to solve this tension. Having said that, there are still several points that should be acknowledged: (1) This tension means that the two traits of universalism and particularism do coexist in academia and scholars. Being committed to the pursuit of truth raises academia above absolute particularism and gives it and its members the potential for universalism. (2) Tensions are part and parcel of democratic life, and, among other things, commitment to democratic life means being ready and able to acknowledge and live with tensions. (3) The particularism of academia is not (at least it does not have to be) statist. Accordingly, academics, even if grounded in their societies, can transcend statist pressures and raise themselves above serving narrow statist interests. This ability is important and plays an important function in my argument in the second part of the book. In a sense, even if academics belong to a class, it is a transnational class, highly equipped to cope with transnational and universal problems, such as those that haunt international politics. (4) To address the tension as best we can means to follow the principles I advocated throughout this book. An engaged academia that acknowledges the tension within itself alongside the democratic dilemmas that engagement raises must commit itself to self-reflexivity, a communal setting, pluralism, and transparency. If academics commit themselves to these principles, they will become theoretician-citizens and academia will be well equipped to engage in a conceptually contested environment.

Theoretician-citizens are theoreticians who assume social and political responsibilities and discharge them in the public sphere and through civil society. They accept these responsibilities having recognized the virtues and merits of theory for providing society with helpful insights for coping with the sociopolitical world, with all its complexities and challenges, a world that is also a conceptually contested environment. These responsibilities must also go hand in hand with the moral understanding that as human beings and citizens theoreticians have a duty and obligation to share their insights with society in a participatory and deliberative fashion through civil society and the public sphere, not through the elitist networks and closed institutional arrangements of the executive establishment. And, finally, to be theoretician-citizens means acting as citizens trained to be circumspect and self-reflexive theoreticians rather than imperious know-all Platonic philosopher-kings.

To engage with the public as theoretician-citizens means considering the sensitivities, preferences, and interests of the public rather than just the members of the closed circles of decision-makers and the related elites who network with them. It involves considering whether or not the public's sensitivities, preferences, and interests are being served and seeing the public often as the universal public, humanity as a whole. That is how we should think about and theorize democracy and processes of democratization and how we must act when forecasting these processes, because these theorizing-based forecasts are most prone to the aforementioned democratic dilemmas. This is also the case with security scholars, who need to beware co-option by the security sectors. No different than theorizing democracy and democratizing, theorizing security must be transparent and away from the heart of darkness. As theoretician-citizens, academics have an obligation to help the public at large by providing insights on security issues, but not through the closed circles of the security sectors with their rules of secrecy. As mentioned above, some leeway is needed vis-à-vis leaving it up to the scholars when to cooperate with the powers and security that be, the circumstances that require they be directly involved with the closed circles of power and security, and when to let the think tank-based scholars serve the state in a kind of delicate division of labor between university and think tank.

Engagement as theoretician-citizen also means making the theorizing process and theory-grounded engagements as transparent as possible. Engaged theoreticians have to explain how their engagement is linked to theory and the role of moral values in shaping their theories and engagements. They must proceed in a spirit of modesty and caution, aware that their engagement is two-faceted. On the one hand, as a continuation of theory, theory-grounded engagement is highly prized, processed information following a thoughtful process of taking and analyzing data in a theory. On the other hand, in the public sphere, the theoretical insights that engagement offers should not be treated as conclusive but as helpful raw material; a single set of data among many other relevant sets, which the public can consult and consider as policies are being shaped. That, after all, is what democratic deliberation is about. Modesty and caution are required both because an elitist trap beckons and because of the particularistic edge of academia, which stems from its interested nature and from theory as the product of theoreticians' standpoints. Hence the call for self-reflexivity and transparency when offering academic advice. This is why academic advice should be treated as one more (important and useful) input into public deliberation, to be evaluated and considered by the public as a whole according to its sensitivities, preferences, and interests. That way the citizens remain sovereign and their own best judges of themselves.

This is true especially for concepts with their definitions and conceptualizations. The normative foundation of theories is most commanding in the context of concepts, namely essentially contested concepts. As we saw earlier, the elements of the sociopolitical world do not fit neatly into human-made concepts. To define is to impose arbitrary delineations on social objects, namely phenomena, processes, and the like. Defining is a bounding practice that involves bounding and rounding: inflating the importance of some differences to create a focus on certain phenomena and processes, while deflating and even ignoring the relevance of other differences so as to draw together various other phenomena and processes. Only thus are definitions possible in the sociopolitical world, which means that definitions are embedded in a normative ground. Consequently, defining is a moral act, and theoreticians need to go through a process of *zooming in, zooming out*, a two-stage epistemological and methodological strategy in which scholars zoom their lens in on particles internal to their theories, namely concepts, and then zoom their lens out by defining and conceptualizing those concepts normatively and with moral sensitivity while taking their impact on the world outside academia into account and keeping a watchful eye on the quality of truth, which is a living entity constructed through the engaged and dynamic processes in which theoreticians play a part.

The zooming in, zooming out process is necessary for conceptual engagement to be accountable for the democratic dilemmas and prevent academic scholars and the wider public from perceiving academic engagement as offering some supreme, know-it-all conceptualization. By ensuring self-reflexivity and transparency, the zooming in, zooming out process can ensure that theoreticians' conceptualizations are sensitive to their own normative foundations, thus also committing academia to pluralism. This means that in addition to advancing the conceptualizations that they prefer for moral reasons, theoreticians should also highlight the essentially contested nature of conceptualization: the manifold legitimate and reasonable possibilities that come into focus when conceptualizing concepts. This would be a modest and conditioned way to engage, or to use Jasanoff's apt terminology, it will be to adopt "technologies of humility" (2003, 2007). This modest and conditioned engagement pays tribute to the power of theory while recognizing its limits. That way, theory-grounded engagement is not to be offered as an all-powerful, conclusive, and know-all form of involvement, as an elitist gift from the ivory tower, but can be received as relevant and helpful raw material to be treated as such and deliberated over by the public.

Theoreticians can only guarantee that the sociopolitical construction of the sociopolitical reality will not take place behind the veil of knowledge by participating sincerely in democratic deliberations as theoretician-citizens through theory-grounded engagement. It is the only way they can ensure openness in discussion and discharge their political and social responsibility to their democratic polities and humanity in general. This applies to practice (engagement) and the kind of bounding practices that should be used (zooming in, zooming out). It also applies to the content of the bounding practices: the content of the definitions to be used in theories and offered to the world outside academia. Zooming in, zooming out guides our efforts to understand the two main concepts dealt with in this book, security and democracy, in moral terms.

I will make one cautious remark regarding the principles of self-reflexivity, transparency, pluralism, and engagement. My proposal so far, the principles I advocate, and the definitions I will propose shortly are all quite close to the deliberative and participatory understanding of democracy. In a sense, my proposal is circular, but not, I hope, tautological. It is circular since it is founded on a participatory and deliberative conceptualization of democracy, which it then attempts to realize and actualize. Nevertheless, it is a virtuous circularity and a logical and reasonable outcome of embracing conceptual politics: democracy and security are essentially contested concepts, drawing from different moral grounds. Those who adhere to the structural and elitist conceptualization of democracy will probably find my proposed measures and definitions unattractive. The ball is now in the court of those who champion elitist democracy and national security to propose alternative schemes for the relations between academia and state and to suggest other definitions of democracy and security (and other relevant concepts). This is the type of disagreement we expect when politics is understood in terms of the parameters of conceptual politics. It is thus a disagreement I can live with and in a spirit of pluralism can even welcome.

Democratic Security

In the early part of the book I suggested that the two main concepts of this book, democracy and security, are joined and interwoven by semantic fields. This is in the sense of being a configured group of words and concepts related to each other by the same subject. I also argued that the analysis of semantic fields and the theoretical framework of essentially contested concepts complement each other, offering us a rich conceptual analysis of the social world. These two analytical perspectives can also account for each other constitutively. One source for the essential contestedness of a concept is the multiplicity of possible and legitimate configurations of the concepts related to it, namely the range of the concept's plausible semantic fields. Likewise, it is the essential contestedness of a concept that allows that concept to slot into different semantic fields, which all refer to the same subject, and at least some of which relate to it reasonably and legitimately. And of course the same thing is applicable to the concepts of democracy and security, which are both essentially contested concepts that jointly form many semantic fields.

These joint analytical perspectives can help us understand the all-inclusiveness of the sociopolitical world: how sociopolitical phenomena are related to the concepts representing them mentally and how different essentially contested concepts are interwoven through connected semantic fields. Different semantic fields combine to form a single conceptually interwoven semantic field, and at least in this sense, the concepts representing sociopolitical phenomena cannot be separated from each other. Arguably the same is true for the sociopolitical phenomena themselves. Consequently, the act of defining in the sense of bounding concepts and delineating them from each other academically appears a heuristically and a methodologically crucial task and an almost senseless Sisyphean ontological labor—another built-in tension of the sociopolitical world that cannot be resolved.

We also find that the concepts (and phenomena) of democracy and security are also intertwined. On the one hand, they are distinctively delineated concepts. On the other hand, in some semantic fields they are intimately linked to the extent of being symbiotically dependent. When we examine democracy and security in terms of semantic fields, the two concepts seem to resemble lichen. Inasmuch as lichen is a composite of algae and fungi that started out as two distinct organisms but combined into a third composited organism, so democracy and security can be separated heuristically but ontologically are a composite of one entity, both conceptually and otherwise. And not unlike algae, fungi, and lichen, there are different ways to relate democracy and security and many semantic fields where the two are symbiotically linked.

The different democratic peace theories link the two concepts of democracy and security and explain how democracy brings security by making wars between democracies less likely (for theoretical and critical discussion, see Wolff and Wurm 2011). The theories argue that democracy advances security and creates a zone of democratic peace. Other observations and theories argue the obverse is true: that democracy undermines security by increasing the likelihood of wars against nondemocracies and encouraging democratic crusades, which, at least under certain circumstances, whip up a moralistic frenzy. Thus, democracy and security can be member concepts from the same semantic fields, together with other concepts. One of these semantic fields is stability, which links democracy and security to other concepts like prosperity, regionalism, dyads, norms, peace, human rights, and so on. Another relevant semantic field containing both democracy and security is the semantic field of instability. Democracy and security are member concepts in this field, alongside concepts such as moralizing, democratizing, checks and balances, rallying round the flag, and so forth.

But it is noteworthy that in the semantic fields above, security is a more central concept than democracy. Democracy relates to security mainly as a concept that explains how security is either strengthened or undermined. Democracy can be understood as an instrument of security, and then it is just a short jump to instrumentalizing democracy in the service of security and justifying models of defensive democracy in which democracy is sacrificed all too easily in the name of security by those who still swear by it. In such cases, the state's security is what is being highlighted, making it a question of *national* security. The state is thus defended and served or disserved by the instrument of democracy, as well as by individual citizens who might find themselves paying the costs and having their rights sacrificed to security. We see that defensive democracy is both too restricted and too permissive. It can easily shed its constitutive democratic values and principles and all too readily legitimize violence. Put differently, a defensive democracy is one that is conceptualized procedurally and minimally, as a structure.

But there are other semantic fields that link democracy and security without instrumentalizing democracy to security's ends; in such semantic fields, democracy assumes center stage while security becomes an instrument in its service and, more important, in the service of democracy's citizens and their rights. After all, democracy's main aim is the well-being of its citizens, at least in its nonstructural conceptions. Similarly, in these semantic fields, security will be conceptualized in line with critical theory or the feminist theory of security or as human security. Thus the two concepts are conceptualized reciprocally, each endowing the other with meanings. In the case of such semantic fields, the conceptual outcome is very different from the semantic field for defensive democracy, which is unhealthily permissive in the way it grants the state executive tools. In the latter semantic fields, legitimacy, as in the legitimacy of the instruments that may be mobilized to defend the citizens, has an important part as well. In terms of adjectives, we aspire to see the adjective "democratic" used to describe "security" in "democratic security," where the subject is the citizen, not the state. This security takes the democratic and human rights of citizens seriously, while democracy takes legitimate measures to secure the life and security of its citizens without denying their rights.

These are the kind of conceptual analyses that we can undertake if we combine the frameworks of essentially contested concepts and semantic fields and apply a dual analytical gaze. In an environment of essential contestedness, the kind of conceptual analysis encouraged here will help us to understand and define democracy and security on a deeper level while committing academia to engagement and its members to serving as a force of theoretician-citizens. By serving their domestic and universal fellow citizens through engagement, theoretician-citizens can help to advance democratic security. They can participate in a civic struggle to achieve participatory and deliberative democracy, emancipatory and humane security, and democratic security, where obstacles to citizens' democratic agency are removed and an intellectual space is opened for criticism and true participation.

Democracy can be fragile, and no one can guarantee success in the civic struggle to promote or even secure it. Nor should we presume the omnipotence of academia. Yet theoreticians do possess certain relevant and vital assets and faculties, making them responsible for engaging the wider public. Democracy is too valuable and important for us to give up. Therefore, while we should not be overly optimistic or presumptuous, neither should we permit pessimism, apathy, and inaction to be taken as acceptable courses for academia.

Appendix ✦ "Megalim Olam"

In October 2012 I was appointed director of the Leonard Davis for International Relations. The Davis Institute is a research institute in the Faculty of Social Sciences of the Hebrew University of Jerusalem. Thus, like many other academics I was given the opportunity to double my academic affiliation, in this case with a university-based think tank. With the responsibility to engage in mind, I contacted Ynet (www.ynet.co.il), one of the largest news sites in Israel and offered them cooperation: I would provide short scholarly articles on matters of international politics and foreign countries, the subjects covered by the international desk, to be published in a special section. The international desk's chief editor, Roi Simyoni, turned out to be an alumnus of my department and was happy to cooperate. We established a section called "Megalim Olam" (Hebrew: "Discovering the World"), where we planned to publish weekly articles of seven hundred to a thousand words on a variety of global and foreign issues. I deliberately approached the most extensively read news outlet. I wanted the articles to be widely accessed and read.

I began to solicit articles from colleagues in Israel and around the world. Needless to say, it was not easy to get academics to write articles and we were unable to publish every week. Keep it in mind that academics work on a different timeline than the daily news world and mostly are not credited by their universities for such publications. Still, there were many academics who were willing to publish in such an outlet. Their reasons were varied: a shared understanding of the responsibility to engage the wider public; a wish to influence the public discourse, feel the satisfaction of immediate publication; or perhaps a desire to be recognized outside the closed academic circle and be publicly credited for their expertise. All this aside, many did agree, and the section was established. The first article was submitted by two of my colleagues from the Department of International Relations, Avraham Sela and Oren Barak, and was published on November

21, 2012, on the last day of Operation Pillar of Defense (the second round in a series of violent Israel/Gaza escalations). It was exactly the same article they had published on Ynet three years before during Operation Cast Lead (the first round). They added only a short preface explaining the verbatim nature of their article and expressing their view of the futility of this second round. This article is actual evidence of the inability of scholarly articles to change the course of history. The first publication did not prevent the second round, and the second publication did not prevent the third, and most devastating, round of violence, Operation Protective Edge, in July 2014. This should help us moderate our expectations of our ability to change history but serves also as an indication that scholars are sometimes insightful and that it is worth trying to bring the voice of academia into the public discourse, encouraging Israelis to stop and think even in the midst of violent conflict.

It did motivate me to approach colleagues and ask them, often repeatedly, to contribute articles. I generally asked them to write on their own area of expertise in a style that was academic and theoretically informed but also publicly accessible, jargon free, and rich with empirical examples. Over the next three years, more than ninety articles were published on a variety of subjects, such as soft power and Japan, Vatican foreign policy, Africa on the rise, democracy in Indonesia, ethics of care, feminism and global justice, justice and asymmetric warfare, the global politics of the Arctic, Jewish diasporas, critical discourses of security, Cuba following Fidel Castro, the quest for autonomy in Catalonia, daily life in Iran, political corruption around the world, cyberwarfare, space diplomacy, the negotiations in Cyprus, the Truth and Reconciliation Commission in Nepal, Turkey's intervention in Syria, the politics of the World Cup, and international financial investments. We received articles by authors from Israel, Canada, Denmark, England, the United States, Colombia, Japan, Spain, and elsewhere. Articles in English were translated into Hebrew by Dr. Mor Mitrani, then a PhD candidate in our department.

"Megalim Olam" became a three-person venture. I solicited articles and edited them so they would follow the general instructions, sometimes asking authors to add examples, clarify points, mellow jargon, and so on. Mor translated articles from English and adapted them for the general public, ready for my final editing. Roi thought up catchy titles and relevant pictures to make the articles attractive, consumable products. However, the catchy titles proved a thorny issue when some of the authors were upset by the titles, finding them simplistic and a sellout for the sake of publicity. This was one indicator of the difference between the writing rationales of academics and those of newspeople. I then made a habit of requesting authors' prepublication approval (at least from writers in Hebrew).

After three years as director of the Davis Institute, I went on sabbatical to the United States, where I wrote much of this book. My successor as director of the institute, Professor Dan Miodownik, has continued the institutional commitment to "Megalim Olam" and left its editing with me. But ironically, the time that I dedicated to developing theoretical and normative arguments to justify "Megalim Olam" left less time for the actual project, and while the articles continued to be published, the flow was dramatically reduced. I have now completed five years of editing and seen about 120 articles published, a total that has left me quite satisfied and no less exhausted.

But apart from narrating the personal narrative and rationale for "Megalim Olam," what can be said about the actual impact on public discourse? For those skeptics among us, the first article on the Gaza rounds of violence by Barak and Sela sums it up. These academic theoreticians did not change the course of history and failed to prevent the follies and immorality of the repeated rounds of violence. In the longer term, we certainly did not achieve the democratic security I call for, since the country and large segments of society keep moving away from democracy and reasoned agency toward silencing dissent and xenophobic and hawkish attitudes and policies. We have not moved a single step closer to peace since "Megalim Olam" was launched and are no closer to the atmosphere of regional reconciliation and rapprochement that we hope for. But if we consider the list of topics covered and the variety of its authors, we can only be impressed by their potential for enriching Israeli public discourse, for making people stop and think, and for raising questions and opening up discussions. Otherwise, we would confront a monologue of ossified conceptions and one-sided hegemony. And if we count the entries to the articles, we see how accessible they are and how "Megalim Olam" has managed to reach far and wide and certainly more people than we would reach through peer-reviewed publications. So something has surely been achieved. People are being exposed to subjects they never thought about, including democracy in the Muslim world (Indonesia and Malesia), successful peace negotiations in protracted conflicts (Colombia and Nepal), alternative discourses of security and ethics (critical and feminist accounts of both), Iranians as human beings and not only enemies, and Africa beyond hunger, corruption, and civil wars. In other words, there is a whole world out there beyond Israel, and lessons to learn about it and from it: Israel is not necessarily the center of the universe, foreign countries and cultures might be more complicated than their public perceptions, and geostrategy is not the only angle through which to watch the world.

Practically all of the articles were read (or at least the articles were entered) by thousands of readers—thirty articles had between 10,000 and 20,000 views, and four had more than 20,000. The record by far, 78,215 views, was set by Dr. Micha'el Tanchum's article published in February 22, 2014, on the Turkish MILGEM project and its strategic and geostrategic implications. The MILGEM project will upgrade the Turkish navy with advanced corvettes equipped with antisubmarine capabilities and a helipad. Tanchum, who is a fellow in the Middle East and Asia Departments at the Truman Research Institute for the Advancement of Peace at the Hebrew University of Jerusalem, is a seasoned writer of commentaries in the international media and expert on Middle East geostrategy. He wrote several articles for "Megalim Olam," all of which were widely read. The Turkish article was the most attractive of all probably because of the strategic implications of the MILGEM project, especially in an era of tensions between Israel and Turkey that were exacerbated by the discovery of gas fields in the eastern Mediterranean. In a country obsessed with strategy, security, and national survival, this is not at all surprising. But it is less easy to guess which articles ranked after Tanchum as popular reading choices. For example, on April 24, 2014, a colleague of mine, Dr. Guy Laron, analyzed the changing trends in global financial investments, showing that investors had returned to the United States and the possible global implications of this change. The article drew 30,217 hits. Another article (February 11, 2014), by Professor Yagil Levy of the Israeli Open University, analyzed Germany's civil service, drawing 29,443 hits. The article appeared during a period of public debate on the Israeli model of military conscription; Levy invited the public to learn from the Germans (always a contested invitation in Israel). This is a perfect example of these articles' potential to engage and widen citizens' horizons for debating the status quo and its alternatives.

This short survey is far from methodologically rigorous. It also lacks key information for effectively comparing the articles, such as how long were they on the homepage and the time of day the articles appeared. Were they published during prime time and for how long? These questions are decided by the homepage editors, and I have no theoretical and methodological tools for analyzing their decisions and answering questions: Did they try to decide which articles will attract readers? Were they interested in attracting readers to the article? What other news items competed for the editors' attention? And so on. For my purposes, the survey is instructive enough, and we can clearly see that an audience exists for scholarly, jargon-free articles. That is not just for articles that usually attract Israelis, namely on security and geostrategy. People are willing to open their minds and read about other issues, which, to borrow terms from critical security studies, can widen and deepen their horizons.

The numbers are impressive; the audience is out there and surely larger than our usual academic readership. And although we are not academically credited for these articles and not cited in a way that aids our promotion, still we accomplish something, and that something is substantially important. We discharge our responsibilities to engage the wider public and perhaps contribute if only a fraction to a more reasoned public discussion and a better world. What more can we reasonably ask for?

For a full list of "Megalim Olam" articles, see http://en.davis.huji.ac.il/commentary-articles-ynet

Notes

Introduction

1. The main exceptions are first-generation constructivists like Nicholas Onuf (1989) and Friedrich Kratochwil (1989). More on that below.
2. I suggest below that political agents try to fixate concepts with one meaning or alternatively empty them of all meaningful meaning. Both these conceptual tactics amount to the same thing in terms of degrading democratic deliberation and contestation.

Chapter 1

1. A more Foucauldian stand would be that those intellectuals are also dominated by a diffused, agentless, and abstract power structure. Here, there is no actual importance in argumentation of any kind. Keith Dowding (2006) justly dubbed this a Foucauldian trap.
2. While it is positivistically tempting to categorically delineate these different aspects of social reality by designating some as dependent variables and others as independent variables, it is hardly ever so in reality. Reality is much fuzzier then positivistic methodological schemes. Rigorous social research is implicated in a social existence that eludes categorical delineations. Hence, for example, social knowledge is produced and reproduced by social practices and rituals, yet at the same time it produces and reproduces them. Variables are heuristically useful, constructed, theoretical entities, but as such, one should remember, they are also but artifacts and, as such, can at times serve as obstacles to a true understanding of social reality. As a matter of fact, theoretical artifacts can themselves sometimes become contested political concepts, and, no less problematic from a positivistic point of view, they may serve as agents in transforming the social reality they supposedly help to heuristically explain.
3. Jennifer Mitzen (2005) captures the ideality of the Habermasian project well, "Of course, the Concert was by no means a realization of the public sphere ideal. Its diplomacy did not embody (or attempt to embody) Habermasian ideals of free publicity and rational communication. But in fairness, no actually existing public sphere today fully embodies these ideals. Power and privilege always matter and

are problems even domestically. The importance of the public sphere concept is as a guide, to determine whether and how a given exercise of power is normatively better or worse than another."

4. Thomas Risse (2000) gives a balanced account of Habermas's notion of the common lifeworld.

5. As argued above, while aiming at hegemony, the most political entrepreneurs usually achieve is public convention. Hegemony implies an absolute and all-embracing framed common sense. Public convention, in contrast, refers to a more limited and partial framed common sense, one that is limited in scope to some sectors of society and partial in its grip on the common sense. Accordingly, rather than using the Gramscian terminology of hegemony and counterhegemony, I use the terms *institutionalized* and *oppositional* public conventions (respectively).

6. On Orwell from an IR perspective, see Hall 2008.

7. Previously (Ish-Shalom 2011b) I treated definitions too loosely by arguing that the act of defining is a feature of the wider public. I think now that the current theoretical move of distinguishing between the act of academic defining and the public and looser act of labeling is appropriate.

Chapter 2

1. For a diachronic analysis of concepts, see Reinhart Koselleck and his conceptual history, for example Koselleck 2006. Christopher Hobson's (2015) excellent book follows the diachronic framework of Koselleck (combining it with the Cambridge school of intellectual history) to study the conceptual history of democracy in IR.

2. William Connolly (1974, 14) and Nicholas Onuf (1989, 4) prefer the notion of cluster concepts.

3. Rawls is the paradigmatic proponent of the importance of the democratic state in the liberal theory of justice (1999a), maintaining his statist perspective even in his *Law of Peoples* (1999b).

4. Other cosmopolitan concerns are global poverty and distributive justice; hence some cosmopolitans stress the moral imperative of having panglobal resource redistribution (see, for example, Singer 1972).

5. This is even more so in the republican conceptualization of democracy. Republicanism stresses that the state belongs to its citizens and that it is of the utmost political importance and ethical virtue for citizens to actively participate in democratic deliberations and contribute to the process of making policy and shaping their shared political life. Liberalism and republicanism share some important features, including a belief in the rational faculties and reasonableness of the citizens. However, there are also some obvious tensions between the republican and liberal theories of democracy. Liberalism focuses on negative liberties and the right not to participate, whereas republican theory gives more weight to the positive liberties and the virtue of participation. It expects a great deal from the individual and does

not shy away from explicitly arguing it. Liberalism is individualistic in orientation, whereas republicanism is communitarian. Thus, although republicanism and liberalism may agree on the mechanisms of participation and deliberations, they are two distinctively divergent conceptualizations of democracy. And the source of their distinctiveness is their different normative groundwork.

Republicanism, even more than liberal democracy, seems to be dependent on the state.

However, James Bohman (2004) argues for cosmopolitan republicanism, due to the embryonic political institutions that take shape on the global level.

6. The triangular form of analysis is arbitrary, and the analysis could have equally been based on four or any other number of components.

7. See also Ken Booth (2005, 2007) and his analysis of security as a derivative concept and Jef Huysmans's (1998) proposal for analyzing security as a thick signifier.

8. Thus Morgenthau, who did at times criticize consequentialist and utilitarian ethics, adopted the Weberian ethics of responsibility (1972, 169–74). See also Barkawi 1998, 159–62; Turner and Factor 1984, 168–69.

9. It is not surprising, then, that Amartya Sen chaired the UN Commission on Human Security that submitted its report on May 2003, calling for a new security framework. See Smith 2005, 53.

10. On global security, see Hough 2004.

11. Feminism is not alone in examining narratives to understand security. See Krebs 2015, which studies the importance of narratives in US security policymaking from a constructivist point of view.

12. On the importance of concrete daily experiences for feminist security studies, see Tickner 1992; Hansen 2000; Blanchard 2003, 1298; Hoogensen and Rottem 2004, 156.

13. Wibben exemplifies the complexity of categorizing the contemporary security studies landscape and the difficulties with delineating one approach from another, since apart from being a feminist, she also draws heavily on poststructuralism (as many feminists do).

Chapter 3

1. For Lebanon's thorny domestic politics, see Barak 2003.

2. The remorseless mutual devastation might have been due to a desire for revenge; see Lowenheim and Heimann 2008.

3. On the Israeli tradition of giving military units and weapons biblical and natural names in an attempt to neutralize them, see Gavriely-Nuri 2010.

4. This technique, the intentional manufacturing of doubt and uncertainty in the public, is sometimes studied under the heading of agnotology (Mirowski and Nik-Khah 2013, 282).

Chapter 4

1. William Connolly argues somewhat similarly but from a poststructuralist perspective (2005)

Chapter 5

1. The idea of zooming in, zooming out concluded my previous book (2013) and pointed to the way theoreticians should think of and discharge their academic responsibility *for* the ramifications of their theories in the world. It led me to my current research on the responsibilities of academia *to* society and is a useful introduction to this part of the book.

2. The precise and nuanced definition in the Correlates of War project is the following: "An interstate war must have: a) sustained combat, involving b) regular armed forces on both sides and c) 1,000 battle fatalities among all of the system members involved." See Sarkees and Schafer 2000, 125.

3. The political stakes in defining an issue as a security issue lies at the heart of the Copenhagen school and its securitization theory. See Buzan, de Wilde, and Wæver 1998.

4. On the nexus of theory and practice in security studies see McSweeney 1999, 148; Booth 2007, 4; Buzan and Hansen 2009, 10, 31; Wibben 2011, 12.

5. The arguments and proposal presented here are mostly relevant to social facts, as they are the sort of facts that are represented by essentially contested concepts and constitute the subject matter of the social sciences.

Chapter 6

1. It should be noted, though, that Kymlicka is not comfortable with the terminology of communities, as he rejects communitarianism. For him communitarianism works against individual autonomy (1995, 163). Thus, he prefers using the terminology of groups. In our context, this issue is of less concern, and by using the terminology of communities I do not undermine individual autonomy. I prefer the terminology of community as it sits better with the Buberian notion of dialogue (see below).

2. On Buber's development from mysticism to existentialism and to dialogue see Friedman 1976; Mendes-Flohr 1989.

3. For a philosophical perspective that heavily influenced Buber's philosophy, see Levinas 1967, 139.

4. Brent Steele (2010a) made a similar point.

Chapter 7

1. The literature on "Mode 2" science (Nowotny, Scott, and Gibbons 2003) recaptures these relations of state and university, arguing in essence that academia has lost its autonomy to a web of complexes, in which state and industry steer, commercialize, and manage the production of knowledge, collapsing the autonomy of academia and the distinction between basic and applied science.

2. Coburn is not alone in this attitude, and social scientists are not its only targets, as can be learned from the questioning of physicist Robert R. Wilson by Senator John O. Pastore in his congressional testimony on April 17, 1969. Senator Pastore kept pressuring Dr. Wilson about the military utility of funding the first accelerator, to which Wilson kept answering in the negative, for example: "It has nothing to do with the military. I am sorry." The dialogue is quoted by Hallam Stevens (2003, 174).

3. This can be seen in and following militarized conflicts, in which think tanks increase their usual productivity and are responsible for voluminous body publications. This, for example, was the case in Israel during and after operation Protective Edge.

Chapter 8

1. Philip Tetlock's ongoing work on forecasting is telling about how difficult forecasting is in the highly complex social world (2005). His studies also reveal that experts are not necessarily better forecasters than nonexperts (Tetlock and Gardner 2015). According to Tetlock, being a superforecaster demands a set of qualities similar to those I ask later from scholars, that is, open-mindedness, carefulness, cautiousness, and self-criticism (2015, 20).

2. Notable exceptions are Australia, Belgium, Greece, and Luxemburg.

3. I do not try to define the bounds of reasonable limits to inequality because those boundaries should be set locally through democratic deliberation and argumentation. However, this answer naturally runs the risk of ad infinitum regress, as the open question still remains who can (and will) participate in this deliberation and the criteria by which we will decide if the unequal participation in the deliberation over the limits to unequal participation will be democratically permissible (i.e., reasonable).

4. Karl Popper also advised conditional predictions, though for epistemological and ontological reasons (Popper 1963, 340).

Chapter 9

1. This understanding of expertise sits well with science and technology studies (STS). See, for example, Latour 1987; Jasanoff 1990, 2005; Pielke 2007; Longino 2002. For STS in IR, see Büger and Gadinger 2007.

2. Transparency is not the only relevant consideration when theorizing the proper regulation of relations between security experts and security sectors. There are other relevant considerations, which, under certain circumstances, can affect this issue. More on that below.

3. Note that because it is centered around transparency, my argument is mainly concerned with university-based security experts. I will have more to say on think tank-based security experts toward the end of this chapter. Accordingly, I generally use the term *academic security experts* and only use the more institutionally accurate but cumbersome term *university-based security experts* when distinguishing those experts from think tank-based security experts.

4. For a radical account of the history and mass psychology of rape, see the seminal study by Brownmiller 1975.

5. This sections draws from Ish-Shalom (2011b). The original article is more nuanced and also presents possible objections that it then proceeds to refute.

6. Barry Buzan captures this dimension of security wonderfully in his book title: *People, States, and Fear* (1983).

7. Later, under Johnson, Rostow replaced Bundy, becoming special assistant to the president for security affairs.

8. That is not to say that theory and ideology are one and the same. The ideological bent is one component of theorizing among other components, such as the academic culture of healthy skepticism (Ish-Shalom 2011b).

9. These are more or less strict across different states.

10. As the introduction explains, my focus in this book is on university-based security experts. However, below, I briefly analyze think tank-based security experts.

11. See also the observation by Niklas Luhmann (1960) regarding the different binary logics in science and politics: in science the binary code is true and not true; in politics it is power and no power.

12. We should be cautious, though, not to overstretch this argument. Academics, especially with tenure, are quite well-off socioeconomically. They are certainly not economically deprived, which can temper their critical edge. But, I wish to argue, surrendering to the temptations of political power can utterly ruin their potentiality for criticism.

13. On the importance of achieving democratic legitimacy for expertise, see Turner 2001, 144–45. Steve Fuller (1992) has similar views in his agenda for social epistemology, which stresses the importance of the accountability of scientists to the public and the need to make knowledge accessible to a society as a whole, and not just the elites (395–97). However, he takes the argument a step too far by arguing that "the persuasiveness of a knowledge claim [is] part of what determines its truth value" (397).

14. On the importance of this question, see also Buzan and Hansen 2009, 63.

15. Transparent argumentation is one of the ethical bedrocks of Habermas's discursive theory of democracy (1984).

16. Note that by being ideal, we can only approach the democratic ideal, drawing closer and closer to it, while never fully attaining it.

17. Regrettably, the notion of enlightenment has been discredited by many post-structuralists.

18. This is true as a general rule. It does not necessarily apply to all think tanks, and there may be many that operate critically and through civil society. We should also consider that the categories of academia and think tanks are ideal types, and in reality some institutions may fall in between.

References

Adler, Emanuel. 1992. "The Emergence of Cooperation: National Epistemic Communities and the International Evolution of the Idea of Nuclear Arms Control." *International Organization* 46 (1): 101–45.
Adler, Emanuel. 1997. "Seizing the Middle Ground: Constructivism in World Politics." *European Journal of International Relations* 3 (3): 319–63.
Adler, Emanuel. 2005. *Communitarian International Relations: The Epistemic Foundations of International Relations*. Abingdon: Routledge.
Adler, Emanuel, and Steven Bernstein. 2005. "Knowledge in Power: The Epistemic Construction of Global Governance." In *Power in Global Governance*, edited by Michael Barnett and Raymond Duvall, 294–318. New York: Cambridge University Press.
Adler-Nissen, Rebecca. 2013. "Introduction." In *Bourdieu in International Relations: Rethinking Key Concepts in IR*, edited by Rebecca Adler-Nissen, 1–23. New York: Routledge.
Akkerman, Tjitske. 2009. "New Wars, New Morality?" *Acta Politica* 44 (1): 74–86.
Alimi, Eitan Y. 2007. *Israeli Politics and the Palestinian Intifada: Political Opportunities, Framing Processes, and Contentious Politics*. New York: Routledge.
Amoureux, Jack L. 2015. *A Practice of Ethics for Global Politics: Ethical Reflexivity*. New York: Routledge.
Amoureux, Jack L., and Brent J. Steele, eds. 2015. *Reflexivity and International Relations: Positionality, Critique, and Practice*. New York: Routledge.
Angliss, Brian. 2007. "Anti-global Heating Claims—a Reasonably Thorough Debunking." https://scholarsandrogues.com/2007/07/23/anti-global-heating-claims-a-reasonably-thorough-debunking/
Anievas, Alexander. 2005. "Critical Dialogues: Habermasian Social Theory and International Relations." *Politics* 25 (3): 135–43.
Apter, David E. 1965. *The Politics of Modernization*. Chicago: University of Chicago Press.
Archibugi, Daniele. 2008. *The Global Commonwealth of Citizens: Toward Cosmopolitan Democracy*. Princeton: Princeton University Press.
Arendt, Hannah. 1960. "Freedom and Politics: A Lecture." *Chicago Review* 14 (1): 28–46.
Aristotle. 2009. *Politics*. Translated by Ernest Barker. New ed. Oxford: Oxford University Press.

Arnett, Ronald C. 1986. *Communication and Community: Implications of Martin Buber's Dialogue*. Carbondale: Southern Illinois University Press.
Avineri, Shlomo. 1968. *The Social and Political Thought of Karl Marx*. London: Cambridge University Press.
Avineri, Shlomo. 1972. *Hegel's Theory of the Modern State*. London: Cambridge University Press.
Avnon, Dan. 1998. *Martin Buber: The Hidden Dialogue*. Lanham, MD: Rowman & Littlefield.
Azaryahu, Maoz. 1986. "Street Names and Political Identity: The Case of East Berlin." *Journal of Contemporary History* 21 (4): 581–604.
Azaryahu, Maoz. 1996. "The Power of Commemorative Street Names." *Environment and Planning D: Society and Space* 14 (3): 311–30.
Baber, Walter F., and Robert V. Bartlett. 2005. *Deliberative Environmental Politics: Democracy and Ecological Rationality*. Cambridge, MA: MIT Press.
Baert, Patrick. 2005. *Philosophy of the Social Sciences: Towards Pragmatism*. Cambridge: Polity Press.
Barak, Oren. 2003. "Lebanon: Failure, Collapse, and Resuscitation." In *State Failure and State Weakness in a Time of Terror*, edited by Robert I. Rotberg, 305–39. Washington, DC: Brookings Institution Press.
Barber, Benjamin. 1984. *Strong Participatory Politics for a New Age*. Berkeley: University of California Press.
Barkawi, Tarak. 1998. "Strategy as a Vocation: Weber, Morgenthau, and Modern Strategic Studies." *Review of International Studies* 24 (2): 159–62.
Barnett, Michael, and Raymond Duvall. 2005. "Power in International Politics." *International Organization* 59 (1): 39–75.
Barry, Andrew. 2006. "Technological Zones." *European Journal of Social Theory* 9 (2): 239–53.
Bates, Thomas R. 1975. "Gramsci and the Theory of Hegemony." *Journal of the History of Ideas* 36 (2): 351–66.
Baudrillard, Jean. 1995. *The Gulf War Did Not Take Place*. Translated by Paul Patton. Bloomington: Indiana University Press.
BBC News. 2010. "Karadzic Defends Bosnian Serb 'Holy' Cause at Trial." http://news.bbc.co.uk/2/hi/europe/8542297.stm
Bell, Daniel A. 2006. *Beyond Liberal Democracy: Political Thinking for an East Asian Context*. Princeton: Princeton University Press.
Berling, Trine Villumsen, and Christian Bueger. 2015. "Security Expertise: An Introduction." In *Security Expertise: Practice, Power, Responsibility*, edited by Trine Villumsen Berling and Christian Bueger, 1–18. New York: Routledge.
Bernstein, Richard J. 1983. *Beyond Objectivism and Relativism: Science, Hermeneutics, and Praxis*. Philadelphia: University of Pennsylvania Press.
Bhaskar, Roy. 2008. *A Realist Theory of Science*. New York: Routledge.
Bieler, Andreas, and Adam David Morton. 2001. "The Gordian Knot of Agency-Structure in International Relations." *European Journal of International Relations* 7 (1): 5–35.

Bjola, Corneliu, and Markus Kornprobst, eds. 2011. *Arguing Global Governance: Agency, Lifeworld and Shared Reasoning*. New York: Routledge.
Blackburn, Simon. 2005. "Reciprocity." In *Oxford Dictionary of Philosophy*, edited by Simon Blackburn, 310. Oxford: Oxford University Press.
Blanchard, Eric M. 2003. "Gender, International Relations, and the Development of Feminist Security Theory." *Signs* 28 (4): 1289–312.
Bohman, James. 2004. "Republican Cosmopolitan." *Journal of Political Philosophy* 12 (3): 336–52.
Booth, Ken. 2005. "Critical Explorations." In *Critical Security Studies and World Politics*, edited by Ken Booth, 259–78. Boulder, CO: Lynne Rienner.
Booth, Ken. 2007. *Theory of World Security*. New York: Cambridge University Press.
Brandist, Craig. 1996. "The Official and the Popular in Gramsci and Bakhtin." *Theory Culture Society* 13 (2): 59–74.
Bridoux, Jeff, and Milja Kurki. 2014. *Democracy Promotion: A Critical Introduction*. Milton Park, Abingdon: Routledge.
Brownmiller, Susan. 1975. *Against Our Will: Men, Women and Rape*. New York: Bantam.
Buber, Martin. 1947. *Between Man and Man*. Translated by Ronald Gregor Smith. London: K. Paul.
Bueno de Mesquita, Bruce, James D. Morrow, Randolph M. Siverson, and Alastair Smith. 1999. "An Institutional Explanation of the Democratic Peace." *American Political Science Review* 93 (4): 791–807.
Büger, Christian, and Frank Gadinger. 2007. "Reassembling and Dissecting: IR Practice from a Science Studies Perspective." *International Studies Perspectives* 8 (1): 90–110.
Büger, Christian, and Trine Villumsen. 2007. "Beyond the Gap: Relevance, Fields of Practice and the Securitizing Consequences of (Democratic Peace) Research." *Journal of International Relations and Development* 10 (4): 417–48.
Burke, Edmund. 1987. *Reflections on the Revolution in France*. Edited by J. G. A. Pocock. Indianapolis, IN: Hackett.
Burton, Michael. 2007. "Between: Stuart Dimmock and Secretary of State for Education and Skills. London: England and Wales High Court (Administrative Court)." www.bailii.org/ew/cases/EWHC/Admin/2007/2288.html
Buttigieg, Joseph A. 1992. Introduction. In *Prison Notebooks*, edited by Joseph A. Buttigieg, 1–64. New York: Columbia University Press.
Buzan, Barry. 1983. *People, States, and Fear: The National Security Problem in International Relations*. Brighton: Wheatsheaf Books.
Buzan, Barry, Jaap de Wilde, and Ole Wæver. 1998. *Security: A New Framework for Analysis*. Boulder, CO: Lynne Rienner.
Buzan, Barry, and Lene Hansen. 2009. *The Evolution of International Security Studies*. New York: Cambridge University Press.
Callaghan, Terry. 2008. "SCANNET Newsletter." http://www.scannet.nu/files/news/newsletter12.pdf
Carroll, Susan J., and Linda M. G. Zerilli. 1993. "Feminist Challenges to Political

Science." In *Political Science: The State of the Discipline II*, edited by Ada W. Finifter, 55–76. Washington, DC: American Political Science Association.

Carta, Caterina. 2014. "Use of Metaphors and International Discourse: The EU as an Idiot Power, a Deceptive Pangloss and a Don Giovanni in His Infancy." *Cooperation and Conflict* 49 (3): 334–53.

C.A.S.E. Collective. 2006. "Critical Approaches to Security in Europe: A Networked Manifesto." *Security Dialogue* 37 (4): 443–87.

Checkel, Jeffrey T. 2001. "Why Comply? Social Learning and European Identity Change." *International Organization* 55 (3): 553–88.

Chernoff, Fred. 2009. "Conventionalism as an Adequate Basis for Policy-Relevant IR Theory." *European Journal of International Relations* 15 (1): 157–94.

Chomsky, Noam. 1970. "Notes on Anarchism." *New York Review of Books* 14 (10) (May 21): 31–35.

Choucri, Nazli. 1978. "Key Issues in International Relations Forecasting." In *Forecasting in International Relations: Theory, Methods, Problems, Prospects*, edited by Nazli Choucri and Thomas W. Robinson, 3–22. San Francisco: W.H. Freeman.

Christensen, Cheryl. 1978. "The Forecasting Potential of International Relations Theories." In *Forecasting in International Relations: Theory, Methods, Problems, Prospects*, edited by Nazli Choucri and Thomas W. Robinson, 52–68. San Francisco: W.H. Freeman.

Clarkson, Carrol. 2003. "'By Any Other Name': Kripke, Derrida and an Ethics of Naming." *Journal of Literary Semantics* 32 (1): 35–47.

Coady, C. A. J. 2004. "Terrorism, Morality, and Supreme Emergency." *Ethics* 114 (4): 772–89.

Coalition on the Academic Workforce. 2012. "A Portrait of Part-Time Faculty Members." http://www.academicworkforce.org/CAW_portrait_2012.pdf

Code, Lorraine. 2006. *Ecological Thinking: The Politics of Epistemic Location*. New York: Oxford University Press.

Cohen, Joshua, and Joel Rogers. 1983. *On Democracy: Toward a Transformation of American Society*. Middlesex: Penguin.

Cohen, Saul B., and Nurit Kliot. 1992. "Place-Names in Israel's Ideological Struggle over the Administered Territories." *Annals of the Association of American Geographers* 82 (4): 653–80.

Collier, David, and Steven Levitsky. 1997. "Democracy with Adjectives: Conceptual Innovation in Comparative Research." *World Politics* 49 (3): 430–51.

Connolly, William E. 1974. *The Terms of Political Discourse*. Lexington, MA: D. C. Heath.

Connolly, William E. 2005. *Pluralism*. Durham, NC: Duke University Press.

Conrad, Joseph. 1989. *Heart of Darkness*. Edited by Ross C. Murfin. Boston: Bedford Books of St. Martin's Press.

Cox, Robert W. 1981. "Social Forces, States and World Orders: Beyond International Relations Theory." *Millennium* 10 (2): 126–55.

Cox, Robert W., and Timothy J. Sinclair. 1996. *Approaches to World Order*. New York: Cambridge University Press.

Dahl, Robert A. 1971. *Polyarchy: Participation and Opposition*. New Haven: Yale University Press.
Davidovic, Jovana. 2016. "Should the Changing Character of War Affect Our Theories of War?" *Ethical Theory and Moral Practice* 19 (3): 603–18.
Davidson, Alastair. 2008. "The Uses and Abuses of Gramsci." *Thesis Eleven* 95 (1): 68–94.
Davis, James W. 2005. *Terms of Inquiry: On the Theory and Practice of Political Science*. Baltimore: Johns Hopkins University Press.
Descartes, René. 1988. *Selected Philosophical Writings*. Translated by John Cottingham, Robert Stoothoff, and Dugald Murdoch. Cambridge: Cambridge University Press.
De Sola Pool, Ithiel. 1978. "The Art of the Social Science Soothsayer." In *Forecasting in International Relations: Theory, Methods, Problems, Prospects*, edited by Nazli Choucri and Thomas W. Robinson, 23–34. San Francisco: W.H. Freeman.
de-Shalit, Avner. 1997. "On Behalf of 'the Participation of the People': A Radical Theory of Democracy." *Res Publica* 3 (1): 61–80.
Diez, Thomas, and Jill Steans. 2005. "A Useful Dialogue? Habermas and International Relations." *Review of International Studies* 31 (1): 127–40.
Dixon, William J. 1994. "Democracy and the Peaceful Settlement of International Conflict." *American Political Science Review* 88 (1): 14–32.
Dodds, Klaus. 2007. "Steve Bell's Eye: Cartoons, Geopolitics and the Visualization of the 'War on Terror.'" *Security Dialogue* 38 (2): 157–77.
Dowding, Keith. 2006. "Three-Dimensional Power: A Discussion of Steven Lukes' *Power: A Radical View*." *Political Studies Review* 4 (2): 136–45.
Drulák, Petr. 2006. Motion, Container and Equilibrium: Metaphors in the Discourse about European Integration." *European Journal of International Relations* 12 (4): 499–531.
Dryzek, John S. 2002. *Deliberative Democracy and Beyond: Liberals, Critics, Contestations*. Oxford: Oxford University Press.
Dryzek, John S., and Christian List. 2003. "Social Choice Theory and Deliberative Democracy: A Reconciliation." *British Journal of Political Science* 33 (1): 1–28.
du Preez, Jan. 2008. "Locating the Researcher in the Research: Personal Narrative and Reflective Practice." *Reflective Practice: International and Multidisciplinary Perspectives* 9 (4): 509–19.
Eagan, M. Kevin, Jr., Audrey J. Jaeger, and Ashley Grantham. 2015. "Supporting the Academic Majority: Policies and Practices Related to Part-Time Faculty's Job Satisfaction." *Journal of Higher Education* 86 (3): 448–83.
Easton, David. 1965. *A Framework for Political Analysis*. Englewood Cliffs, NJ: Prentice-Hall.
ECLA (Economic Commission for Latin America). 1971. *Development Problems in Latin America: An Analysis by the United Nations Economic Commission for Latin America*. Austin: Published for the Institute of Latin American Studies by the University of Texas Press.
Elster, Jon. 1998. *Deliberative Democracy*. Cambridge: Cambridge University Press.

Engelstad, Ericka, and Siri Gerrard. 2005. "Challenging Situatedness." In *Challenging Situatedness: Gender, Culture and the Production of Knowledge*, edited by Ericka Engelstad and Siri Gerrard, 1–26. Delft: Eburon.

Enoch, David. 2004. "Some Arguments against Conscientious Objection and Civil Disobedience Refuted." *Israel Law Review* 36 (3): 227–52.

Etzioni, Amitai. 2007. *Security First: For a Muscular, Moral Foreign Policy*. New Haven: Yale University Press.

Eyal, Gil. 2002. "Dangerous Liaisons: The Relations between Military Intelligence and Middle Eastern Studies in Israel." *Theory and Society* 31 (5): 653–93.

Fierke, K. M. 2007. *Critical Approaches to International Security*. Cambridge: Polity Press.

Finnemore, Martha, and Kathryn Sikkink. 2001. "Taking Stock: The Constructivist Research Program in International Relations and Comparative Politics." *Annual Review of Political Science* 4:391–416.

Floyd, Rita. 2011. "Can Securitization Theory Be Used in Normative Analysis? Towards a Just Securitization Theory." *Security Dialogue* 42 (4–5): 427–39.

Flyvbjerg, Bent. 1998. *Rationality and Power: Democracy in Practice*. Chicago: University of Chicago Press.

Fraser, Nancy. 1990. "Rethinking the Public Sphere: A Contribution to the Critique of Actually Existing Democracy." *Social Text* 25–26: 56–80.

Freeden, Michael. 1996. *Ideologies and Political Theory: A Conceptual Approach*. Oxford: Clarendon Press.

Freeman, John R., and Brian L. Job. 1979. "Scientific Forecasts in International Relations: Problems of Definition and Epistemology." *International Studies Quarterly* 23 (1): 113–43.

Friedman, Maurice S. 1976. *Martin Buber: The Life of Dialogue*. 3rd ed. Chicago: University of Chicago Press.

Frost, Mervyn. 1996. *Ethics in International Relations*. Cambridge: Cambridge University Press.

Fuller, Steve. 1992. "Social Epistemology and the Research Agenda of Science Studies." In *Science as Practice and Culture*, edited by Andrew Pickering, 390–428. Chicago: University of Chicago Press.

Gaddis, John L. 1992–93. "International Relations Theory and the End of the Cold War." *International Security* 17 (3): 5–58.

Gale, Fred. 1998. "Cave 'Cave! Hic Dragones': A Neo-Gramscian Deconstruction and Reconstruction of International Regime Theory." *Review of International Political Economy* 5 (2): 252—83.

Galeotti, Anne Elisabetta. 2007. "Relativism, Universalism, and Applied Ethics: The Case of Female Circumcision." *Constellations* 14 (1): 91–111.

Gallie, W. B. 1956. "Essentially Contested Concepts." *Proceedings of the Aristotelian Society* 56: 167–98.

Gappa, Judith M., Ann E. Austin, and Andrea G. Trice. 2007. *Rethinking Faculty Work: Higher Education's Strategic Imperative*. San Francisco: Jossey-Bass.

Gavriely-Nuri, Dalia. 2008. "The 'Metaphorical Annihilation' of the Second Lebanon War (2006) from the Israeli Political Discourse." *Discourse & Society* 19 (1): 5–20.

Gavriely-Nuri, Dalia. 2010. "Rainbow, Snow, and the Poplar's Song: The 'Annihilative Naming' of Israeli Military Practices." *Armed Forces and Society* 36 (5): 825–46.

Geis, Anna, and Wolfgang Wagner. 2011. "How Far Is It from Königsberg to Kandahar? Democratic Peace and Democratic Violence in International Relations." *Review of International Studies* 37 (4): 1555–77.

Giddens, Anthony. 1984. *The Constitution of Society: Outline of the Theory of Structuration*. Berkeley: University of California Press.

Gill, Stephen. 1990. *American Hegemony and the Trilateral Commission*. New York: Cambridge University Press.

Gill, Stephen, ed. 1993. *Gramsci, Historical Materialism and International Relations*. New York: Cambridge University Press.

Gill, Stephen, ed. 2012. *Global Crises and the Crisis of Global Leadership*. New York: Cambridge University Press.

Gilligan, Carol. 1982. *In a Different Voice: Psychological Theory and Women's Development*. Cambridge, MA: Harvard University Press.

Givati, Moshe. 2007. "That Was No War." *Haaretz*, March 19.

Goldfarb, Jeffrey C. 2006. *The Politics of Small Things: The Power of the Powerless in Dark Times*. Chicago: University of Chicago Press.

Graeber, David. 2002. "The New Anarchists." *New Left Review* 13: 61–73.

Graeger, Nina. 1996. "Environmental Security?" *Journal of Peace Research* 33 (1): 109–16.

Gramsci, Antonio. 1971. *Selections from the Prison Notebooks*. Edited and translated by Quintin Hoare and Geoffrey N. Smith. New York: International Publishers.

Gramsci, Antonio. 1992. *Prison Notebooks*. Vol. 1. Translated by Joseph A. Buttigieg and Antonio Callari. European Perspectives. New York: Columbia University Press.

Gramsci, Antonio. 1996. *Prison Notebooks*. Vol. 2. Translated by Joseph A. Buttigieg. European Perspectives. New York: Columbia University Press.

Gramsci, Antonio. 2007. *Prison Notebooks*. Vol. 3. Translated by Joseph A. Buttigieg. New York: Columbia University Press.

Gross, Michael L. 2010. *Moral Dilemmas of Modern War: Torture, Assassinations, and Blackmail in an Age of Asymmetric Conflict*. New York: Cambridge University Press.

Gurevitch, Zali. 2001. "Dialectical Dialogue: The Struggle for Speech, Repressive Silence, and the Shift to Multiplicity." *British Journal of Sociology* 52 (1): 87–104.

Gusterson, Hugh. 1996. *Nuclear Rites: A Weapons Laboratory at the End of the Cold War*. Berkeley: University of California Press.

Gusterson, Hugh. 2015. "Ethics, Expertise and Human Terrain." In *Security Expertise: Practice, Power, Responsibility*, edited by Trine Villumsen Berling and Christian Bueger, 204–27. New York: Routledge.

Guzzini, Stefano. 2000. "A Reconstruction of Constructivism in International Relations." *European Journal of International Relations* 6 (2): 147–82.

Guzzini, Stefano. 2005. "The Concept of Power: A Constructivist Analysis." *Millennium* 33 (3): 495–521.

Guzzini, Stefano. 2013. "Power Analysis." In *Bourdieu in International Relations: Rethinking Key Concepts in IR*, edited by Rebecca Adler-Nissen, 79–92. New York: Routledge.

Habermas, Jürgen. 1984. *The Theory of Communicative Action*. Vol. 1: *Reason and the Rationalization of Society*. Translated by Thomas McCarthy. Boston: Beacon Press.

Habermas, Jürgen. 1987 *The Theory of Communicative Action*. Vol. 2: *Lifeworld and System*. Translated by Thomas McCarthy. Boston: Beacon Press.

Habermas, Jürgen. 1989. *The Structural Transformation of the Public Sphere: An Inquiry into a Category of Bourgeois Society*. Translated by Thomas Burger with the assistance of Frederick Lawrence. Cambridge, MA: MIT Press.

Habermas, Jürgen. 1993. *Justification and Application: Remarks on Discourse Ethics*. Translated by Ciaran P. Cronin. Cambridge, MA: MIT Press.

Habermas, Jürgen. 1998. *Between Facts and Norms: Contributions to a Discourse Theory of Law and Democracy*. Translated by William Rehg. Cambridge, MA: MIT Press.

Hacking, Ian. 1999. *The Social construction of What?* Cambridge, MA: Harvard University Press.

Hall, Ian. 2008. "A 'Shallow Piece of Naughtiness': George Orwell on Political Realism." *Millennium* 36 (2): 191–215.

Hamati-Ataya, Inanna. 2011. "The 'Problem of Values' and International Relations Scholarship: From Applied Reflexivity to Reflexivism." *International Studies Review* 13 (2): 259–87.

Hamati-Ataya, Inanna. 2013. "Reflectivity, Reflexivity, Reflexivism: IR's 'Reflexive Turn'—and Beyond." *European Journal of International Relations* 19 (4): 669–94.

Hansen, Lene. 2000. "The Little Mermaid's Silent Security Dilemma and the Absence of Gender in the Copenhagen School." *Millennium* 29 (2): 285–306.

Hansen, Lene. 2011. "Theorizing the Image for Security Studies: Visual Securitization and the Muhammad Cartoon Crisis." *European Journal of International Relations* 17 (1): 51–74.

Hansen, Lene, and Ole Wæver, eds. 2002. *European Integration and National Identity: The Challenge of the Nordic States*. New York: Routledge.

Haraway, Donna. 1988. "Situated Knowledges: The Science Question in Feminism and the Privilege of Partial Perspective." *Feminist Studies* 14 (3): 575–99.

Harding, Sandra G. 1986. *The Science Question in Feminism*. Ithaca, NY: Cornell University Press.

Harding, Sandra G. 1991. *Whose Science? Whose Knowledge? Thinking from Women's Lives*. Ithaca, NY: Cornell University Press.

Harding, Sandra G. 1993. "Rethinking Standpoint Epistemology: What Is 'Strong Objectivity?'" In *Feminist Epistemologies*, edited by Linda Alcoff and Elizabeth Potter, 49–82. New York: Routledge.

Harding, Sandra G. 1998. *Is Science Multicultural? Postcolonialisms, Feminisms, and Epistemologies*. Bloomington: Indiana University Press.

Hawkesworth, Mary E. 1996. "Knowers, Knowing, Known: Feminist Theory and Claims of Truth." In *Gender and Scientific Authority*, edited by Barbara Laslett, Sally G. Kohlstedt, Helen Longino, and Evelynn Hammonds, 75–99. Chicago: University of Chicago Press.

Heeren, John. 1971. "Karl Mannheim and the Intellectual Elite." *British Journal of Sociology* 22 (1): 1–15.

Hegel, Georg Wilhelm Friedrich. 1942. *Hegel's Philosophy of Right*. Translated by T. M. Knox. Oxford: Clarendon Press.

Heilbroner, Robert L. 1963. *The Great Ascent: The Struggle for Economic Development in Our Time*. New York: Harper & Row.

Held, David. 2010. *Cosmopolitanism: Ideals and Realities*. Cambridge: Polity Press.

Henderson, Bill. 2006. "Runaway Global Heating." http://www.countercurrents.org/cc-henderson300906.htm

Herman, R. D. K. 1999. "The Aloha State: Place Names and the Anti-conquest of Hawaii." *Annals of the Association of American Geographers* 89 (1): 76—102.

Hermann, Charles F. 1972. *International Crises: Insights from Behavioral Research*. New York: Free Press.

Heywood, Andrew. 1994. *Political Ideas and Concepts: An Introduction*. London: Macmillan.

Hobson, Christopher. 2011. "Towards a Critical Theory of Democratic Peace." *Review of International Studies* 37 (4): 1903–22.

Hobson, Christopher. 2015. *The Rise of Democracy: Revolution, War and Transformations in International Politics since 1776*. Edinburgh: Edinburgh University Press.

Hobson, Christopher, and Milja Kurki. 2011. "Introduction: The Conceptual Politics of Democracy Promotion." In *The Conceptual Politics of Democracy Promotion*, edited by Christopher Hobson and Milja Kurki, 1–15. New York: Routledge.

Hoffman, Stanley. 1977. "An American Social Science: International Relations." *Daedalus* 106 (3): 41–60.

Hoogensen, Gunhild, and Svein Vigeland Rottem. 2004. "Gender Identity and the Subject of Security." *Security Dialogue* 35 (2): 155–71.

Hopf, Ted. 2013. "Common-Sense Constructivism and Hegemony in World Politics." *International Organization* 67 (2): 317–54.

Hough, Peter. 2004. *Understanding Global Security*. New York: Routledge.

Huber, Daniela. 2015. *Democracy Promotion and Foreign Policy: Identity and Interests in US, EU and Non-Western Democracies*. Basingstoke: Palgrave Macmillan.

Huntington, Samuel P. 1996. *The Clash of Civilizations and the Remaking of World Order*. New York: Simon & Schuster.

Hurka, Thomas. 2005. "Proportionality in the Morality of War." *Philosophy & Public Affairs* 33 (1): 34–66.

Hutchings, Kimberly. 2008. "1988 and 1998: Contrast and Continuity in Feminist International Relations." *Millennium* 37 (1): 97–105.

Huysmans, Jef. 1998. "Security! What Do You Mean? From Concept to Thick Signifier." *European Journal of International Relations* 4 (2): 226–55.

Intergovernmental Panel on Climate Change. 2007. "Climate Change 2007: Synthesis Report. Summary for Policymakers." http://www.ipcc.ch/pdf/assessment-report/ar4/syr/ar4_syr_spm.pdf

Ish-Shalom, Piki. 2006a. "Theory Gets Real, and the Case for a Normative Ethic: Rostow, Modernization Theory, and the Alliance for Progress." *International Studies Quarterly* 50 (2): 287–311.

Ish-Shalom, Piki. 2006b. "The Triptych of Realism, Elitism, and Conservatism." *International Studies Review* 8 (3): 441–68.

Ish-Shalom, Piki. 2010. "Political Constructivism: The Political Construction of Social Knowledge." In *Arguing Global Governance: Agency, Lifeworld and Shared Reasoning*, edited by Corneliu Bjola and Markus Kornprobst, 231–46. New York: Routledge.

Ish-Shalom, Piki. 2011a. "Conceptualizing Democratization and Democratizing Conceptualization: A Virtuous Circle." In *The Conceptual Politics of Democracy Promotion*, edited by Christopher Hobson and Milja Kurki, 38–52. New York: Routledge.

Ish-Shalom, Piki. 2011b. "Defining by Naming: Israeli Civic Warring over the Second Lebanon War." *European Journal of International Relations* 17 (3): 475–93.

Ish-Shalom, Piki. 2011c. "Theoreticians' Obligation of Transparency: When Parsimony, Reflexivity, Transparency and Reciprocity Meet." *Review of International Studies* 37 (3): 973–96.

Ish-Shalom, Piki. 2011d. "Three Dialogic Imperatives in International Relations Scholarship: A Buberian Program." *Millennium* 39 (3): 825–44.

Ish-Shalom, Piki. 2012. "Conceptualizing Democratization and Democratizing Conceptualization: A Virtuous Circle." In *The Conceptual Politics of Democracy Promotion*, edited by Christopher Hobson and Milja Kurki, 38–52. New York: Routledge.

Ish-Shalom, Piki. 2013. *Democratic Peace: A Political Biography*. Ann Arbor: University of Michigan Press.

Ish-Shalom, Piki. 2015. "Zooming In Zooming Out: Reflexive Engagements." In *Reflexivity and International Relations: Positionality, Critique, and Practice*, edited by Jack L. Amoureux and Brent J. Steele, 83–101. New York: Routledge.

Israeli Broadcasting Authority. 1998. "Nakdi Briefing (20 July)." http://www.iba.org.il/Chairman/Doc/DOC226235.pdf

Israel Government. 2006a. "Decision 258: Operation 'Sachar Holem'—IDF Retaliation against Hezbollah's Attack out of Lebanon, Jerusalem (12 July)." http://www.pmo.gov.il/Secretary/GovDecisions/2006/Pages/des258.aspx

Israel Government. 2006b. "Decision 342: Payment of Salaries in the North and Compensations for Indirect Harms, Jerusalem, (July 30)." http://www.pmo.gov.il/Secretary/GovDecisions/2006/Pages/des342.aspx

Jackson, Patrick Thaddeus. 2011. *The Conduct of Inquiry in International Relations: The Philosophy of Science and Its Implications for the Study of World Politics*. New York: Routledge.

Jasanoff, Sheila. 1990. *The Fifth Branch: Science Advisers as Policymakers*. Cambridge, MA: Harvard University Press.

Jasanoff, Sheila. 2003. "Technologies of Humility: Citizen Participation in Governing Science." *Minerva* 41 (3): 223–44.
Jasanoff, Sheila. 2005. *Designs on Nature: Science and Democracy in Europe and the United States*. Princeton, NJ: Princeton University Press.
Jasanoff, Sheila. 2007. "Technologies of humility." *Nature* 450 (7166): 33.
Joseph, Jonathan. 2008. "Hegemony and the Structure-Agency Problem in International Relations: A Scientific Realist Contribution." *Review of International Studies* 34 (1): 109–28.
Kahn-Nisser, Sara. 2011. "Toward a Unity of Ethics and Practice: Interpreting Inclusion and Diversity." *International Studies Review* 13 (3): 387–410.
Kaldor, Mary. 1999. *New and Old Wars: Organized Violence in a Global Era*. Stanford, CA: Stanford University Press.
Kaldor, Mary. 2006. *New & Old Wars*. 2nd ed. Cambridge: Polity Press.
Kant, Immanuel. 1969. *Foundations of the Metaphysics of Morals*. Translated by Lewis White Beck. New York: Macmillan; London: Collier Macmillan.
Katzenstein, Peter J. 1996. *The Culture of National Security: Norms and Identity in World Politics*. New York: Columbia University Press.
Kearns, Robin A., and Lawrence D. Berg. 2002. "Proclaiming Place: Towards a Geography of Place Name Pronunciation." *Social & Cultural Geography* 3 (3): 283–302.
Kibrik, Roee. 2016. "Sovereignty as It Should Be: Theoretical Gaps and Negotiations for Peace in Israel/Palestine." *International Negotiations* 21 (3): 440–72.
Klein, Bradley S. 1994. *Strategic Studies and World Order: The Global Politics of Deterrence*. Cambridge: Cambridge University Press.
Kymlicka, Will. 1995. *Multicultural Citizenship: A Liberal Theory of Minority Rights*. Oxford: Oxford University Press.
Kober, Avi. 2008. "The Israel Defense Forces in the Second Lebanon War: Why the Poor Performance?" *Journal of Strategic Studies* 31 (1): 3–40.
Kohanski, Alexander S. 1982. *Martin Buber's Philosophy of Interhuman Relation: A Response to the Human Problematic of our Time*. Rutherford, NJ: Fairleigh Dickinson University Press; London: Associated University Presses.
Korn, Dan. 1994. *Time in Gray*. Tel Aviv: Zmora-Bitan, Publishers (in Hebrew).
Kornprobst, Markus, Vincent Pouliot, Nisha Shah, and Ruben Zaiotti, eds. 2008. *Metaphors in Globalization: Mirrors, Magicians and Mutinies*. New York: Palgrave Macmillan.
Koselleck, Reinhart. 2006. "Crisis." Translated by Michaela W. Richter. *Journal of the History of Ideas* 67 (2): 357–400.
Kratochwil, Friedrich V. 1989. *Rules, Norms, and Decisions: On the Conditions of Practical and Legal Reasoning in International Relations and Domestic Affairs*. Cambridge: Cambridge University Press.
Kratochwil, Friedrich V. 2007. "Re-thinking the 'Inter in International Politics." *Millennium* 35 (3): 495–511.
Krauthammer, Charles. 2001. "The Bush Doctrine." *Weekly Standard*, June 4.

Krebs, Ronald R. 2015. *Narrative and the Making of US National Security*. Cambridge: Cambridge University Press.
Kripke, Saul A. 1980. *Naming and Necessity*. Cambridge, MA: Harvard University Press.
Kubal, Timothy, J. 1998. "The Presentation of Political Self: Cultural Resonance and the Construction of Collective Action Frames." *Sociological Quarterly* 39 (4): 539–54.
Kuklick, Bruce. 2006. *Blind Oracles: Intellectuals and War from Kennan to Kissinger*. Princeton, NJ: Princeton University Press.
Kurki, Milja. 2010. "Democracy and Conceptual Contestability: Reconsidering Conceptions of Democracy in Democracy Promotion." *International Studies Review* 12 (3): 362–86.
Laslett, Barbara, Sally Gregory Kohlstedt, Helen Longino, and Evelynn Hammonds. 1996. Introduction. In *Gender and Scientific Authority*, edited by Barbara Laslett, Sally Gregory Kohlstedt, Helen Longino, and Evelynn Hammonds, 1–16. Chicago: University of Chicago Press.
Lasswell, Harold D. 1958. *Politics: Who Gets What, When, How*. New York: Meridian Press.
Latour, Bruno. 1987. *Science in Action: How to Follow Scientists and Engineers through Society*. Cambridge, MA: Harvard University Press.
Lebel, Udi. 2007. "Civil Society versus Military Sovereignty: Cultural, Political, and Operational Aspects." *Armed Forces & Society* 34 (1): 67–89.
Lepgold, Joseph. 1998. "Is Anyone Listening? International Relations Theory and the Problem of Policy Relevance." *Political Science Quarterly* 113 (1): 43–62.
Lev, Ori. 2004. "Review: Michael Walzer's *Arguing about War*." *Logos* 3 (4). http://www.logosjournal.com/lev_walzer.htm
Levinas, Emmanuel. 1967. "Martin Buber and the Theory of Knowledge." In *The Philosophy of Martin Buber*, edited by Paul Arthur Schilpp and Maurice S. Friedman, 133–50. La Salle, IL: Open Court.
Levine, Daniel. 2011. "International Theory and the Problem of Sustainable Critique: An Adornian-Biblical Parable." *Borderlands* 10 (1): 1–41.
Levine, Daniel. 2012. *Recovering International Relations: The Promise of Sustainable Critique*. New York: Oxford University Press.
Lippmann, Walter. 1955. *Essays in the Public Philosophy*. Boston: Little, Brown.
Longino, Helen E. 2002. *The Fate of Knowledge*. Princeton, NJ: Princeton University Press.
Löwenheim, Oded. 2008. "Examining the State: A Foucauldian Perspective on International Governance Indicators." *Third World Quarterly* 29 (2): 255—74.
Löwenheim, Oded. 2014. *The Politics of the Trail: Reflexive Mountain Biking along the Frontier of Jerusalem*. Ann Arbor: University of Michigan Press.
Löwenheim, Oded, and Gadi Heimann. 2008. "Revenge in International Politics." *Security Studies* 17 (4): 685–724.
Luhmann, Niklas. 1960. *The Political System*. New York: Alfred A. Knopf.
Lukes, Steven. 2004. *Power: A Radical View*. 2nd ed. New York: Palgrave Macmillan.

Lupovici, Amir. 2014. "The Limits of Securitization Theory: Observational Criticism and the Curious Absence of Israel." *International Studies Review* 16 (3): 390–410.

Lustick, Ian S. 1993. *Unsettled States, Disputed Lands: Britain and Ireland, France and Algeria, Israel and the West Bank–Gaza*. Ithaca, NY: Cornell University Press.

Lustick, Ian S. 1999. "Hegemony and the Riddle of Nationalism." In *Ethnic, Conflict and International Politics in the Middle East*, edited by Leonard Binder, 332–59. Gainesville: University Press of Florida.

Luxemburg, Rosa. 1961. *The Russian Revolution, and Leninism or Marxism?* Ann Arbor: University of Michigan Press.

Malesevic, Sinisa. 2008. "The Sociology of New Wars? Assessing the Causes and Objectives of Contemporary Violent Conflicts." *International Political Sociology* 2 (2): 97–112.

Mannheim, Karl. 1952. *Essays on the Sociology of Knowledge*. Edited by Paul Kecskemeti. London: Routledge and Kegan Paul.

Mansbridge, Jane J. 1970. *Beyond Adversary Democracy*. Chicago: University of Chicago Press.

Maoz, Zeev, and Bruce Russett. 1993. "Normative and Structural Causes of Democratic-Peace, 1946–1986." *American Political Science Review* 87 (3): 624–638.

Marx, Karl. 1994. "A Contribution to the Critique of Hegel's Philosophy of Right: Introduction." In *Karl Marx: Early Writings*, edited by Joseph J. O'Malley and Richard A. Davis, 57–70. Cambridge: Cambridge University Press.

McGann, James G. 2007. *Think Tanks and Policy Advice in the US: Academics, Advisors and Advocates*. Oxon: Routledge.

McGann, James G., and Robert K. Weaver, eds. 2002. *Think Tanks and Civil Societies: Catalysts for Ideas and Action*. Rev. ed. New Brunswick, NJ: Transaction Publishers.

McMahan, Jeff. 2006. "On the Moral Equality of Combatants." *Journal of Political Philosophy* 14 (4): 377–93.

McSweeney, Bill. 1999. *Security, Identity and Interests: A Sociology of International Relations*. Cambridge: Cambridge University Press.

Mearsheimer, John J., and Stephen M. Walt. 2013. "Leaving Theory Behind: Why Simplistic Hypothesis Testing Is Bad for International Relations." *European Journal of International Relations* 19 (3): 427–57.

Mendes-Flohr, Paul R. 1989. *From Mysticism to Dialogue: Martin Buber's Transformation of German Social Thought*. Detroit: Wayne State University Press.

Meyer, Thomas, with Lewis Hinchman. 2007. *The Theory of Social Democracy*. Cambridge: Polity Press.

Millikan, Max F., and Walt W. Rostow. 1957. *A Proposal: Key to an Effective Foreign Policy*. New York: Harper & Brothers.

Milošević, Slobodan. 1989. "St. Vitus Day Speech. June 28." http://www.slobodan-milosevic.org/spch-kosovo1989.htm

Mirowski, Philip, and Edward Nik-Khah. 2013. "Private Intellectuals and Public

Perplexity: The Economics Profession and the Economic Crisis." *History of Political Economy* 45, suppl. 1: 279–311.

Mitzen, Jennifer. 2005. "Reading Habermas in Anarchy: Multilateral Diplomacy and Global Public Spheres." *American Political Science Review* 99 (3): 401–17.

Modelski, George. 1987. *Long Cycles in World Politics.* Seattle: University of Washington Press.

Mohanty, Chandra Talpade. 2003. "'Under Western Eyes' Revisited: Feminist Solidarity through Anticapitalist Struggles." *Signs* 28 (2): 499–535.

Morgenthau, Hans J. 1946. *Scientific Man vs. Power Politics.* Chicago: University of Chicago Press.

Morgenthau, Hans, J. 1972. *Science: Servant or Master?* New York: New American Library, distributed by Norton.

Müller, Harald. 2004. "Arguing, Bargaining and All That: Communicative Action, Rationalist Theory and the Logic of Appropriateness in International Relations." *European Journal of International Relations* 10 (3): 395–435.

Muravchik, Joshua. 1991. *Exporting Democracy: Fulfilling America's Destiny.* Washington, DC: AEI Press.

Mutz, Diana Carole. 2006. *Hearing the Other Side: Deliberative versus Participatory Democracy.* Cambridge: Cambridge University Press.

National Center for Educational Statistics. 2001. *Digest of Education Statistics 2000.* Washington, DC: Department of Education.

Newman, Edward. 2004. "The 'New Wars' Debate: A Historical Perspective Is Needed." *Security Dialogue* 35 (2): 173–89.

Newman, Peter. 2007. "A Carbon Neutral Country. What Would It Take for Australia to Become a Leader in Greenhouse?" http://archive.dea.org.au/~deaorg/archive_site/node/161

Nietzsche, Friedrich. 1968. *The Portable Nietzsche.* Edited and translated by Walter Kaufmann. New York: Viking Press.

Norwegian Nobel Committee. 2007 "Press Release: The Nobel Peace Prize for 2007." http://www.nobelprize.org/nobel_prizes/peace/laureates/2007/press.html

Nowotny, Helga. 2003. "Dilemma of Expertise: Democratising Expertise and Socially Robust Knowledge." *Science and Public Policy* 30 (3): 151–56.

Nowotny, Helga, Peter Scott, and Michael Gibbons. 2003. "Introduction. 'Mode 2' Revisited: The New Production of Knowledge." *Minerva* 41 (3): 179–94.

Okin, Susan, M. 1989. "Reason and Feeling in Thinking about Justice." *Ethics* 99 (2): 229–49.

Onuf, Nicholas Greenwood. 1989. *World of Our Making: Rules and Rule in Social Theory and International Relations.* Columbia: University of South Carolina Press.

Oren, Ido. 2006."Can Political Science Emulate the Natural Sciences? The Problem of Self-Disconfirming Analysis." *Polity* 38 (1): 72–100.

Oren, Ido. 2009. "The Unrealism of Contemporary Realism: The Tension between Realist Theory and Realists' Practice." *Perspectives on Politics* 7 (2): 283–301.

Orwell, George. 1961. *1984*. New York: New American Library.
Parekh, Bhikhu. 1992. "The Cultural Particularity of Liberal Democracy." *Political Studies* 40 (issue supplement): 160–75.
Pateman, Carole. 1970. *Participation and Democratic Theory*. New York: Cambridge University Press.
Payne, Rodger A. 2007. "Neorealists as Critical Theorists: The Purpose of Foreign Policy Debate." *Perspectives on Politics* 5 (3): 503–14.
Peoples, Columba. 2008. "Decoding Ballistic Missile Defense: Semiotics and the Power of the Image in American Ballistic Missile Defense." *Social Semiotics* 18 (1): 17–31.
Peoples Columba, and Nick Vaughan-Williams. 2010. *Critical Security Studies*. New York: Routledge.
Pielke, Roger A. 2007. *The Honest Broker: Making Sense of Science in Policy and Politics*. New York: Cambridge University Press.
Popper, Karl. 1963. *Conjectures and Refutations: The Growth of Scientific Knowledge*. London: Routledge.
Potter, Elizabeth. 2006. *Feminism and Philosophy of Science: An Introduction*. New York: Routledge.
Pouliot, Vincent. 2007. "Sobjectivism": Toward a Constructivist Methodology." *International Studies Quarterly* 51 (2): 359–84.
Prichard, Alex. 2010. "Deepening Anarchism: International Relations and the Anarchist Ideal." *Anarchist Studies* 18 (2): 29–57.
Prichard, Alex. 2012. "Anarchy, Anarchism and International Relations." In *The Continuum Companion to Anarchism*, edited by Ruth Kinna, 96–108. London: Continuum.
Przeworski, Adam. 1999. "Minimalist Conception of Democracy: A Defense." In *Democracy's Value*, edited by Ian Shapiro and Cassiano Hacker-Cordón, 23–55. Cambridge: Cambridge University Press.
Puchala, Donald J. 2005. "World Hegemony and the United Nations." *International Studies Review* 7 (4): 571–84.
Putnam, Robert. 1988. "Diplomacy and Domestic Politics: The Logic of Two-Level Games." *International Organization* 42 (3): 427–60.
Putnam, Robert D. 2000. *Bowling Alone: The Collapse and Revival of American Community*. New York: Simon & Schuster.
Pye, Lucian W. 1966. *Aspects of Political Development*. Boston: Little, Brown.
Rada, Moran. 2007. "There Was War, 'Now the Boys above Are Calmer.'" http://www.ynet.co.il/articles/0,7340,L-3378473,00.html
Rawls, John. 1993. *Political Liberalism*. New York: Columbia University Press.
Rawls, John. 1999a. *A Theory of Justice*. Rev. ed. Cambridge, MA: Harvard University Press.
Rawls, John. 1999b. *The Law of Peoples*. Cambridge, MA: Harvard University Press.
Rich, Andrew. 2004. *Think Tanks, Public Policy, and the Politics of Expertise*. Cambridge: Cambridge University Press.
Riedel, Eibe. 2007. "The Human Right to Social Security: Some Challenges."

In *Social Security as a Human Right: Drafting a General Comment on Article 9 ICESCR—Some Challenges*, edited by Eibe Riedel, 17–28. Berlin: Springer.

Risse, Thomas. 2000. "Let's Argue!": Communicative Action in World Politics." *International Organization* 54 (1):1–39.

Robinson, Fiona. 1999. *Globalizing Care: Ethics, Feminist Theory, and International Relations*. Boulder, CO: Westview Press.

Rorty, Richard. 1989. *Contingency, Irony, and Solidarity*. Cambridge: Cambridge University Press.

Rosenau, James N. 2003. *Distant Proximities: Dynamics beyond Globalization*. Princeton, NJ: Princeton University Press.

Rostow, Walt W. 1961. *The Stages of Economic Growth: A Non-communist Manifesto*. Cambridge, MA: Cambridge University Press.

Rostow, Walt W. 1964. *View from the Seventh Floor*. New York: Harper & Row.

Rostow, Walt W. 1988. *Essays on a Half Century: Ideas, Policies, and Action*. Boulder, CO: Westview Press.

Russell, Bertrand. 1956. *Logic and Knowledge: Essays, 1901–1950*. London: G. Allen & Unwin; New York: Macmillan.

Santora, Marc. 2007. "Global Warming Starts to Divide G.O.P. Contenders." *New York Times*, October 17.

Sarkees, Meredith Reid, and Phil Schafer. 2000. "The Correlates of War Data on War: An Update to 1997." *Conflict Management and Peace Science* 18 (1): 123–44.

Scanlon, T. M. 1998. *What We Owe to Each Other*. Cambridge, MA: Belknap Press of Harvard University Press.

Schelling, Thomas, C. 1960. *The Strategy of Conflict*. Cambridge, MA: Harvard University Press.

Schlag, Gabi, and Anna Geis. 2017. "Visualizing Violence: Aesthetics and Ethics in International Politics." *Global Discourse: An Interdisciplinary Journal of Current Affairs and Applied Contemporary Thought* 7 (2–3): 193–200.

Schmitt, Carl. 2007. *The Concept of the Political*. Expanded ed. Translated by George Schwab. Chicago: University of Chicago Press.

Schumpeter, Joseph A. 1962. *Capitalism, Socialism and Democracy*. 3rd ed. New York: Harper Torchbooks.

Schuster, Jack H., and Martin J. Finklestein. 2006. *The Academic Faculty: The Restructuring of Academic Work and Careers*. Baltimore: Johns Hopkins University Press.

Sen, Amartya. 2000. *Development as Freedom*. New York: Anchor Books.

Sending, Ole Jacob. 2015. *The Politics of Expertise: Competing for Authority in Global Governance*. Ann Arbor: University of Michigan Press.

Seymour, David M. 2010. "From Auschwitz to Gaza: Ethics for the Want of Law." *Journal of Global Ethics* 6 (2): 205–15.

Sheehan, Michael. 2005. *International Security: An Analytical Survey*. Boulder, CO: Lynne Rienner.

Shenhav, Shaul R. 2004. "Once upon a Time There Was a Nation: Narrative Conceptualization Analysis. The Concept of 'Nation' in the Discourse of Israeli Likud Party Leaders." *Discourse & Society* 15 (1): 81–104.

Shenhav, Shaul R. 2005a. "Concise Narratives: A Structural Analysis of Political Discourse." *Discourse Studies* 7 (3): 315–35.
Shenhav, Shaul R. 2005b. "Thin and Thick Narrative Analysis: On the Question of Defining and Analyzing Political Narratives." *Narrative Inquiry* 15 (1): 75–99.
Shenhav, Shaul R. 2006. "Political Narratives and Political Reality." *International Political Science Review* 27 (3): 245–62.
Shenhav, Shaul R. 2015. *Analyzing Social Narratives*. New York: Routledge.
Silberstein, Laurence J. 1989. *Martin Buber's Social and Religious Thought: Alienation and the Quest for Meaning*. New York: New York University Press.
Singer, Peter. 1972. "Famine, Affluence, and Morality." *Philosophy and Public Affairs* 1 (3): 229–43.
Smith, Dorothy E. 1987. "Women's Perspective as a Radical Critique of Sociology." In *Feminism and methodology: Social Science Issues*, edited by Sandra G. Harding, 84–96. Bloomington: Indiana University Press; Milton Keynes: Open University Press.
Smith, James A. 1991. *Idea Brokers: Think Tanks and the Rise of the New Policy Elite*. New York: Free Press.
Smith, Steve. 2005. "The Contested Concept of Security." In *Critical Security Studies and World Politics*, edited by Ken Booth, 27–62. Boulder, CO: Lynne Rienner.
Sofer, Roni. 2007. "Final: The Campaign in the North Will Be Called War." http://www.ynet.co.il/articles/0,7340,L-3378190,00.html
Steele, Brent J. 2010a. "Irony, Emotions and Critical Distance." *Millennium* 39 (1): 89–107.
Steele, Brent J. 2010b. "Of 'Witch's Brews' and Scholarly Communities: The Dangers and Promise of Academic Parrhesia." *Cambridge Review of International Affairs* 23 (1): 49—68.
Steele, Brent J. 2013. *Alternative Accountabilities in Global Politics: The Scars of Violence*. New York: Routledge.
Stevens, Hallam. 2003. "Fundamental Physics and Its Justifications, 1945–1993." *Historical Studies in the Physical and Biological Sciences* 34 (1): 151–97.
Stone, Diane. 1996. *Capturing the Political Imagination: Think Tanks and the Policy Process*. New York: Frank Cass.
Sylvester, Christine. 2013. "Experiencing the End and Afterlives of International Relations/Theory." *European Journal of International Relations* 19 (3): 609–26.
Tetlock, Philip E. 2005. *Expert Political Judgment: How Good Is It? How Can We Know?* Princeton, NJ: Princeton University Press.
Tetlock, Philip E, and Dan Gardner. 2015. *Superforecasting: The Art and Science of Prediction*. New York: Crown Publishing.
Thomas, Caroline. 2001. "Global Governance, Development and Human Security: Exploring the Links." *Third World Quarterly* 22 (2): 159–75.
Thomas, Caroline, and Peter Wilkin, eds. 1999. *Globalization, Human Security, and the African Experience*. Boulder, CO: Lynne Rienner.
Tickner, Arlene, and Ole Wæver, eds. 2009. *International Relations Scholarship around the World*. London: Rutledge.

Tickner, J. Ann. 1988. "Hans Morgenthau's Principles of Political Realism: A Feminist Reformulation." *Millennium* 17 (3): 429–40.

Tickner J. Ann. 1992. *Gender in International Relations: Feminist Perspectives on Achieving Global Security*. New York: Columbia University Press.

Tickner, J. Ann. 2005."What Is Your Research Program? Some Feminist Answers to International Relations Methodological Questions." *International Studies Quarterly* 49 (1): 1–21.

Turner, Stephen. 2001. "What Is the Problem with Experts?" *Social Studies of Science* 31 (1): 123–49.

Turner, Stephen P., and Regis A. Factor. 1984. *Max Weber and the Dispute over Reason and Value: A Study in Philosophy, Ethics, and Politics*. London: Routledge and Kegan Paul.

Umbach, Paul D. 2007. "How Effective Are They? Exploring the Impact of Contingent Faculty on Undergraduate Education." *Review of Higher Education* 30 (2): 91–123.

United Nations. 2000. Security Council Resolution 1325. http://www.un.org/womenwatch/osagi/wps/#resolution

Vermes, Pamela. 1988. *Buber*. New York: Grove Press.

Villumsen, Trine, and Christian Buger. 2010. "Security Expertise after Securitization: Coping with Dilemmas of Engaging with Practice." Paper presented at the Annual Conference of the International Studies Association, New Orleans, LA, February 17–20.

Vuori, Juha A. 2010. "A Timely Prophet? The Doomsday Clock as a Visualization of Securitization Moves with a Global Referent Object." *Security Dialogue* 41(3): 255–77.

Wæver, Ole. 1996. "The Rise and Fall of the Inter-paradigm Debate." In *International Theory: Positivism and Beyond*, edited by Steve Smith, Ken Booth, and Marysia Zalewski, 149–85. New York: Cambridge University Press.

Wæver, Ole. 1998. "The Sociology of a Not So International Discipline: American and European Developments in International Relations." *International Organization* 52 (4): 687–727.

Walt, Stephen M. 1991. "The Renaissance of Security Studies." *International Studies Quarterly* 35 (2): 211–39.

Walt, Stephen M. 2005. "The Relationship between Theory and Policy in International Relations." *Annual Review of Political Science* 8: 23–48.

Walt, Stephen M. 2012. "Theory and Policy in International Relations: Some Personal Reflections." *Yale Journal of International Affairs* 7 (2): 33–43.

Waltz, Kenneth N. 1959. *Man, the State, and War: A Theoretical Analysis*. New York: Columbia University Press.

Waltz, Kenneth N. 1979. *Theory of International Politics*. New York: McGraw-Hill.

Weber, Martin. 2005. "The Critical Social Theory of the Frankfurt School, and the 'Social Turn' in IR." *Review of International Studies* 31 (1): 195–209.

Weber, Max. 1949. *The Methodology of the Social Sciences*. Edited and translated by Edward A. Shils and Henry A. Finch. Glencoe, IL: Free Press.

Weber, Max. 1958. *Essays in Sociology*. Edited and translated by Hans Gerth and C. Wright Mills. New York: Oxford University Press.

Weldes, Jutta. 1996. "Constructing National Interests." *European Journal of International Relations* 2 (3): 275–318.

Weldon, S. Laurel. 2006. "Inclusion and Understanding: A Collective Methodology for Feminist International Relations." In *Feminist Methodologies for International Relations*, edited by Brooke A. Ackerly, Maria Stern, and Jacqui True, 62–87. New York: Cambridge University Press.

Wendt, Alexander. 1992. "Anarchy Is What States Make of It: The Social Construction of Power Politics." *International Organization* 46 (2): 391–425.

White House. 2002. "The National Security of the United States." September 17. http://www.whitehouse.gov/nsc/nss.pdf

Wibben, Annick T. R. 2011. *Feminist Security Studies: A Narrative Approach*. New York: Routledge.

Wiener, Antje. 2014. *A Theory of Contestation*. Berlin: Springer.

Wight, Colin. 2006. *Agents, Structures and International Relations: Politics as Ontology*. Cambridge: Cambridge University Press.

Wilkin, Peter. 2002. "Global Poverty and Orthodox Security." *Third World Quarterly* 23 (4): 633–45.

Williams, John. 2015. *Ethics, Diversity, and World Politics: Saving Pluralism from Itself?* Oxford: Oxford University Press.

Winkler, Carol. 2008. "Encroachments on State Sovereignty: The Argumentation Strategies of the George W. Bush Administration." *Argumentation* 22 (4): 473–88.

Winograd Commission. 2008. "Reports." http://www.vaadatwino.gov.il/

Wyn Jones, Richard. 2005. "On Emancipation: Necessity, Capacity, and Concrete Utopias." In *Critical Security Studies and World Politics*, edited by Ken Booth, 215–35. Boulder, CO: Lynne Rienner.

Wolfers, Arnold. 1952. "'National Security' as an Ambiguous Symbol." *Political Science Quarterly* 67 (4): 481–502.

Wolff, Jonas. 2012. "The Conceptual Politics of Democracy Promotion in Bolivia." In *The Conceptual Politics of Democracy Promotion*, edited by Christopher Hobson and Milja Kurki, 119–30. New York: Routledge: 2011.

Wolff, Jonas, and Iris Wurm. 2011. "Towards a Theory of External Democracy Promotion: A Proposal for Theoretical Classification." *Critical Dialogue* 42 (1): 77–96.

Wolin, Sheldon S. 2004. *Politics and Vision: Continuity and Innovation in Western Political Thought*. Princeton, NJ: Princeton University Press.

Young, Iris M. 1981. "Towards a Critical Theory of Justice." *Social Theory and Practice* 7 (3): 279–302.

Young, Iris M. 1986. "Impartiality and the Civic Public: Some Implications of Feminist Critiques of Moral and Political Theory." *Praxis International* 5 (5): 381–401.

Index

Adler, Emanuel, 30, 186
Alliance for Progress, 156, 167, 171
America, 35, 50, 84, 85, 97, 114, 129, 138, 139, 147, 156, 157, 182, 186. *See also* United States
American Anthropological Association, 186
Anarchist, 50–51, 55
Archibugi, Daniele, 52
Arendt, Hannah, 19, 20, 100
Aristotle, 49
Avnon, Dan   124

Balkans, 78, 85–87
Barak, Oren, 205, 207
Battle of Kosovo, 87
Baudrillard, Jean, 70, 115
Bernstein, Richard, 26
Bint Jbail, 73
Booth, Ken, 59–60, 213n.7, ch.2
Bosnia-Herzegovina, 86
Bounding practices (definition and working), 10–11, 34, 41, 43, 68, 69, 89, 159, 176, 195, 201
Bourdieu, Pierre, 5, 29, 176, 187
Brodie, Bernard, 110
Buber, Martin, 12, 118, 122–28, 214n.2, ch.6
Bueno de Mesquita, Bruce, 162–63, 166
Bundy, McGeorge, 110, 182, 216n.7, ch.9
Burke, Edmund, 49
Burton, Michael, Judge, 82
Bush, George, W., 6, 85, 91

Buzan, Barry, 62, 64, 216n.6, ch. 9

Campbell, David, 63–64
Capability approach, 61, 65, 114
Castro, Fidel, 206
Chomsky, Noam, 50
Clinton, Bill, 161
Coady, C. A. J., 112
Coburn's amendment, 138–39
Coburn, Tom, 139
Cohen, Adar, 88
Cold War, 111, 182, 183, 186
Conceptual politics, 7, 8, 11, 68, 70, 97–103, 196, 201
Connolly, William, 4, 5, 22, 107, 212n.2, ch.2, 214n.1, ch.4
Constructivism / politically-tuned constructivism, 2–4, 24–26, 90–92, 97–101, 195
Cox, Robert, 41, 58–59, 135–36, 158–59, 197
Critical theory, 9, 42, 114, 119, 135, 203

Definitions, 9–10, 39–41, 43–46, 105–16, 195–201
Democracy, different conceptualizations and theories, 6, 46–56, 154–163, 201–4
 Communitarian, 51, 55, 167
 Cosmopolitan, 51–52, 55
 Deliberative/participatory/liberal, 6, 40, 47–48, 53–54, 102, 160–61, 166–68, 170–73, 188–89, 197–98, 201

239

Democracy (*continued*)
  Elitist/structural/conservative, 6, 40, 48–49, 54, 161–62, 166–67, 197, 201, 204
  Republican, 212–13n.5, ch.2
  Socialist, 50, 55, 167
Democratic peace theory, 42, 56, 110, 157–58, 162–63, 169, 189, 202–3
de-Shalit, Avner, 102
Democratic security, 11, 13, 201–4
Denali/Mount McKinley, 35
Deontology, 60–62, 65, 90, 112, 114
Der Derian, James, 63
Descartes, René, 115
Dialogue, 8, 10–12, 27–28, 97, 103, 117–31
Dilthey, Wilhelm, 123
Dual analytical gaze, 2, 7, 12, 20, 93, 97, 103, 148, 152, 177, 191, 194, 196, 204

Easton, David, 19
Edry, Yaakov, 77
Engaged academia, 1, 2, 7–13, 17, 20, 31, 92, 97–103, 146, 204, 209
English school, 100, 120
Ethics of care, 62, 206
Ethics of responsibility, 59, 64, 213n.8, ch.2
Essentially contested concepts (characteristics), 16–17, 22–24, 43–68, 69–93, 105–16
Eyal, Gil, 186

Falsifiability, principle of, 153
Feminism, 119, 141, 178–81, 206
First Lebanon War, 80–81
Forecasting, 151–73
Frankfurt school, 60–61, 65
Freeden, Michael, 44–45, 57, 61
Frege, Gotlob, 36
Fuller, Steve, 216n.13, ch.9

Gallie. W.B., 1, 4, 21–22, 44–47
Gavriely-Nuri, Dalia, 72

Gaza, 206–7
Giddens, Anthony, 110
Gilligan, Carol, 62
Giuliani, Rudolph, 84
Gore, Al, 81–85, 89–91
Gramsci, Antonio, 1–7, 17–21, 30–31, 32–34, 69–70, 79–81, 91–93, 196
Gramsci-like vernacular, 83–84, 89–91
Grandfather paradox, 151–52, 172
Grossman, David, 74
Grossman, Uri, 74
Gurevitch, Zali, 33
Gusterson, Hugh, 184–85

Habermas, Jürgen, 7–9, 26–33, 69, 89–93, 101–3, 110, 216n.15, ch.9
Habermas-like vernacular, 83–84, 89–91
Hacking, Ian, 43
Halutz, Dan, 74
Hansen, Lene, 62, 64
Haraway, Donna, 178
Harding, Sandra, 126, 178–80
Hawkesworth, Mary, 98
Hegel, Georg Wilhelm Friedrich, 165
Hegemony, 17–21
Held, David, 52–53
Hezbollah, 71–73, 76
Hobson, Christopher, 7, 70, 212n.1, ch.2
Hoopoe, 79
Human Terrain System (HTS), 186, 187, 192
Huntington, Samuel, 161
Huysmans, Jef, 63–64, 213n.7, ch.2

Intergovernmental Panel on Climate Change (IPCC), 81–84, 89
Iraq War, 6, 113, 158, 186
Israel, 36, 38–39, 70–81, 88, 97, 136, 147, 183, 186, 205–9
Israel Defence Forces (IDF), 70, 73–75, 79, 81, 88

Jackson, Patrick, 107
Jasanoff, Sheila, 171, 200
Johnson, Lyndon, B., 171, 186, 216n.7, ch.9

Kant, Immanuel, 60–61, 90, 181
Karadžić, Radovan, 85–86, 90–91
Kennedy, John F., 155–56, 171, 182, 186
Kerala/DAWN model, 167
Kissinger, Henry, 110
Kratochwil, Friedrich, 30–31, 211n. 1, intro.
Krauthammer, Charles, 158
Kripke, Saul, 36–37
Kripkean labeling by naming, 37–39, 77, 80–81
Kuklick, Bruce, 110
Kurki, Milja, 7, 70
Kymlicka, Will, 12, 118, 120, 122, 214n.1, ch.6

Laron, Guy, 208
Lasswell, Harold, 31
Lebanon, 70–72, 76, 213n.1, ch.3
Levinas, Emanuel, 63–64, 214n.3 ch.6
Levy, Yagil, 208
Lomborg, Bjørn, 85
Luhmann, Niklas, 216n.11, ch.9
Lukes, Steven, 18, 33
Lustick, Ian, 5, 18, 80

Mannheim, Karl, 134
Maoz, Zeev, 157
Marx, Karl, 156, 166
McCain, John, 84
McKinley, William, 35
Mearsheimer, John, 113–14
Megalim Olam, 205–9
MILGEM project, 208
Milošević, Slobodan, 87, 89, 91
Miodownik, Dan, 207
Mitrani, Mor, 206
Modernization theory, 155, 158–61, 171, 182

Morgenthau, Hans, 49, 54, 161, 213n.8, ch.2
Muravchik, Joshua, 158
Mutz, Diana, 48

Nakdi Briefing, 79
Nasrallah, Hassan, 73
National Science Foundation, 139
Neo-Gramscianism, 24, 33
Nietzsche, Friedrich, 106
Nussbaum, Martha, 61

Obama, Barack, 35, 85
Objectivity/strong objectivity, 58, 109, 111, 141–42, 165–66, 178–81
Okin, Susan, 62
Olmert, Ehud, 74–75, 81
Onuf, Nicholas, 19, 23, 30–31, 212n.2, ch.2
Operation Cast Lead, 206
Operation Pillar of Defense, 206
Operation Protective Edge, 206, 215n.3, ch.7
Oren, Ido, 113, 156–57, 182
Organic intellectuals, 18–19, 33
Orwell, George, 51, 77, 212n.6, ch.1

Paine, Rodger, 113
Palestine, 79–80, 122, 136
Palestinian sunbird, 79–80
Parekh, Bhikhu, 51, 167
Peretz, Amir, 74, 77
Pluralism, 10–12, 46–47, 97, 100–103, 117–22, 125–31, 164, 179, 196–201
Pollard, Jonathan, 183
Popper, Karl, 153, 215n.4, ch.8
Positivism, 9, 41–42, 58, 111, 114, 121, 141, 178, 211n.2, ch.1
Poststructuralism, 8–9, 58, 62–67, 114–15, 119, 213n.13, ch.2, 214n.1, ch.4, 217n.17, ch.9
Prebisch, Raúl, 159, 167
Putnam, Robert, 156–57, 160–62, 166, 182

Quisisana clinic, 1–2, 7, 23, 89, 103, 117, 146, 166, 173, 177, 196

Rawls, John, 12, 20, 22, 100–101, 113, 117–19, 164, 212n.3, ch.2
Realism, 49, 58–62, 64–67, 113–14, 119–20, 125, 138
Relativism, 10, 26, 63, 66–67, 114, 118, 128
Republika Srpska, 86
Responsibility, 7, 10, 12, 31, 48, 52, 54, 59, 92–93, 97–103, 111, 114, 140, 145, 149, 155, 163, 170, 173, 188–90, 196–201, 209
Rhetorical capital, 34–36, 87
Romney, Mitt, 84
Rorty, Richard, 127–28
Rostow, Walt, 110, 155–56, 159–60, 162, 167, 171, 182, 186, 216n.7, ch.9
Russell, Bernard, 36–37
Russett, Bruce, 169

Scanlon, T.M., 101
Schelling, Thomas, 110, 183
Schmitt, Carl, 19
Schumpeter, Joseph, 49, 162, 166
Second Lebanon War, 36, 38–39, 70–77, 89, 91
Securitization, 66, 82, 84, 175–77, 181, 188, 190–94, 214n.3, ch.5
Security (conceptualization and different schools), 56–67
  Critical, 60, 65, 192, 203
  Feminist, 62–63, 66, 179–80, 192, 203
  Human, 60–61, 65–66, 192, 203
  Realist, 58–59, 64
  Poststructuralist, 63–64, 66
Sela, Avraham, 205, 207
Self-reflexivity, 10–11, 97–103, 119, 122, 125–26, 131, 141, 166, 172, 175, 178–79, 196–201

Semantic field, 6, 11, 42–47, 53–57, 64–68, 146, 201–4
Sen, Amartya, 61, 213n.9, ch.2
Sending, Ole Jacob, 176
Sheehan, Michael, 64
Simmel, Georg, 123
Simyoni, Roi, 205
Smith, Steve, 64
Social semiotics, 34
Standpoint theory/epistemology, 9, 98–99, 112, 125, 141, 154, 158, 170, 178–80, 183, 185, 197–99

Tanchum, Micha'el, 208
Theoretician-citizen, 10, 12, 103, 134, 152, 169–73, 177, 184, 189–204
Thomas, Caroline, 61
Tönnies, Ferdinand, 119
Transparency, 11–12, 97–103, 122, 136, 140–42, 144–49, 176–84, 191–201, 216nn.2,3, ch.9
Trump, Donald, 85
Truth, 26, 114–19, 124, 128, 131, 140, 197, 200

United Nations, 61
United Nations Economic Commission for Latin America (ECLA), 159, 180
UN Security Council Resolution 1325, 180
UN Security Council Resolution 1701, 72
United States, 31, 35, 52, 85, 139, 155–56, 182–83, 206. *See also* America

Verta, Adam, 88
Von Bismarck, Otto, 156

Walt, Stephen, 59, 113
Waltz, Kenneth, 59
Weber, Max, 19, 59, 107–8, 213n.8, ch.2

Wibben, Annick, 62–63, 66, 213n.13, ch.2
Wiener, Antje, 31
Wilkin, Peter, 61
Williams, John, 100–101
Winograd, Eliyhau, 74
Winograd Commission, 74
Wittgenstein, Ludwig, 36
Wolfers, Arnold, 57

Wolin, Sheldon, 106–7
Wyn Jones, Richard, 60

Ynet, 205–9
Young, Iris Marion, 62

zooming in, zooming out, 12, 58, 105–16, 127, 178, 200–201, 214n.1, ch.5